Praise for *The Australian Way of Parenting*

Previously published as *Into the Rip*

"When American journalist Dami[...]
New York Times bureau chief, he d[...]
risk activities are normal—even [...]
minating parenting guide, a take[...]
industrial complex, and a deep study of contrasts between the
Australian and American minds. It made even a wimp like me
consider heading into the sea."

—Pamela Druckerman, *New York Times*
bestselling author of *Bringing Up Bébé*

"*Into the Rip* is a beautiful tale of one family trying to figure things
out—and, at the same time, a brilliant synthesis of a century of
psychological science on how all of us can learn to dive headfirst
into challenges, grow and adapt, and ultimately do well in life."
—Angela Duckworth, *New York Times* bestselling author of *Grit*

"*Into the Rip* is absolutely terrific. It's a gripping story that gets
the science of risk right. I haven't seen any other writings about
my work and the study of risk that are like this, integrated with a
powerful story well told."

—Paul Slovic, author of *Perception of Risk*, founder
and president of Decision Research, and professor
of psychology at the University of Oregon

"It often takes a stranger's eyes to see our own country clearly.
By plunging into the Sydney surf, Damien Cave peered into the

Australian soul. What he found there—courage, grit, community—is welcome news when our lives and our core values have never seemed so precarious."

—Geraldine Brooks, Australian American journalist
and novelist of the Pulitzer Prize–winning *March*

"Damien Cave's *Into the Rip* is many books in one—a beautiful memoir of his family's years living in Australia, a deeply reported exploration of how we approach risk, pain and safety in the 21st century, and a sometimes painful examination of American life and American assumptions. Even if everyone doesn't end up surfing in the South Pacific after reading this book, they will be convinced of something much more important: that changing the way we live today is possible, necessary, exhilarating."

—Suzy Hansen, Pulitzer Prize finalist
author of *Notes on a Foreign Country*

"Absolutely genuine. A lively mix of history, philosophy, science, reportage—and an honest, heartfelt memoir of the joys and miseries of parenting. I learned a lot from it."

—Dan Kois, author of *How to Be a Family* and host
of the podcast *Mom and Dad Are Fighting*

"Damien Cave does an excellent job of deconstructing the phenomenon of trauma and risk to understand why some people are more vulnerable than others. His experience in war zones must have given him crucial insights into the topic."

—Sebastian Junger, *New York Times* bestselling
author of *Tribe* and *Freedom*

"A thrilling examination of self and family, risk and reward, failure and triumph, in ways both big and small. Cave's vivid exploration of risk-taking told through the ages mixed with his own experiences as a parent, partner, and perspicacious journalist will make you devour this book—and then slam it shut, look inside yourself, and want to be a better person."

—Dionne Searcey, author of *In Pursuit of Difficult Women*

PARENTING
LIKE AN

ONE FAMILY'S QUEST
TO FIGHT FEAR AND DIVE
INTO A BETTER, BRAVER LIFE

DAMIEN CAVE

Published by Sourcebooks
P.O. Box 4410, Naperville, Illinois 60567–4410
(630) 961-3900
sourcebooks.com

Originally published as *Into the Rip* in 2021 in Australia by Scribner, an imprint of Simon
& Schuster Australia. This edition issued based on the paperback edition published
in 2021 in Australia by Scribner, an imprint of Simon & Schuster Australia.

Library of Congress Cataloging-in-Publication Data

Names: Cave, Damien, author.
Title: Parenting like an Australian : one family's quest to fight fear and
 dive into a better, braver life / Damien Cave.
Other titles: Into the rip
Description: Naperville, Illinois : Sourcebooks, [2023] | "Originally
 published as Into the Rip in 2021 in Australia by Scribner, an imprint
 of Simon & Schuster Australia. This edition issued based on the
 paperback edition published in 2021 in Australia by Scribner, an imprint
 of Simon & Schuster Australia"--Title page verso. | Includes
 bibliographical references.
Identifiers: LCCN 2022047807 (print) | LCCN 2022047808
 (ebook) | (trade paperback) | (pdf) | (epub)
Subjects: LCSH: Parenting--Australia. | Americans--Australia. | National
 characteristics, Australian. | Australia--Social life and customs.
Classification: LCC HQ755.8 .C428 2023 (print) | LCC HQ755.8 (ebook) |
 DDC 649/.10994--dc23/eng/20221107
LC record available at https://lccn.loc.gov/2022047807
LC ebook record available at https://lccn.loc.gov/2022047808

Printed and bound in the United States of America.
VP 10 9 8 7 6 5 4 3 2 1

For Diana, Balthazar, and Amelia, my
tutors in risk and a well-lived life

Contents

Introduction

Our journey to Australia began in Manhattan, on a typical summer afternoon in a Midtown office building. I was sipping burnt black coffee in the *New York Times* cafeteria with a friend when she asked what I wanted to do next. I was an editor on the national desk, she was running the *Times*'s global expansion efforts, and I told her I wasn't really sure but that I was almost ready to go out again—to get back into the field.

"How about Australia?" she said. "Now."

It was the summer of 2016, and the company was anxious about its future, convinced that financial stability required an expanded presence and more subscribers from around the world, especially places where we already knew we had readers—including Australia.

"Don't you want someone Australian?" I asked.

"We need someone who understands the *Times* already. You should apply."

I returned to my desk, distracted and out of breath. Should I apply? My wife, Diana, and I were just coming up on two years back in New York after various stints interstate and abroad. Our son, Baz, and daughter, Amelia, were thriving in their bilingual public school, and Diana had just received a promotion at the digital media company where she'd been trying to advance. We were working nonstop and rushing like ambulance drivers to meet the most mundane daily appointments, like breakfast and bedtime, but wasn't everyone? I could hardly imagine telling our parents we might move so far away. They believed we were finally settling down after hopscotching from San Francisco to New York, then to Baghdad, Miami, Mexico City, and Brooklyn.

Still. Australia.

That night, I met Diana for dinner at Babbo, Mario Batali's throwback Italian bistro in lower Manhattan. As usual, I was late. I was also nervous: how would I even bring up the idea of another move? And the truth was, Diana and I had been fighting a lot. Too much stress, not enough time, for the kids or ourselves. Babbo was our first dinner out alone in months, and we'd made the reservation a while ago, thinking it would be a good way to reconnect.

When I arrived, Diana was at the bar, tapping away on her phone, wearing a black dress with tall black boots—the consummate New Yorker.

"Hey," she said, smiling. "So there you are."

The things that often made me crazy about the city—the lack of time for anything but work, the sense of superiority seeping out of the superrich—she brushed off like a light rain. New York, she often said, was the place where she felt most comfortable because there was always someone richer, poorer, or crazier, and it was now the city I was about to ask if she might want to leave. Again.

Best to plunge right in.

"So this weird thing came up at work today."

She looked at me with suspicion.

In a dark corner near the bar, as we ate, I explained what happened. Even as I heard myself talking, I felt torn. I wanted to go but was that a sign of bravery or cowardice? I was no fan of New York but doubted my instincts. *Is the city the problem or is it me?*

My job with the *Times* had led to all our other moves, and with Diana finding her feet at home, I knew I owed her the right to decide on this one. Expecting her to nix the idea, I reminded myself that it would be a lot easier to just stay. Big deal, I wasn't happy—we lived in a city of ambition, not bliss. I had a good job. I was co-leading a new, diverse team charged with covering race in America and helping out with breaking news. Diana was managing a group of video journalists focused on social justice and millennials.

Leaving might be great, I thought—or it could be a misguided dodge that would hurt us financially as we stepped away from the higher pay scales of New York. It might even push Diana and I further apart. I'd seen the pattern before with other journalism couples: an international move, separation, divorce.

I looked to Diana for guidance. She nodded and said little as I talked, but when I finished, she surprised me.

She recalled the fun she had many years earlier as a visiting student at the University of Technology in Sydney.

"That was the best year of my life," she said. "I think we should go for it."

This is a book about taking one big risk—a move to the other side of the earth—that led to an exploration of many others and, ultimately, a dramatic change in how we live as a family. It's a book that began with a question Australia forced us to ask: what would life be like if we actively embraced more of what scares and excites us, with our children, with each other, and with those we barely know? It is also just a story of two parents trying to raise decent kids…two supposedly brave parents who needed more help with risk-taking and community than they thought.

Diana and I came to Australia in early 2017 somewhat blinkered, with the loud voices of American-made bravado. We were convinced Sydney would be easy compared with some of our previous assignments—Baghdad during the worst year of the war, Mexico City in the midst of a violent drug conflict. We weren't at the strongest point in our marriage, but like a lot of New Yorkers, we saw ourselves in the best possible light, as high achievers who yelled too much only because America was hard and our work was important. We needed a change, and Australia presented itself. Maybe we even believed our new country would be lucky to have us. Isn't that the American way? To assume that we're the ones with lessons to share?

But Australia, one of the safest countries in the world, frightened us in ways we never expected. It found us wanting, not special—that was the first sign we'd gotten something wrong. The country did not throw open its arms; it demanded that we play along socially and physically, disrupting realms of our life we had long ignored. Up to that point, doing scary things had always involved work and big decisions. Do you raise your hand to cover the war? Do you quit your job before you have a new one?

Australia made us look at everything else. The mantras that Diana and I took with us wherever we moved (choose the bigger adventure, do what the place does best) became enormous challenges for our entire family in Australia, where our bodies, minds, schedules, and even our identities were tested.

It started with the water and our children. Within a few weeks of our arrival, the public school they attended had a "swim carnival," where all the kids took a day off from school to compete in the pool, in every stroke, including the butterfly. There were winners and losers, and fear was not an excuse—there was no getting out of the competition. That should have been a hint of what was to come, but I missed it as I tried to make sense of the other aquatic activity all around us. In those early days, I often found myself stopping and staring with awe at children who were knee-high and mastering the tumultuous ocean, surfing, swimming, and joining a program called Nippers that made them mini lifesavers in training.[i]

There seemed to be clubs for all these activities. There seemed to be no drop-off-and-go activities. Parents volunteered to push their own children and those of their neighbors into the surf. Nippers, in particular, was a family affair, time consuming, frightening, thrilling. And extremely popular. I couldn't quite work out why that was the case at first, but I could sense that there was something deep and meaningful in the combination of fear, nature, family involvement, and community spirit.

For both children and adults, what I witnessed was the surrender of control, the embrace of risk, trust, and the insistence on collective action—all of which run counter to the trends of our time. In so much of Western culture, we have drifted into a cycle of self-centered self-protection. We seek physical comfort and total psychological security. We have prioritized attention, feelings, and speech, not good conduct. Our phones and algorithms promise connection but serve up isolation. Every day, we choose convenience over uncertainty, overvaluing pleasure and ignoring what being challenged has to teach.

When we think about risk, if we think about it at all, we tend to treat it as an individual act, a choice each of us makes—to climb a mountain, to become a soldier. Or risk is something we let others manage, whether in finance or government. We push risk aside, insisting that total safety is an unqualified good. We expect fear to be solved with money, but the more prosperous we become, the more anxious and depressed. We insure our lives and property even as we destroy the planet's future. We have fewer children, who we try harder to protect, even as we poison them with worry and self-regard.

Do we even notice that we have entirely overcomplicated everything? How do we live stronger and better—as individuals, families, and communities?

These were the questions I had in mind when we left the first phase of Trump's America in early 2017. I thought my queries would fade with time and distance. As it turned out, we landed in a place that helped me answer them. Australia fed my curiosity, humbled me, and provided clues to mysteries I'd been trying to understand since my own childhood.

This is not a book, however, with a one-word title that aims to solve everything with pithy anecdotes and psychological studies. Risk is too big and messy a topic for any one-size-fits-all formula, which is also true of parenting, so my approach is more reflection than equation. I've tried in my own way to merge insights from science, history, and everyday life in a country that, from an American perspective, stands out for its moderation.

That attribute can be hard to defend or even see very clearly. When Australians ask me to help them make sense of America today, as they often do, I remind them that our history is filled with extremes—from revolution to civil war, from civil rights to our current hyperpolarized moment. What that means is that sometimes we see the middle with disdain. To many Americans, compromise feels like defeat and moderation like a lukewarm bath. It's not a place that we think we'd enjoy.

But Australia and other democracies that live more often in the middle, with both politics and the risks of everyday life, represent a calmer, less anxious alternative with lessons that can make America happier and healthier.

The first lesson, I think, has something to do with humor and humility. I'm often struck by how quick Australians are to make jokes at their own country's expense. Whenever I praised the country's approach to risk, they'd laugh. *Risk? We're not risk-takers!* They're the first ones to tell you their country is too cautious and compliant, from the arts (where government grants go mostly to big and well-established institutions) to business (where there is less tolerance for failure than there is in, say, Silicon Valley).

Those are indeed areas where Australia's leaders could and should do more to encourage a greater tolerance for risk. But that's only a corner of the national portrait. There's a lot that the Australians I've met—maybe because they are so tough on themselves—tend to overlook. For one thing, they underestimate the value of Australia's approach to risk management in life's most consequential areas, such as driving, banking, public health, and parenting, where policy and behavioral norms have found an equilibrium between recklessness and overprotection. For years, it has had some of the world's safest roads, and its immunization rates are among the highest in the world—for COVID-19 and many other infectious diseases.

What I've also seen and come to admire is the way that people here live with a connection to the landscape and each other that makes physical and social fear a speed bump, not a stop sign. In my experience, from the remote, red-dirt Outback of northwestern Australia to the cold-water coastline of southern Tasmania, Australians are by and large an optimistic people, inclined toward adventure, trust, and fraternal, unpretentious acts of boldness that they often see as little more than community common sense. If they underestimate their own risk-savvy norms and the benefits that grow from their buoyant approach, it's probably for two reasons: first, because Australia's culture of collective bravery and resilience *is* gradually weakening, as it is in other parts of the developed world; and second, because anything familiar enough to be taken for granted rarely looks extraordinary.

Australians, I've concluded, are in the odd position of getting risk (and parenting) mostly right most of the time without really noticing. Maybe this book, which was published first in Australia, will help correct that. But if that's the case, it may only be because it's not just me—a mildly neurotic American—who picked up on the fact that there is wisdom in the Australian way. I did, of course, also seek out expertise. Because my interest centered on risk in family life (rather than, say, finance), I prioritized psychologists and other social scientists—people like Martin

Seligman, the founder of positive psychology, Gerd Gigerenzer, a German maestro of risk and intuition, Brock Bastian, Australia's optimistic expert on the power of pain, and Angela Duckworth, the author of *Grit*. Their work and the lengthy interviews I did with them helped me better understand what we were experiencing and what could be learned from an approach to parenting (and life) that treats risk as communal and worth learning to manage.

I found that their personal stories were as useful as their research. This was also true for other deep thinkers I was lucky enough to connect with, from Aboriginal elders to anthropologists to historians, firefighters, oyster farmers, epidemiologists, pro surfers, terrorism victims in Christchurch, New Zealand, and fellow members of the surf lifesaving club in our Sydney suburb of Bronte.

When I started this book, I didn't expect quite so many teachers. I intended to explore Australia's approach to the ocean, and I imagined combining our family's experiences, interviews with experts, and memories from my earlier experiences with risk, especially covering the war in Iraq for the *New York Times*. Those elements still form the book's backbone. But then more news interrupted.

Between the time I started and finished, the world's experience of risk (along with my own) expanded exponentially. I was just starting to get a handle on the surf, for example, when an Australian white supremacist attacked two mosques in Christchurch. Never could I have imagined covering a mass shooting in a country so safe and idyllic, a place where many of the attacker's victims had moved for refuge. It forced me to look beyond the everyday risks I'd been exploring, confront the biases that can blind societies to public risks, and recognize that sometimes the bravest acts as parents and citizens involve taking a chance on each other when all we want to do is hide.

A few months later, I found myself in the middle of another tragedy—suiting up in fireproof gear to cover the most catastrophic bushfires ever recorded in Australian history. Monsters of heat and flame fueled by climate change, an existential risk if there ever was one, the blazes were fought mostly by Australian volunteers in their own communities.

And then, of course, there was COVID-19. The longer the global health disaster wore on, the more it exposed a deep divide in how people and nations approach risk, trust, and responsibility. In the United States, especially in the first year of COVID, the virus magnified the dysfunctional tendencies that have been gaining momentum for decades. So many of the realities I just accepted as part of American life—destructive political divisions, rebelliousness against the state, and rampant inequality—have contributed to the deaths of more than one million Americans.

The most confusing and heartbreaking cases involved people who refused to be vaccinated for reasons of conservative politics or "freedom" only to die from COVID. But I also had my share of intense arguments with left-leaning friends who insisted that keeping children out of school made sense even after the data showed the risks of serious illness for kids was low while the consequences of shuttered classrooms was high.

From my distant vantage point, it all reflected a very American approach to uncertainty and peril. In the United States, with its cult of individualism, a person's approach to risk is often seen as a marker of one's cultural and political identity. Consensus is rarely rewarded, even among experts, and when shared responsibility and freedom clash, many Americans choose reckless liberty while others insist on total risk elimination. It's that old clash of extremes.

Australia's experience has been very different because, I came to understand, its approach to risk is very different. In general, the response has been more cautious, collective, and nimble, leading to much better results. When outbreaks arose, deaths were kept to a minimum—at about one-tenth of the death rate in America, as of mid-2022—through strict lockdowns and the solidarity of a diverse population that repeatedly chose, as I wrote in the *Times*, "short-term pain for collective gain." Trust in one another, a driver of public health compliance that kept death rates low in many countries, saved tens of thousands of lives in Australia.

Competence in state and local government played an important role, but ultimately the culture—egalitarian, pragmatic, optimistic, and interdependent—kept the country healthy. And that culture is what our very American family had little choice but to try and adopt.

Long before the coronavirus hit, I was fascinated by the tension between individualism and collectivism in Australia and in the United States. Two colonial frontier nations settled with the same language and British backstory seemed to have diverged. With guns, healthcare, education, and wages, the United States prioritized personal freedom and competition while Australia chose another path to—what? Communitarianism? Fraternalism? Democratic socialism?

I wasn't sure what to call the Australian way, and I knew there were elements of what I admired that could be found in other countries, too, but I found myself obsessed with the intangible and meaningful norms that held together a country that seemed to be a distant cousin to where I grew up. I wanted to explore the underlying values—the way decisions were made about risk and reward at the family and community level.

What I failed to realize at first was that I could not investigate such things from a comfortable journalistic distance. I needed to "get amongst it" as much as I could, which turned out to be harder than expected. In my early forties, I was used to being relatively good at the things I knew how to be good at. Australia made me learn how to be a terrible beginner at every new thing I tried.

As much as the ocean scared me, harder still were the demands of Australian togetherness. I was an ambivalent newcomer to what Australians call mateship, craving connection even as I questioned the social pressure to conform and Australia's insistence that "tall poppies" be cut back down to size. I had a hard time not talking about my own job or someone else's. When people went out of their way to help me, I sometimes resented the fact that I was expected to do the same. The Australians I met, whether they knew I was a journalist or not, couldn't help but demand that I integrate—no celebration of achievements was allowed without self-deprecating humor. I had to understand their sports (or is it sport?) and the minutiae of their history. Even when they said something discriminatory, I was supposed to just laugh, not argue, because being offended by a joke was apparently worse than saying something offensive.

Maybe it was all so jarring because I arrived in Sydney at a distant extreme. I was more serious, isolated, and myopic than I wanted to admit—overworked, overweight, eager to win every Twitter debate, not so quick to get to know new friends. Like a lot of Americans, I guess I thought I could separate myself from the trajectory of my country, or at least the parts I didn't like. But in reality, I was (to borrow from Graham Greene) just as much of an ugly American as the next guy. Wasn't I also wasting time on what didn't matter—social media righteousness, the latest Netflix show, pleasing a boss—all while ignoring or blaming others for the greater dangers emerging? Existential dangers? Democracy dangers? I could smell the gangrene all around. It took a long time for me to see I was as infected as everyone else.

Eventually, I realized that I didn't just need to explore what worked in Australia or what was different. I needed to examine, interrogate, and change the nation inside myself and my family.

In that quest, I kept returning to a couple of touchstones. One was my experience of the war in Iraq. On the ground, working from the *Times*'s Baghdad bureau when car bombs and urban combat were a daily occurrence in 2006 and 2007, the war was a master class in risk and community. On the geopolitical level, it was a stark example of American hubris.

Further back, there was my upbringing. My parents were baby boomers from New York suburbs who sought utopias that were never found. My mother was an artist and a musician who succumbed to drugs, and she died just before I went to Iraq after she was hit by a car crossing the street to her halfway house. My father eventually found Jesus. They were among the many who divorced in the '70s and '80s, and my childhood was shaped first by my father's lefty Woodstock vibes, then later by his and my stepmother's Christian evangelical parenting, which arose at the moment when the Moral Majority surged.

Journalism became my way of avoiding social movements of any kind. Through reporting, I could explore any interest and be thrown into things I might never have encountered without having to sign up myself. But pursuing the goal of journalist as neutral observer also made me a lonely island. I became an expert in keeping life at a safe distance.

By the time I got to Sydney, all I really knew how to do was work. After nearly twenty years in journalism, I knew how to tell other people's stories, even in the tragedies of war and natural disasters. But my notebook and my camera were a shield shined with privilege: if it got too tough, I could leave and write about something else. I was doing more observing than actual living. What little life I had outside work was stuck on repeat. Wherever we lived, I always ran the same distance, ate the same kinds of food, took the same kinds of vacations. The friendships I had built as a younger man were weak, mainly because of a lack of effort from me, and I often felt unsure about what I was aiming for. As a parent. As a husband. As a citizen. All these insecurities I just ignored, until Australia forced me to square up to them.

Australians seemed to be more comfortable with serendipity and commitment. They wanted—no, expected—my physical presence at activities that had nothing to do with work or productivity, from school barbecues to sport and Nippers to book and ideas festivals. At first I thought it might just be where we landed in Sydney, but census and survey data show that, compared with Americans, Australians are less lonely,[ii] more likely to have joined a community group or club,[iii] more likely to agree with the statement "most people can be trusted." And 94.4 percent of Australians report being able to get support in times of crisis from people living outside their household.

The disease of disconnection is still here and might be getting worse, but it's a stage 1 or 2 condition, not a full-blown terminal illness. Despite declines, Australians' real-life social networks of friends and family are larger, and Australians spend more time than Americans cultivating those connections.[iv]

Nippers and surf lifesaving—a national volunteer movement without equal worldwide, with 315 surf clubs around Australia that have saved thousands of lives—represent one way the country continues to cohere.[v] From run-down to übermodern, from well run to troubled, the clubs themselves are magnets of community built into the sand and dunes. Worldwide, roughly 40 percent of the population lives within one hundred kilometers of an ocean.[vi] In Australia, roughly 85 percent live within half that distance.[vii]

Geography and culture are always hard to disentangle, but seeing how Australians interacted with the water, through my kids and eventually my own humiliating attempt to participate, made me look with fresh eyes at where we had landed and at my own priorities. Our new home seemed to be a place where physical risk and other admirable attributes—modesty, resilience, and benevolence—were inseparable and complementary, with each reinforcing the other.

I hadn't thought much about those virtues until I realized how much I needed them in a world that continues to grow riskier and more demanding of courage and collective action with each passing month. Australia offered both a critique along with a path toward hope, maybe even revival. And it all started with a counterintuitive approach to risk, with teaching children to manage danger, with diving into the rip currents of life—partly for fun and fulfillment but mostly so we can all learn to make better, braver decisions in every swell of the unexpected.

ONE

Arriving in Australia

A history of risk; Pascal's triangle; too much "pathological prudence"?

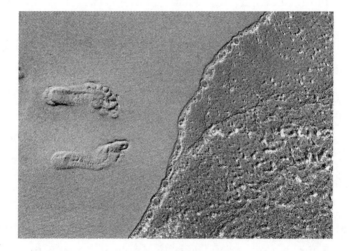

The Nippers swim assessment took place on a cool spring day, warm in the sun, freezing in the shade, on the campus of an all-girls Anglican school in what felt like an Australian secret garden. It was a world unto itself and entirely unfamiliar. Even before we found a parking spot, I could see a flood of families with swim-ready children in tight Speedos rushing toward a narrow stairway that seemed to cut through a brick wall covered in foreign flowers.

I paused at the entrance with Diana, Baz, and Amelia to let the foot traffic ease. I could hear splashing and squealing from the outdoor pool. The parents looked like they'd come from a schooner. One, two, three sets of mothers and fathers walked past, their stomachs too flat, their straw hats too stylish, their chatter routine—as if it was entirely normal to have hundreds of children swimming outside three months before the summer.

"Find our people," Diana had said when I came to Sydney for the first time to find a place to live. *Were these our people?*

I had my doubts. At the pool, my first impression was harder to deny: *no, they were not our people.* The bodies there lacked the middle I brought with me from New York. Little things everyone had, like towel ponchos, I'd never seen before. Just the range of goggle styles and swimsuit colors astounded me. No wonder they called them costumes, or what was the Sydney abbreviation again—*cossies*?

I stood there in a daze, confused, intrigued, and nervous. We had the wrong clothes, the wrong accents, and we were clearly out of our comfort zones. Diana, the family introvert who nonetheless managed everything, stretched into the gap. She immediately found someone she knew—Woz, Amelia's Nippers coach, a bearded bear of a man with a daughter the same age as Amelia, who had just turned seven. He was wearing a green sun visor and a white moisture-wicking shirt that identified him as an "age manager," a phrase I would have otherwise associated with geriatrics. But in a weird twist of fate, for Diana, he was an old friend; she'd known Woz twenty years ago, during her semester studying in Sydney. We'd been to his house for dinner a few nights earlier.

"Can she swim a hundred meters?" Woz asked.

We all looked at Amelia, the unpredictable, often-stubborn baby of the family in a rainbow bathing suit. Four laps of the pool. She shrugged, jumped in, and started swimming. Up and down she went, her little body twisting and splashing.

"Aw, she's gonna be fine," Woz said. She finished easily.

Her older brother by seventeen months, Baz, short for Balthazar, was next. He had to swim 150 meters, two more laps than his sister. We figured he'd be fine. He'd taken swimming lessons when we lived in Mexico. The day he turned four, he rode a bike on two wheels the first time he tried. His strong little body always seemed to work well with a physical challenge.

"Go!" came the shout, and he was in. He finished two laps as Diana and I swiveled our heads to take in the scene, but with the third, another boy had caught up and bumped into him. Baz looked up. The other boy's arm whacked him again as he passed. I winced. *Just keep going.* It wasn't a race, and there was no malice in the incident. But after a few more strokes, Baz stopped at the opposite end and got out of the pool. When he turned to look at us, Diana and I shook our heads and mouthed the word "No."

He walked slowly toward us, looking angry. He'd never been very good with unpredictability, even as a baby. He buried his face in my hip and burst into tears. When I tried to comfort him—"Hey, it's okay. You can try again"—he hardened, flopping down on the grassy hill near the pool, pulling his knees into his chest, and refusing to give it another shot.

"I'm not doing it," he said. "I'm not."

His dark eyes narrowed. He was only eight years old, and he looked too serious for his age.

"You just need to try again," I told him.

"No," Baz said again, tensing up, like a coil. "I'm not doing it."

I looked around. No one seemed to take much notice of us. Not the six-year-old twins twisting goggles out of their hair; not the blond moms with their big sunglasses; not the awkward twelve-year-olds chasing each other with the first buds of attraction. But I had a hunch that a very public dispute with American accents would change that. It felt like the kind of place where we were one shout from being closely watched.

Baz lifted his head out of his arms. I could see the gap between his two front teeth.

"I just want to go home," he said.

I hated seeing him fail. Even more, I hated that we didn't belong. As a reporter, I was used to awkward situations; as a father, I hated the sensation that everyone else knew what they were doing except for me, and now, my boy.

I looked at him sitting there, an unmovable boulder. Baz, my type A wonder of intensity, the one who adapted easily when we moved to Mexico City, then New York, was shivering, wet, wrapped in a fluffy striped towel, wearing the baggy little-boy swim trunks that no serious swimmer would touch. But he was not a serious swimmer. That was the problem. *Does he need to be? Really?*

Diana and I tried one more time to persuade him.

"You can do this," I told him. "Just get back in and try again."

"No."

"How about if you do it, we go get an ice cream after this."

"No. I can't do this. I can't!"

He was convinced, fixed in place, and scared. Diana took a deep breath, turned, and found the coach for Baz's Nippers group, Al, a dad with dark hair and a deep voice who looked like he used to play professional rugby. Later I found out that he actually had been a pro player, but at the time, all I could see was that his calves were the size and shape of footballs.

"What happens if Baz doesn't pass?" Diana asked.

"Then he can't do Nippers," Al said. "We need to know he'll be safe."

My stomach tightened when I heard that. I'd seen Nippers once at Australia's most iconic beach, Bondi, with kids running around the sand in neon and throwing themselves into the waves. It looked silly and ridiculous, like some beachfront circus act of synchronized childhood, but Al's warning made me think it was something else—at least for our particular beach. We were not in big, easy Bondi. Our kids would be doing Nippers, whatever it was, in a smaller, rougher spot where the waves were bigger, the rips stronger, the rocks sharper.

"If you can swim in Bronte, you can swim anywhere." Wasn't that the slogan? I'd been too busy at work to pay much attention, but I did recall hearing someone call it one of Australia's most dangerous beaches, maybe the most dangerous, which made me wonder as I stood there by the pool, *How on earth is that sort of thing even measured?*

We'd been in Australia for about six months. For the first time, I felt completely thrown off and uncertain about how to proceed. If Baz didn't pass or if he quit, he would be accepting failure in what already felt to me like a boys-and-banter kind of country where wimping out would not be welcome. But then I pictured the waves, slamming into the sharp stones and the sand, throwing my little boy around like a rag doll. Surprising even myself, I was scared—I wanted to protect him. Like Baz, I wanted to run away too, all the way back to Brooklyn or somewhere else more intellectual where the demands on my children did not include a need to prove they could handle a dangerous stretch of the Pacific Ocean.

I turned to Diana and could see she was having similar thoughts. Her eyes had that dazed look that she must have seen in mine—we were both surprised. We were supposed to be better at this. We were former war correspondents for the *New York Times*. We'd both moved around a lot, and we thought of ourselves as risk seekers who were up for anything. Better yet, we saw ourselves as risk assessors who had learned how to both be careful and overcome fear with calm calculation. We knew firsthand that even in the world's most dangerous places, on any given day, most people are fine. We were the parents who laughed at the mothers who kept their toddlers from slides at playgrounds and refused to give their kids any candy. We thought we'd worked pretty hard to reject the helicopter parenting of upper-middle-class America.

Or had we? In Australia of all places, we were forced to question our assumptions and how we had come to see ourselves in comparison to the only people we'd thought mattered—other Americans. As we walked back to the car with a daughter who would soon be thrown into Nippers and a son who might not—we knew he'd get another chance later but we weren't sure he'd pass—I barely said a word. All four of us were quieter than usual. There was something that scared us about Australia and something in ourselves we weren't sure we understood.

The first time I flew into Sydney, as the plane circled above the coast at sunrise, I realized I'd never seen a city so in love with the sea. Every home, every building, seemed to have an ocean view. It was like other places we'd been—San Francisco, Istanbul, Miami—but somehow more concentrated and more kinetic. Waves thundered against tall rocky cliffs that turned into dramatic urban hillsides rolling inward toward green, leafy parks and the harbor's sandy coves with sailboats bobbing in peace. Hefty ferries of green and yellow crisscrossed the middle of the urban blue bay, leaving wakes of white that looked like trails of sprinkled sugar. Even the office towers of the central business district looked close enough to the water to draw an ocean reflection.

When Mark Twain visited in 1895, he compared the shape of Sydney Harbor to a maple leaf, calling the shimmering expanse "the wonder of the world."[i] For my own first impression, I didn't need a North American reference point to feel just as awestruck. The dramatic dark blue harbor amazed me with its size and hidden corners, its Double Bay, Rose Bay, Watsons Bay.

On the ground, I was no less smitten and just as out of place as Mr. Twain. I'd never been to Australia before. I was there to get organized ahead of our family move. It was late January of 2017, winter in New York, summer in Sydney, and I was exhausted, pale, and anxious. Donald Trump had just been inaugurated, and the *Times* office was still filled with whispers about what the election revealed about the country and ourselves. There were conversations in the hallways about whether we needed to open new bureaus in "Trump's America," whether we'd under-estimated how much racism would define the results, whether we'd all relied too heavily on our own digital prognosticator, "the needle," showing that Hillary Clinton was the heavy favor-ite to win.

To my New Yorker eyes, Sydney was an escape—it was as if I'd time traveled to an entirely different mood. With just one twenty-four hour journey, I was transported from doubt to trust. People were still smiling and getting along. In every neighborhood I visited in my dash around the city to find a school, a home, and an office, I stared in amazement at simple things that had died out in most of America long ago, like local butcher shops and gas stations where you could pump before you paid. The architecture felt British, but all that brick didn't seem to belong in such a strange, beguiling place where no one questioned you for walking through the city barefoot, where the water and a warm breeze seemed to peek around every corner like a waving neighbor.

That was certainly the case in Bronte, the hilly, coastal suburb in Sydney's east where we happened to end up after I lucked into a rental there that someone else had abandoned. I'd chosen the neighborhood mostly because it wasn't too far from the airport and the local primary school had a Spanish teacher, which meant my children would not totally lose the language they'd grown up with in Miami (where they were born), in Mexico City (where we lived for four years), and in Brooklyn (where they attended a bilingual public school). I also felt like I'd won the lottery: the house was just a ten-minute walk from the beach. The landlord even accepted my proposal for discounted rent.

I flew back to New York and stayed just long enough to work out a place to store all our belongings. We weren't sure we'd stay for more than a couple of years. Since shipping everything would take forever, the four of us arrived in Sydney for good on the first of March without much of anything. Besides clothes, all we carried were a few rolled-up photos and vintage Cuban movie posters, two wool rugs from Oaxaca, and Wolfie, a giant stuffed wolf that Amelia begged us not to abandon. Wolfie took up a duffel bag all on her own.

The drive to Bronte was relatively short, and Diana and the children were quiet. I was excited to see what they would make of my choice. The house wasn't exactly luxurious. The floors and windows were grimy when the real estate agent showed it to me, the gray carpeting upstairs was already starting to buckle, and there was no backyard, but the place was larger than our apartment in Brooklyn, and it allowed for a glimpse of the ocean from our upstairs balcony. When we pulled our stuff inside, Diana and the kids seemed pleased.

Our new home was almost entirely empty except for a couch, a small dining table, and three beds. Looking around, our voices echoing off the walls, it was clear that we were starting from scratch. New house. New country. New life. Without knowing what it would entail, that was what I wanted. But I was worried that the kids would face a tough transition. The one thing I loved about New York was their school, so when we visited Bronte Public School a week after our arrival, I was already on edge.

When we heard that our timing meant we would have to figure out what grade would work best, I hesitated. They had already done six months of school, Baz in second grade, Amelia in first grade, which meant they could stay at that level or jump ahead. Baz was born in February, squarely within the boundaries for what the Australians call "year three," so that was an easy one, but for Amelia, it was tougher. She was born in July: she would either be one of the oldest in first grade or the youngest in second.

Diana and I looked at each other. I could see certainty in her dark brown eyes. "We choose the bigger adventure," she said, relying on that phrase that guided us through previous moves and dilemmas. We pushed them both up a grade.

The first few months were a whirlwind of figuring out a new place. It rained every day for a month, making us wonder about the amazing Sydney weather we'd heard about. We bought a car and nearly took off the side mirrors on every journey as we struggled with driving on the left side of the road. Mostly, though, we eased through the routine we'd gotten used to after so many relocations. Get a new phone. Find the grocery store. Work out banking. Buy and assemble IKEA furniture, preferably without a knockdown, drag-out argument.

We'd gotten pretty good at moving—neither Diana nor I had lived anywhere for more than five years at a time—and the rhythms of setting up a new house in a new place seemed to bring us back together in ways New York never had. Novelty and motion seemed to be good for us.

Diana knew Australia better than me, even if her experience

of Sydney occurred as a broke university student many years earlier, so she was the first to scrutinize our surroundings with context. The place looked richer, she said. More diverse, more globally connected.

As was often the case, I looked at our new home mostly through the lens of work. I was opening the first *Times* bureau in Australia since World War II. I had just a few weeks to find employees, get an office going, and assign or write a wide enough range of stories to show that we were committed to seriously covering the country and the region. I figured I could win over my bosses and our new Australian audience with overwork, as I always had. Plus, I'd done what I could to prepare, speaking to novelists, reading history books, watching movies like *The Castle*.

But it wasn't enough. I started out with a few bogus assumptions, mostly based on a lingering bias that told me the way things worked in America should be how they work everywhere. When I tweeted about tips—asking if people really didn't tip in Australia and if that might explain my experience with slow restaurant service—I took it right on the chin. A tsunami of replies hit back on Twitter, explaining that while Australians do tip a little when they want, the country's high minimum wage—cemented into law before just about every country in the Western world—aimed to create a society where workers didn't have to rely on the largesse of strangers for survival. That was not something I had considered. Point taken.

Beyond gratuities, I was also confused by the Australian habit of sitting in the front seat of taxis, creating less of a chauffeur vibe, the swearing on broadcast television, and, of course, there was the drinking.

Some of my earliest lessons in the Australian way involved boozy meals. I mostly remember my introduction to the practice, a lunch in the city's center at a restaurant with Scandinavian design and perfectly cooked meat. The foreign policy expert who had proffered the invite ordered a bottle of wine and then another, killing the afternoon's productivity as we talked of neighborhoods and children as much as actual work. I left, blinded by a warm sun slicing between office towers, stressed about what I needed to get done.

Then Diana got a ticket in the mail for $600 after a camera caught her making some kind of illegal turn. Neither of us could believe the dollar amount. Diana, who rarely did anything wrong while driving, was angry. I was intrigued. *Is Australia laid-back or rigid?* Unlike other places where I'd been a newcomer, there was no language barrier. Australia was just a place I couldn't read.

The country's political discourse was also confusing. On one hand, Australia was a haven for immigrants, where the prime minister at the time, Malcolm Turnbull, often bragged of multicultural success and a wide-open welcome for skilled workers, students, and refugees. Nearly half of Australia's twenty-five million people had been born abroad or had at least one parent born abroad. On the other hand, Australia's offshore detention program for asylum seekers trying to arrive by boat violated every rule of decency and international human rights, leading to regular scolding from the United Nations.

The appeal of Australian family life was much easier to grasp. I kept running into Australians who had lived the expat life in London, Jakarta, Singapore, and New York, who all told me they couldn't wait to get back to Australia to raise their kids. It wasn't hard to see why. The climate and culture let kids be kids. Every morning, I saw small children walking to school alone. Every Friday, Baz and Amelia joined the entire school for sports. Cricket, soccer, basketball, swimming—as second and third graders, they traveled and competed against other schools for most of the day as part of their public-school curriculum. And every week, they came home full of energy and stories.

In New York, they barely had a half hour of recess. In Sydney, they had triple that, plus sports. I was starting to think my love for their Brooklyn school had been misplaced. Not that the teachers in Bronte were trying to win me over. They absolutely were not.

"There's nothing wrong with losing," Baz's teacher told me after his team suffered a blowout in Australian Rules football, which the school pushed him to play. I was wondering why she didn't guide him toward what he knew and loved—soccer. But with her standing before us in black workout pants, her hands on her hips, I could see there was no use asking; she just assumed we'd understand the value of a completely new sport where he would go on to lose nearly every single game he played.

The school also required a lot more public speaking compared with their school in Brooklyn—and parents were actually expected to be around. School assemblies were frequent multiple-hour affairs, well attended by mothers and fathers from all professions, some in suits, others in work boots and the high-visibility neon that seemed to be a mark of laborer pride. I made sure to go, but I often earned dirty looks for answering emails on my phone. (Apparently this was a school that didn't care about my *important work*. No one asked about my job.) It was there, in the gym that smelled of sausage, after the kids sang the Australian anthem emphasizing that the nation was "girt by sea," that we first heard about Nippers. A mom with a short blond bob brought it up, followed by a half dozen others.

"You're signing them up for Nippers, right?"

"You have to sign them up for Nippers."

"You know what they would love? Nippers."

By that point, I'd worked out that it was something fun involving the ocean. It took me a little longer to learn that Nippers is a unique cultural creation common enough to be loved without being deeply studied. Volunteers, mostly other parents who have trained as lifesavers (aka lifeguards), run the program at each of Australia's surf clubs—the community centers that appear on most of the country's beaches. Every year, they enroll around sixty-two thousand kids from ages five to fourteen, and the numbers have been growing even when competition with screens has led to declines in participation rates for other sports and physical activities. That helped explain why everyone wanted us to do it—Nippers was gaining momentum.

Only trouble was, we hadn't been in the water much, since we arrived in autumn and Nippers began in the spring. And no one explained what Nippers actually involved. It was like a lot of the Australian journalism I was reading—there was an assumption of knowledge. People were expected to be up to speed with no need for background. I couldn't tell if that was a journalistic tic or a sign of some broader national attribute. Maybe a preponderance of trust in the reader? Perhaps compulsory voting meant everyone paid closer attention to the intricacies of public policy? Or maybe journalists and their sources were just talking to each other.

It made me search for additional entry points. With Nippers, we were invited in.

Well, sort of. After lunch one day, I wandered down to the Bronte surf club to sign up Baz and Amelia. I looked around the two-story brick building sitting right up against the beach, trying to work out where or when someone would be there to help. All I could see was crumbling concrete, rust, and a sign that said the water temperature was seventeen degrees Celsius. I typed the number into my phone: a chilly sixty-three Fahrenheit. A few days later, I stopped by again and found a woman with long reddish hair sitting at a computer in a room with no windows.

"Is this where I can sign up for Nippers?" I asked.

She pointed to a pile of papers without looking away from the screen.

"There's a swim test," she said, keeping her eyes on her computer. "Next week."

"That's fine," I said, trying to sound cheerful.

They were young, and I doubted they'd be pushed beyond their limits.

Looking back, I probably should have paid more attention to her gruff warning and demeanor.

Clearly, for whatever reason, I had miscalculated. After Baz quit the test, I thought about what went wrong. I suppose I was too confident in Baz's abilities. I never expected to have to help him recover from a sporting setback, and given the higher-than-anticipated standards required just to get into Nippers, maybe I'd also underestimated the whole endeavor—both the ocean and what Australia would demand from our children and from me.

I decided to more closely examine our surroundings, starting with the sea I'd first noticed from the plane. I was closer now. I often ran along the coastal walk between Bronte and Bondi, and after Baz's swim test, the view shifted from a vista to photograph to something rougher and more tangible. My kids had never gone swimming past where they could stand, in any ocean, anywhere. They were just eight and seven. Forced to imagine Baz and Amelia being pushed into Bronte proper, I realized that I needed to study what they would be up against, as if it were a bully or enemy army.

All along Sydney's eastern coast, large swells rolled in regularly, making it look like there were trains under the surface. In some areas, the waves seemed to break far out back, while at other times, they crashed on the sand or into cliffs that made the water explode into a burst of white. It was loud, deafening in its dissonance. Whenever and wherever I looked, the water was in constant motion, bashing against the land as if at war. Advance, retreat, advance.

But instead of being pushed away, the Australians around me seemed drawn to it. Nippers was one scene in a lengthy episodic drama. The beaches were packed at sunrise, no matter how heavy the surf or rough the conditions. I saw surfers jumping off the rocks to get to waves the size of two-story homes and swimmers and spearfishing men and women far from shore in areas where (I discovered from the news) sharks were sometimes seen.

Looking at the ocean, trying to figure out what to do with Baz, I was surprised by the gap between the boldness of my

Australian neighbors and my own dithering. I'd always thought the appetite for risk was elemental—either you're the kind of person who jumps out of planes and goes to war or you're not. If I had to define it for myself, I would have said that a risk is anything that scares and excites us at the same time, if we're paying close attention. Big or small, risks are life's imaginable uncertainties—the adventures, disasters, windfalls, or accidents that humans have a role in anticipating and shaping. Given that their outcomes depend partly on skill and knowledge, not just luck, maybe risks are the ultimate tests of our humanity.

But in Sydney, I could see that our responses to those tests can be as varied as the weather and the tides. Each of us is not just strong or weak, brave or neurotic. Culture and context also shape what we see as risky and dangerous or normal and manageable.

I kept trying to picture Baz and Amelia in the waves. They were new. Maybe they just had a lot to learn. Clearly I did too. And if how we engage with risk is shaped over time—if our fears in particular grow from what we're taught and what we absorb from those around us—then I knew I needed to start at the very beginning. *What have I been taught about risk, maybe without noticing? What have we all been taught?*

Risk is as old as life itself, and for as long as *Homo sapiens* have walked the earth, we've been forced to make decisions involving uncertainty and danger to ourselves and our offspring. The urge to fight, freeze, or flee that I saw in Baz by the pool is built into our evolutionary DNA. Our early ancestors passed on the genes of the very cautious and the very brave—those who avoided the lion at the watering hole or slayed the big cat and cooked it up for dinner. Humanity has always held the potential to manage the most severe and most minor risks with bravery, cowardice, or everything in-between.

But what about once we gathered into larger groups and societies, in different places, with different cultures and more sophisticated threats? How much of our approach to risk is shared, how much is distinctive, and how much comes from our particular time and place?

Most scholars start their accounts of risk with games of chance, noting that nearly every ancient society seemed to have enjoyed some kind of gambling—cards originated in Asia; the Aztecs bet on board games; dice, originally played with a knuckle bone known as an astragalus, have been found at archaeology sites across Europe and in Egyptian tomb paintings from 3500 BC.[ii] But it's not until 1661 AD that the word *risk*, as a noun applied to mass experience, appears in the English language.[iii] It is believed to have come from a classical Latin word, *resect*, with the sense of a rock, crag, or reef that cuts—alluding to the hazards of the sea.

It has also been argued that risk's roots can be found in the Latin word for fortune (*resicum*) and an Arabic word (*rizq*), which can mean blessing. But in 1661, the *Oxford English Dictionary* tells us, the word was defined as "peril, jeopardy, danger, hazard, chance." Four of those synonyms trigger anxiety and dread. From the very birth of the English word, when it was first applied to what anyone might experience, our sense of "risk" was weighted toward fear.

In seventeenth-century England, there was a lot of "peril, jeopardy, danger, hazard, chance." Human life had always been precarious, but a greater concentration of people meant a multiplication of risk—a population boom at the time produced more homelessness and destitution. In the palace, smallpox killed the heir to the throne in 1612, pushing ahead the arrogant King Charles I, whose belief in his own divine right led to a civil war in 1642. There were also recurrent crop failures, an outbreak of the bubonic plague in 1665 that killed 15 percent of London's population, and a fire that destroyed most of the city's buildings a year later.[iv] Risk was everywhere, and few people could have connected it with reward.

I remembered some of these details from when I first encountered the seventeenth century at university, in an honors seminar focused on Western civilization. I can still see myself at a heavy wooden table trying to make sense of it all, leaning back in spindly chairs that creaked like they'd come from 1620s Paris. Every week, my professor, a tall, regal woman with a crown of white curly hair and a classics PhD from Harvard, gave us a new book or two from the period to digest with a dozen classmates. Among the more famous Englishmen like Thomas Hobbes and John Locke was a singular Frenchman: Blaise Pascal.

All these writers were trying to grapple with the extremities of their time and the momentous doubt science and mathematics had begun to cast on traditional religion. But Pascal, a philosopher-scientist of the highest order, he was my favorite. I greatly admired the humility and existential angst in his essays, or "Pensées." I was especially fond of a passage of his that called for humankind to see its own importance in context—as something between a speck in the universe and a mighty colossus.

"For after all what is man in nature?" he wrote. "A nothing in regard to the infinite, a whole in regard to nothing, a mean between nothing and the whole; infinitely removed from understanding either extreme."

In the end, he concluded with a plea for moderation: "Let us then know our limits. We are something, but we are not all."[v]

I'd forgotten how much I admired that.

Returning to Pascal for his humanity and intellect, I also discovered something I'd missed entirely—Pascal had been a giant of risk analysis, one of the first people to work out the basics of probability. In 1654, working with a lawyer from Toulouse named Pierre de Fermat, he changed the way the world would assess risk for centuries to come by solving a problem known as "the points."[vi] It involved a game of chance with bouncing balls where six goals were needed to win, with the question: How do you divide the rewards if the game is interrupted when one player is ahead?

The person who introduced the problem in 1494, Luca Pacioli, insisted that fairness and mathematics required that the pot be divided according to past tosses.[vii] So in the game to six, if one player had three points and the other had one, the leading player deserved three times the winnings of the person losing.

Pascal and Fermat approached the challenge in different ways, but together they proposed a 180-degree turn in perspective. They sought a solution by calculating all the possible future outcomes. They created a method to look ahead at what would probably happen.

Pascal's breakthrough involved making such calculations easier, partly by creating a triangle of numbers that captured what to expect from each new throw of the ball.[viii] Or think of a coin toss. If you throw the coin three times, there is only one combination that will yield three heads (HHH), but there are three that will deliver two heads and one tail (HHT, HTH, THH), along with three more that give one head and two tails (HTT, THT, TTH), and one for all tails (TTT). This is the pattern "1, 3, 3, 1" in the third row of Pascal's triangle, as seen below (the top row is considered the zero row for counting purposes).

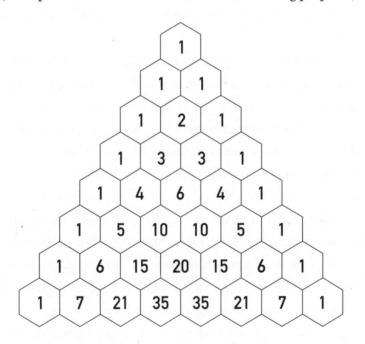

Pascal's analysis was an early example of using expected values (what you can expect to happen, based on some kind of action), which would become the basis for the first treatise on probability by Christiaan Huygens, a Dutch physicist, in 1657. Today, weather forecasts, economic models, insurance, and casinos all rely on what Pascal and Huygens developed.[ix]

But being able to calculate the odds of possible outcomes had consequences beyond the practical or corporate: once we felt we could assess the odds, we began to feel we could control and even beat them. The tool of calculation became a tool of mastery and dominion. Pascal, the sickly son of a tax officer, helped create the conditions for a belief—and the expectation—that through our own mental efforts, we can predict and manage even the most complex hazards. Humans are exceptional because we can calculate. Toward perfection! Toward safety! And so the notion of a "calculated risk" was born.

While it was far beyond me to calculate all the possible outcomes of my children's interactions with the ocean, I still drew some comfort from the idea of Pascal's triangle. It was visual proof of what I wanted to believe—that the chance of harm was small and with lessons and experience would grow smaller. My anxieties could (usually) be contained in this cool lattice of logic. But Pascal's own confidence didn't last. At the peak of his career, he fled from reason back to faith, to an extreme Catholic sect called the Jansenists, who argued that human knowledge and scientific investigations were useless; all that mattered was God.[x] Even that was somehow reassuring. Pascal embodied his times—the inflection point when God died and modernity began—and if he could have his doubts about rational thought and lose touch with moderation, then I could forgive my own inconsistency.

Risk, after all, is more stressful than fortune or fate or divine providence. When you don't believe God is pulling all the strings or laying out the safety net below, the scales are lifted from your eyes, and all you've got is reason and intuition to calm your fears.

At least in the American conception of risk, where each of us is responsible for whatever happens in our lives, the way risk elevates reason and choice feels like an enormous burden. A frightening burden. No wonder so many people (especially those of us without much faith or mathematical genius) are hesitant to try new and risky endeavors—we believe we're responsible for anything that might go wrong, in a world of "peril, jeopardy, danger."

That seemed to be what Pascal couldn't get out of his head: the sudden weight of responsibility dropped on us all. Indeed, he is most famous today for the wager to which his name has been attached, in which he reasoned that the odds favor belief in God, even though God's existence cannot be definitively proven. Looking back now, I think he was trying to soothe himself with what amounts to risk mitigation. If you live as if God exists, he reasoned, you avoid the worst-case scenario of eternal damnation; if you're wrong and there is no God, you lose nothing. The safest bet is the bet on God.

Pascal's wager is where religion and calculation meet. It was an existential attempt to reduce anxiety, just like his entire life—just like all our lives. Maybe that's what early modernity taught us all: risk begins with fear, followed by a search for control and peace of mind.

But what did humanity actually do with risk's new burden of responsibility?

After college, I became a reporter because I hate sitting at a desk all day and I like to ask questions. So I started calling some of the people whose work I'd been studying. Historian Emily

Nacol's *An Age of Risk* explores how early ideas of risk shaped Enlightenment thinkers. When I gave her a call at the University of Toronto, she argued that British philosophers like Locke and Hobbes contributed to the discussion of risk in early modernity by doing the same thing Pascal did but on a broader scale: they focused on the probability of future outcomes, not for individuals playing games but for all of society.

Locke believed every citizen has a responsibility and a right to guard against the emergence of oppression.[xi] Using the metaphor of a ship taking many turns to follow the wind (the ocean is a constant presence in early risk theory), he called for the masses to assess the conditions and calculate; citizens have a right to rebel preemptively if their captain is heading toward cruelty or danger. Locke accepted risk as a reality of modern life and emphasized the need for anticipatory action: "Men can never be secure from Tyranny, if there be no means to escape it, till they are perfectly under it: And therefore it is, that they have not only a Right to get out of it but to prevent it."[xii]

Nacol told me that Hobbes, however, had a very different view of risk.

"Hobbes is the weird outlier in my book because he wants to displace it," she said. "He sees uncertainty as the most negative thing we can ever experience."[xiii]

In *Leviathan*, Hobbes made clear that he was a pessimist. The life of man, he wrote, is "solitary, poor, nasty, brutish, and short."[xiv] He put forward the idea of a strong sovereign because he saw unpredictability as a threat, a boil to be lanced, rather than a boat trip to be managed.

"Men," he wrote, "desire security above all things."[xv]

According to Nacol, various elements of the Locke-Hobbes tension still play out today. Some institutions push risk management outward to many people, as Locke did, expecting them to make choices on their own or together in groups. Others take a top-down approach—à la Hobbes—granting greater control to authorities who enforce obedience or nudge the public toward better behavior.

The dichotomy often appears in public health debates. Should cigarettes be banned, or should they just have safety labels giving people the information they need to make decisions of their own? But on a personal level, Nacol said, most people just want whichever approach reduces risk to zero so they do not have to think about it.

"One thing that's been true since the idea of risk was born is that humans are not very good at risk calculations," she said. "We all want to get rid of it. What's different is how, and I do think a lot of people are seeking elimination. How do we displace risk entirely?"[xvi]

That seemed to be how I was feeling about the ocean—I craved a guarantee of safety even though I knew the odds were in our favor. It felt like a relatively new development for me. Was it tied to having kids? To having more education or wealth? Thinking of Baz and Amelia, I could hear a familiar phrase in my head—*I want to give you the life I never had*. I asked Nacol if our societal safety seeking might be tied to class, money, and children. "You should look at the rise of insurance in early modernity," she told me. "It's a way of calculating and thinking ahead; but it is also about profit."

Nacol pointed me to a historian of science named Lorraine

Daston, who was a bit of an insurance obsessive. Her book *Classical Probability in the Enlightenment* picked up where Nacol's left off. Instead of focusing on the well-known theorists of the time, Daston dug into the documents and details of the era, creating a portrait of fits and starts in the way reason and math were applied to real-world risks, from sinking ships to young parents suffering unexpected death.

The section on life insurance, which emerged in eighteenth-century London, was surprisingly fascinating.[xvii] As Daston explained with geeky zeal, it was the form of insurance that offered a public debut for the calculations of probability that Pascal and others had developed, but it was also, at its core, a product of privilege, parental responsibility, and anxiety. It was the first time humans sold financial security and rewarded caution on a societal level.

The company that set the template was the Equitable, or in its full version, the Society for Equitable Assurance on Lives and Survivorships.[xviii] Formally established in 1762, the Equitable was led and shaped even before it was incorporated by a mathematician named James Dodson, who sought to remove any hint of gambling from the business. When he published his first table of premiums in 1756, life insurance lived in the underworld: people bet on whether someone who owed money would die before paying.

The Equitable's offering was different. Families could buy equity in the company to protect themselves from economic decline in the case of unexpected death. The prospectus explained that the system was based on Dodson's new science of mortality tables, because "although the lives of men separately taken, are uncertain, yet in an aggregate of lives [life expectancy] is reducible to a certainty."[xix] As is the case with insurance today, the fees from those who turned out not to need an early payout would fund payments to those who did. The sudden death of a breadwinner would not force children to go hungry.

Even in such an academic tome, there was a suggestion that modern risk management had a parental angle. Curious about that, I emailed Daston, a professor who teaches in the United States and in Germany. We agreed to meet over video chat. With her book-strewn office in Berlin behind her and graying hair in her eyes, she told me that early insurers were selling more than just a new financial product.

"They're selling a vision of security," she said, "which previously would have been unimaginable."[xx]

In her view, the Equitable's salesmen and clients were part of a broader cultural shift toward the emergence of a self-conscious middle and upper-middle class determined to give their children a better, safer life than their own.

Daston put her finger on the difference between luck and risk while hinting at an early version of helicopter parenting's connection to control and self-belief: "These were the spokesmen for a meritocracy where hard work and talent, not winning the lottery, were the surest way to advancement; for a secure social order in which the well-off today would not find themselves poor tomorrow; for a sense of familial responsibility so strong that it reached beyond the grave."

I recognized the urge. In 2010, while I was covering the earthquake in Haiti that killed more than two hundred thousand people, an older colleague joked that I'd better have good life insurance. Until then, I didn't realize I could or should think of protecting my family postmortem, but when I got back to Miami, Diana and I rushed to buy a policy and I remember feeling proud. My own parents never had much money growing up, and the payout, in the case of my untimely death, amounted to more than I could ever imagine earning. Sitting in our Miami kitchen, watching Baz sleep in his infant swing, I liked the idea of all that security flowing to my loved ones. And apparently, I was just the latest customer in a long line of emotional safety seekers.

Daston told me that when life insurance first emerged, even pastors jumped on board, actively promoting companies like the Equitable to their parishioners. A century or so after Pascal fled to religion, religion sought solace in probability. It signaled a much broader shift in risk management, with the duty of care pushed down to parents.

To be fair, the risks were shared among many. Life insurance represented a pragmatic and creative collectivism of sorts, but with a new aspect: the relationship was purely transactional. By the end of the eighteenth century, class had indeed become a part of the modern risk equation. In order to benefit from others, you had to be able to pay—the best parents are those who cough up whatever it takes to protect their children forever, the insurance industry told the world.

There's nothing wrong with trying to protect our children from our own untimely death, of course, but the Equitable also set in motion a dynamic that insists no one can ever be too careful. The company's leaders promised cold calculation, but according to a mathematical consultant's report from 1771, they were cautious in every way, using the mortality table with the shortest life spans to reduce the length of potential payouts and charging even more for any sort of behavior deemed risky, from drinking to travel.[xxi] And the safety of the company was paramount. Even when 60 percent of the firm's assets were considered "surplus," even when its own calculations found that most of its money would never be needed, it did not pay out dividends as it had promised.

The model of exorbitant fees in exchange for calm soon became the industry standard. Along the way, the Equitable's original selling point—a product based on statistics and logic—was tossed aside. Math no longer ran the business. Decisions were made based on fear and the promise of money creating emotional security.

Daston gave the paradigm a label that stuck with me long after I read it: "pathological prudence."[xxii]

In the end, I couldn't let Baz quit Nippers before he'd even begun. I didn't want to give in to pathological prudence. Knowing more about the origins of risk and parental anxiety, I started to see Baz's failure as an opportunity to learn more about ourselves, Australia, and maybe even human nature.

We had a month until Nippers officially started in late October. On the next sunny Saturday, Baz and I went to the pool that would be our testing ground, Bronte Baths, a thirty-meter stretch carved from the rocks at Bronte's southern end.

I'd read somewhere that the pool had an illustrious history. Poking around on government websites that seemed surprisingly eager to document local swimming achievements, I discovered it was the place where the Australian crawl earned its name, with a boy not much older than Baz. In 1898, a ten-year-old named Alick Wickham, who had recently moved to Sydney from the Solomon Islands, entered a two-lap race and wowed the crowd with a stroke none of them had seen before. [xxiii] At the time, competitive swimmers pulled themselves along on their sides, sliding through the water using a scissor kick. But according to the International Swimming Hall of Fame, Wickham swam facing forward with his head held fairly high. He threw his arms into the water with his elbows bent and kicking up and down with his feet, prompting George Farmer, a well-known Sydney swimming coach, to shout, "Look at that kid crawling!"

Some historians argue the stroke is ancient, and others insist Indigenous Americans introduced the crawl to the West during a race in London in 1844.[xxiv] But the Australian "crawl" from Bronte caught on and spread. With a handful of adjustments, it's the stroke used in every freestyle contest at the Olympics today and what most swim lessons teach.

Baz didn't know or care about any of that. Walking down to the water, his dark eyes glaring at me, he was as surly as he had been when we left his first attempt to pass the test.

"Just do a few laps, and I'll time you so we know what you need to do," I told him.

I tried to sound encouraging. Later on, I learned about all the swim coaches and classes in Sydney at the pools that are nearly as common as basketball hoops in New York. But I was unaware and American: I thought swim lessons were for beginners, while training for a swim test was an individual act.

"You need to know that you can get better at something," I told my son.

He walked a few steps behind me the entire way, trying to slow us down. A stroll that should have taken five minutes edged close to fifteen. At the pool, he crossed his arms and stared straight ahead in silence, refusing to jump in.

"You're lucky because so many things in life come easy to you," I told him. "So this is hard. So what? It will be good for you to learn how to do something that's hard."

No response.

I tried a softer sell. "It will feel so great if you do it. Seriously."

Still nothing. We stood there together for a few minutes, maybe less, until my patience reached its limit. I was starting to get worried about him in the water, any water, any time.

"You need to get in the pool. I need to know you can do this."

He turned, looked me straight in the eyes, and screamed, "NO!" He's always had a loud voice, ever since his first cry. When I cut the umbilical cord after he was born and he let out his first yell, it sounded like he had an amplifier hidden somewhere in his chest. I'd gotten used to it as he got older, but I never liked it—especially not when he broke it out in public.

I chuckled at first, that awkward laugh my own father had often used to buy a moment to think. But really, I was furious. So I picked up my son and threw him into the pool.

"Swim," I yelled.

It felt like something my dad would have done, but the sink-or-swim method didn't appear to be common practice in Bronte. I could feel the other parents around me staring. Far too angry to look back at them, I pulled out my phone so I could time Baz going back and forth. The first lap, he kept his head out of the water, sobbing loud enough for me to hear. I watched him without looking around. It took him less than a minute. The second lap, he swam head down, crawling at a comfortable pace.

When he got out, we were both a shade below nuclear. We walked over to the beach where Diana and Amelia were swimming in an area called the bogey hole. Protected from the surf by piles of rocks, it was where the toddlers and youngest children could swim with some degree of safety. Baz put down his goggles and ran into the water. Laughing and splashing around, he suddenly looked smaller and younger. I wanted to give him a hug.

"He's so tough to deal with," I told Diana, sitting next to her on the sand.

As I explained what happened, I couldn't tell if she felt I'd handled it all wrong, and I wasn't sure either. Maybe he wasn't being stubborn. Maybe he was just afraid.

"Don't worry about it," Diana said. "There's a lot to learn." Diana was always a rule follower, the eldest daughter of Cuban immigrants who rarely needed hard boundaries to be well behaved. She was happy with the way she'd been parented and figured we'd repeat it even if our kids were less obedient than she had been.

I was more uncertain, probably because I was the product of an inconsistent parenting style that often shifted from hands-off and encouraging to overbearing and judgmental. As a father, I had no idea what to keep from my past and what to abandon. Unsure of when to push and when to protect, I didn't feel like I belonged with the always-nurturing crowd or the get-tough dads who never showed their emotions.

In New York, I found that I was yelling, a lot—when Baz and Amelia fought like siblings do, when they resisted doing something new, and when they did not obey my commands. I blamed work stress, which also led to a lot of yelling with Diana, who often felt her own needs, career, and life came second. When we went to a restaurant, I instinctively took the best seat at the table. When I wanted to exercise, I did, without thinking of the timing or how it would affect her plans.

As both a partner and a parent, I lacked peripheral vision—I could be as oblivious as a blind and untrained Labrador, breaking things without intent. Dealing with Baz in particular, I often felt raw and hurt because my attempts to solve problems rarely seemed to match up with whatever was going on in his head. Even as I was literally throwing Baz into the deep end, I felt like I was the one drowning, grabbing for air or solid land. All I knew how to do was keep trying. All I wanted to do was loosen up.

So a few days later, I dragged Baz to the pool again after he finished school. It was a glorious spring day, sunny and warm but not too warm, colored with the golden light Australia sells to potential tourists.

Baz was in a slightly brighter mood. He seemed to accept that a swim was inevitable, that no amount of resistance would work. When we got to the pool, he moved slowly, but he put on the goggles we'd bought without any pressure from me. The goal this time would be to swim farther, not necessarily faster. To get him to a point where he didn't tire out too early. The water sparkled, sun glazed and silver over navy blue.

"All right," I told him, "this time, I'm coming in with you."

"Really?"

"Yeah, why not?"

I dived in. Splashing into the pool felt like jumping into a tray of melting ice. My body stiffened. Baz carefully walked in after me and shivered. I just tried to breathe. We started swimming. Baz, naturally competitive, seemed to think we were racing. Suddenly he started moving much faster than he did before, while I breaststroked next to him.

"Good," I said, trying to sound like a coach. "Keep going."

After two laps, he asked to take a break. With some pushing from me, we decided to aim for two more. I stayed at one end as he went back and forth. It felt good to see him striving. When he really tried, he seemed to be swimming as well as some of the other kids his age on the day he failed his test. He didn't seem to hate it either, though I did notice that he kept his head above water too often. And he was still too slow.

At home afterward, I reported our progress to Diana.

"Maybe we should have them take some lessons," she said.

It felt a little like defeat, but lessons were common in Australia long after children learned the basics. Another parent had told Diana about a couple of options, one at a nearby university, another outdoors in Bondi at a place called Icebergs. The next day, she made a few calls. The indoor pool was booked. Baz and Amelia enrolled with the Mermaid Swim Academy at Icebergs—not exactly a name to be welcomed. Diana bought them each a wet suit.

At first, they were nervous and resistant. It was yet another new thing, yet another new teacher. But the pool was a post-card, perched on Bondi's southern end, draped in sunlight, with bikini-clad women sunbathing alongside men with six-pack abs while retirees with gray hair on their chests took turns swimming laps. I'd never seen any place like it.

Once Baz and Amelia got into the pool with two or three other kids, they listened to and obeyed their cheerful instructors. Amelia, who used to scream through every swim lesson when she was a toddler in Mexico, seemed to be a natural, her arms entering the water at what looked to me like the perfect angles, her face turning at just the right moment before snapping back under. Seeing Baz behave like a stellar student as well, crawling forward, I was struck with a mix of pride and shame. Pride in his efforts, shame because I still believed his success or failure fell squarely on my shoulders, yet he was better off without me.

I asked one of the swim teachers if she thought Baz would be able to do 150 meters.

"Oh yeah," she said. "Definitely."

After a few lessons, Diana discovered that the woman who ran the swim school, known only as Jo Mermaid, had a connection to the local surf club community, enough to be trusted with Nippers swim tests. That meant Baz could do his swim assessment at Icebergs after one of his lessons. The following Tuesday, at around 4:00 p.m., I got a text from Diana with just two words: "He passed."

At home, Baz smirked when I asked him how it felt to triumph after failing, hinting that it felt better than he wanted to admit. For a moment, I felt like slightly less of a paternal failure. I guess the pushing worked? Or maybe it was the letting go, allowing someone else to teach him? Regardless, there was something powerful in seeing him conquer a new fear and realize that he was more capable than he'd thought.

It felt like we'd made a family discovery. There was something out there that we wanted to chase, for him and for all of us. To be part of a club, to learn about the ocean, to become, what? Brave? Aquatic? Australian?

TWO

Nippers

How we became so fragile; Martin Seligman and the
problem of self-esteem; the Americans start surfing

On the first Sunday of Nippers, we were all clueless but curious enough not to complain. We rose early, ate breakfast, and collected the necessary gear: wet suits, goggles, colored swim caps (green for Baz, orange for Amelia), and bright pink Lycra rash guards or rashies that I guessed were meant to help the children be easily seen and tracked in the rough water. As we approached the beach, we could see a mix of clouds and sun, with choppy seas and waves taller than our children.

"I don't want to go," Baz said.

"I'm scared," said Amelia.

"You're going to be fine," I told them. "Keep moving."

Bronte Beach is small, just a few hundred meters across, sitting at the bottom of a narrow gully with rocks and homes on each side and the Bronte Baths pool carved into a cliff at the southern end. It's less touristy than Bondi, a couple of kilometers north, and more dangerous. Only Tamarama—the beach between Bondi and Bronte—has a higher frequency of rescues and drownings. On some summer days, there are more than one hundred people saved across all three beaches, which sit in the same local council.

None of them looked anything like where I played as a child on the Atlantic coast, with its long, flat barrier islands that make every section of surf look like another. Bronte is a geological vortex. On any given day, there are steep drop-offs into the water that come and go with shifting sands. Swells from the south deliver waves that sometimes climb over four meters or thirteen feet, and there are always wrenching rip currents where the water from wave after wave races back out to sea, sometimes in a clear and obvious direction, other times with great, confounding turbulence.

Our first Sunday for Nippers appeared to be entirely average: the waves were chest-high from trough to crest, slamming into the shore; the rips were strong; the tidal line in the sand was jagged, like it had been drawn by an angry two-year-old scribbling with a pen.

When we reached the surf club entrance, Amelia found her group right away. She recognized a few girls from her school, including a few friends, which distracted her enough to smile. Baz's squad had more strangers and more boys whose bodies, even at such a young age, looked built for the water, with wide shoulders, narrow waists, and long torsos.

His instructors were Al, whom we'd met at Baz's first swim trial, and a skinnier dad named Guy. Both were around my age but healthier, with fewer wrinkles on their foreheads and less body fat. They introduced themselves and checked names off a list.

"All right, boys, today we're doing to do a little water and a little sand," Al said.

A circle of mothers and fathers in yellow Bronte caps surrounded them and nodded. A handful of other parents wore bright orange rashies that said "water safety" in big, important black letters.

The day began with something called flags. All the boys lie down flat, side by side, facing the ocean. About twenty meters or yards behind them, parents planted pieces of rubber hose in the sand. When Al gave them the signal, the boys popped up, ran, and grabbed a piece of hose. With each contest, more of the hoses were taken away.

Baz took to it relatively quickly. He made it through the first few rounds, enough to give him a little confidence. From there, they ran to the pool where they swam a lap, ran up the stairs to a cliff behind the pool, then back down for another lap. Run, swim, run. Run, swim, run. By the third turn, Baz was dragging but in the middle of the pack. He didn't seem entirely miserable.

Amelia's under-sevens class for girls was louder and generally more fun; they still seemed to be in a more playful phase of the program. Her coach, Woz, Diana's old friend, and his deputy, Ollie, led the girls through a relay race in the sand, and then they swam circles in the bogey hole. Many of the girls—there were about fifty of them in all—gathered between activities, chatting and laughing before screaming their way into the cold water.

I was proud of Baz for surviving with minimal complaining. I was proud of Amelia for throwing herself all the way into the task. I felt like I'd just watched some elaborate national ritual with rules and codes I couldn't decipher. Afterward, as we walked back up the hill toward home, I asked the kids what they thought.

"It was actually more fun than I expected," Amelia said.

I looked at Baz.

"It was okay."

The following week, and the one after that, Nippers became more grueling. Craig "Bettsy" Betts, the Nippers director, whom I rarely saw without the serious look of a skipper at sea, was imperturbable, deciding each Sunday morning whether the conditions warranted boldness or caution. In general, he leaned toward action. Baz and Amelia started with small swims into big waves, leading to longer swims and boards out past the breakers and back in. The children may have looked small and fragile—some could barely tie their shoes—but each week, they defied that categorization.

I did not really understand the point of all these drills until I discovered that the official name for the Nippers program was "junior lifesaving." I had figured the goal was to make Baz and Amelia the best they could be, as individuals, like that old U.S.

Army ad from when I was young. In fact, the kids were learning to get in and out of the water as quickly and safely as possible so they could help others do the same.

Along the way, as Bettsy put it, Nippers aimed to "teach our young boys and girls a love of the ocean and the importance of becoming surf proficient." I'd never heard the word *proficient* used as often as I did at the surf club; I may not have heard it at all before I came to Australia, where I learned that the word emerged in the late sixteenth century from the Latin term for advancing. It felt to me like there was optimism there; maybe whatever fears we had could be conquered by advancing, one step or wave at a time.

Nippers did not begin with such philosophical ideas. It was formally organized in the 1960s as a way to bolster the surf life-saving ranks when they started losing members to surfing and the counterculture,[i] when the "me" generation of my parents decided it wasn't cool. The clubs were hardly perfect back then. As Douglas Booth and other historians have pointed out, a lot of them were run by rowdy chauvinists with far less interest in lifesaving than in messing around with their mates.[ii] According to the surfers, the "clubbies" were basically thuggish jocks (and there's still a pretty strong strand of that gruff conformity within the institution now).

But many surf clubs have changed more than their critics realize. The old culture has been diluted by an influx of new members. Women were admitted in 1980 and have taken on leadership roles;[iii] half of Bronte's board of management now consists of women.

Nippers also took off and has continued to grow in strength.

Kids now make up about 35 to 40 percent of Australia's 176,000 surf club members, and with parents signing up alongside them, many clubs are now dominated by families. This is a return to form—some of the first photos from Bronte's surf club, taken around the turn of the twentieth century, show men in old-fashioned swimsuits and young boys around Baz's age standing in the foreground on the sand.[iv] Intergenerational teaching was baked in from the start.

For my kids, Nippers was their first experience with communal parenting. They were learning from the dads and moms of their friends, on land and in the water. In Sydney, parents were expected to be there every week and to participate, even if, like me, they had no idea what they were doing.

The social aspect of it all was as intimidating as the water. It took a while for Diana and me to find our people. We avoided the parents who looked like Instagram influencers, with outfits and straw hats that made them look like the human equivalent of fine wicker chairs. But a lot of the parents were neighbors, and quite a few of those I eyed warily on that first day at the pool turned out to be warm and friendly. On more than one occasion, I met fathers who admitted they knew as little as I did about what was going on.

It soon became apparent that Baz was far from the only one who struggled. Every Sunday, without fail, I saw children in tears, panic in their eyes, eager to skitter away from their instructors. One cool morning, I even saw a father carry his crying son into the ocean much as I threw Baz in the pool, except this particular boy was bigger and older, his gangly legs dragging through the water as he tried to thrash himself free. *Is that...abuse? Or*

angry love? I could easily imagine places in America where someone would have reported that dad for child abuse. In Bronte,
everyone shrugged. The social norms, that swirl of unspoken
psychological expectations that defines life in any community,
produced an appreciation for collective coaxing.

Mothers and fathers who barely knew each other worked
like a coordinated sales team to goad small children into the dangerous Pacific with every trick they could imagine.

"You don't want to be the only one who doesn't get in there,
do you?"

"Aw, come on. You can handle this."

"Just do it once."

Those were the parents Diana and I ended up talking to
most—the smiling and demanding types, maybe because they
calmed our nerves with their optimism. Whether it was Ollie
and Tammy, whose daughter, Saskia, was becoming one of
Amelia's closest friends, or a few of the other dads from Baz's
group, they were ones who trusted that their kids would survive
and learn to appreciate the challenging experience, the ones who
just wanted their kids to try hard, make peace with fear, embrace
the challenge that nature presented, and have a bit of fun.

Each week, though, the Nippers age managers pushed the
kids deeper and further, and our job as motivational parents
became a little harder. Baz and Amelia never really wanted to go
beyond where they had gone before. Even with the other kids,
there was always something they didn't want to do, usually a
long swim past the break. The ocean was never still or easy to
manage. Neither were the little ones in pink Lycra.

One Sunday when the weather and the water had warmed,

Diana found herself playing the role of extracurricular parent when she took on a girl with strawberry blond hair. Woz had been watching her, softly encouraging her with each activity. But when the girls moved on to their third swim and she was the only one still dry, he pushed a little harder.

"You gotta swim if you're in Nippers."

She shook her head. Diana had just successfully convinced a whining Amelia to give it a go, so she decided to help.

"It's beautiful in there!" she said, bending down to the girl's level to maximize enthusiasm. "Think of how great you'll feel!"

The little girl stared at Diana, her hair tangled and messy. "I was sick on Friday," she said.

"But not today, right?"

"I vomited."

I laughed when I heard the exchange. For Diana, it was a rare defeat. For Nippers too. Week after week, the collective push toward risk seemed to work. More and more of the kids completed most of the tasks most of the time. They persisted despite waves crashing on shore with the weight of anvils (each cubic meter of water weighs about a ton) and rip currents that seemed to yank them sideways or out to sea at the pace of an Olympic swimmer. In many cases, I saw a sudden transformation in their eyes—first squinting with fear, then focused straight ahead, alert and engaged.

Witnessing their courage, I felt my own cowardice more deeply. On my runs, I no longer viewed the waves as killers, but I was still lost on how to navigate them. I would hear people point out a rip, and I'd look at the water and see nothing but messy surf. Part of the reason I was drawn to other parents was because

I appreciated their expertise. I didn't trust myself to help Baz or Amelia. I was trusting the group because I had no choice.

I mostly hid all this insecurity. I started to think of Sunday mornings as a version of Michael Caine's famous quote: "Be like a duck, calm on the surface but always paddling like the dickens underneath."[v]

The worst moments were when Baz or Amelia cried and begged me not to make them do something, a swim or a trip out with the boards. I hated seeing them so emotional and wondered how a yes or no would affect their mood for the rest of the day. What also got me was when they just took on some crazy task without me even noticing.

On one occasion, about halfway through the Nippers season, which runs October through March, Amelia just disappeared. She was next to me, then she was gone. It was a windy Sunday, around low tide, when the rocks seem to jut from the earth like the tips of giant spears. She had grown used to using the boards in the bogey hole by then, but now a handful of them were heading out into the ocean. Deep into the ocean.

When I figured out where she was, she was following a bunch of the other girls but a few dangerous seconds behind. I saw her running straight out with a board, paddling over a small wave, but then getting picked up, flipped over, and dropped by the larger set wave that followed. The powerful whitewash rolled her in near the rocks. When she finally came up, her thick brown hair a knot of salt and sand, she ran to me, crying and coughing.

"I don't want to go again, Daddy. Don't make me go again."

She looked small but strong, with the same dark skin and broad shoulders as her mother. I hugged her and consoled her until she calmed down, mostly to give myself more time to think. *Should she go back out?*

"You can do this, Amelia," I told her. "It's hard but you'll feel better if you try again."

She shook her head side to side with unmistakable clarity. The other girls were starting to head back in; maybe we missed our moment. Or was I being softer because she's a girl?

The following week, she was back on the board, a little more cautious but alert, focused, and determined. Watching her push into a wave as big or bigger than the one that knocked her back last time, I thought of William Blake, the darkest of the Romantic poets, the only one I really liked: Amelia had moved from innocence to experience.

Baz's returns to shore were sometimes even more violent, with several departures and returns leading him or the board into the sandy shore with a body slam of complete discombobulation. Sometimes he came up fighting tears, but the other kids and instructors seemed to ignore those moments. No one made fun of anyone for crying, nor did anyone aim to erase the pain. They just treated it as a passing squall.

With time, Baz learned to enjoy the occasional dumping and rolling. Thankfully, I could also see that his body wasn't quite as easily broken as I had imagined.

In his case, there were two clear signs that Nippers was producing progress and confidence. First, when we went to the beach for fun, in Bondi or Bronte, he bodysurfed near the shore, looking specifically for the waves that would rinse him into the sand and coming up smiling. Second, he started surfing.

He took his first few lessons as Nippers ramped up that

November. In New York that week, if I'd been there, I would have been managing coverage of another mass shooting. A gunman in all black had opened fire on parishioners at a rural Texas church, killing twenty-six people. For some reason, that seemed to be a risk Americans were willing to tolerate.

In Sydney, I went to watch Baz at Bondi, where the waves looked far less frightening with my son riding them to shore, smiling and loving it. Suddenly Nippers felt (to both of us) less torturous and more like a skill worth acquiring for fun and thrills.

A few Sundays later, Diana and I stopped by the surf club in the main gathering space with the gray carpet and the photos of lifesaving champions on the walls. We waved to a few of the parents we recognized and tried to deconstruct the scene. In the broader universe of club members, some people seemed to fit the Australian stereotype of Sydney's Eastern Suburbs: bankers and blonds in "Bronte Carlo." But there was also a dad with curly hair who came from Colombia (I'd heard him tell someone else), along with Asian families, Lebanese families I'd met previously, and, based on their accents, a few Europeans and Americans.

Some of the most active Australians in the club, I later learned, had a prior connection to the Australian military, which made more sense once I discovered the club's history. Others were nurses, doctors, teachers, construction workers, lawyers, therapists, pub owners, and animators. If we'd talked about politics—and we didn't—I have no doubt the range of views would have swung across the spectrum.

It was if the very American problem of disappearing community groups and lost goodwill, identified by Robert D. Putnam's book *Bowling Alone*, from 2000, never caught on.[vi] Togetherness, reciprocity, trust, fun—they were all relatively easy to find in Sydney, from lawn bowling clubs and pub trivia nights to swimming groups. And for families, Nippers was the most accepted welcome point.

The parents, us included, were a self-selected group that shared a love of the ocean and a desire to put our children through the paces of aquatic boot camp. That's how I thought of Nippers as our first summer season wore on in early 2018: combat training for tiny tots. What I was still trying to understand by the end, though, was to what extent boot camp rigor was the goal.

Nippers was not cruel or reckless—it was not tough for toughness's sake. Most of the time, there seemed to be a search for hearty but not ridiculous adventure. Every Sunday in Bronte, the ocean heaved and receded with a different rhythm and force, and the Nippers crew adjusted. The decisions shifted with conditions. Sometimes the leaders of the program decided to add extra lifesavers and really go for a challenge, never at the beach's outer edges by the rocks but somewhere in the moderate middle. Sometimes they avoided a surge of danger, heading to the pool, not the ocean, where the kids swam until they were exhausted.

It was the kind of place where the adults in charge kept a straight face no matter what happened, where every unexpected development—including the occasional child rescue—was taken in stride. Instead of seeking only individual satisfaction or acting in opposition to risk, trying to resist or eliminate it, the entire program, with hundreds of children, seemed to move within the natural risks around them almost like a school of fish. On my most philosophical days, it felt to me as if they were not asserting dominion over nature (which one Aboriginal writer later told me was the greatest sin of Western civilization). Rather, they were trying to gain the local knowledge that was needed to survive and thrive within it—accepting that the danger and the sublime flow together for all living things.

On one of the last Sundays of our first Nippers season, a little over a year after we arrived in Australia, I saw how that commitment could evolve. With the ocean pumping out beach-combers a few meters high, the kids didn't go in that day. It was too dangerous, Al said. The swells and rips left the beach com-pletely closed, so he walked the boys over to a corner of the sand and started talking about the stonefish—it resembles a rock but is the most venomous fish in Australia, with spiky fins that inject poison into your feet if you step on one. It can be fatal. On the pain scale, it usually ranks as a ten out of ten, with an agony that lasts for hours. Some victims have compared the experience to crucifixion.

I'd heard of the fish, like I'd heard of Australia's deadly spi-ders. What I didn't realize was that, along with the blue-ringed octopus, which can fit in the palm of your hand and leave you paralyzed, the toxic little fish lives in rocky ocean pools—like the ones by the bogey hole. Like the ones all our kids played in.

Al left out the crucifixion comparison but not much else. "Venom…death…poison." I heard all those words and more as he talked about both the blue-ringed octopus and the stone-fish. My mouth fell open. The children listened. They all simply nodded. They stayed calm. Al stayed calm. He simply shared the facts, crouching down so the boys could hear him, bouncing on those giant rugby calves.

What I noticed first was the respect the boys reserved for Al's guidance, and then I thought about what he left out. He did not tell the boys to avoid the rock pools. He did not try to scare them into staying away. Instead, he assumed, correctly, that they would play where the stonefish lived because the coast was a glorious playground, and they couldn't help themselves. It was a given: nature holds mostly rewards, with a few hazards too. A good life requires bravery.

I tried to picture the scene in Brooklyn or California. I couldn't do it. I kept thinking of the summer camp we had sent Baz and Amelia to in Park Slope, Brooklyn, where parents with high paying careers would freak out every year because their children, some older than our own, swam in knee-high water with one adult per child. So many of the people we had encountered in Miami and in Brooklyn were both terrified of physical danger for their children and desperate to keep them perpetually happy and worthy of praise. There were soccer games where no one kept score, teachers who, afraid of offending someone, told us that they had no role to play in helping children deal with discussions around race even as protests filled the streets. When anyone dared talk about an uncomfortable subject or something a child was not excellent at, they stepped in a little closer and whispered as if the sound of something difficult might ruin them.

Watching the boys finish with Al, I realized how much of life can be lost to fear and avoidance. Rural and working-class families deal more regularly with risk because they must, but for everyone else, a deeper divide opened up before me. I started to think that a lot of comfortable white-collar parents believed they had risen above anything that might make their children feel or look weak, scared, or confused. In the most extreme cases, parents of means treated hardship with low-level disgust, as something they didn't have time for, as if an extended struggle was beneath them. And especially if there wasn't a "productive" end—a fancy degree, a good job—why bother with such unpleasantness?

Eager to appear perfect, they let their children stay fragile by avoiding imperfection.

What created that cycle of protection and fragility? As the early history of risk has shown, some of it arrived with modernity, which intensified parental fear with the burden of secular responsibility and put caution, children, and wealth together on the same aspirational pedestal.[vii] The pressure to buy safety began with merchant-class parents and pastors pushing life insurance in the eighteenth century, and that was followed by a boost from popular culture. The Romantic poets of the nineteenth century more or less invented the idea of childhood innocence with their "cult of the child." Theater, advertising, art, and children's books all built on the modern belief in a blissed-out youth, which brought a mix of benefits and costs.

The gains for children at the time are well known and undeniable. By the 1880s, child labor was outlawed in England, and universal public education was becoming standardized.[viii] Other countries followed a similar path. But along with greater attention to the condition of children came more prudence and even higher expectations. By the first few decades of the twentieth century, when my grandparents were born, mothers and fathers with stable incomes were expected to guide their children toward upward mobility and the finer things in life, from classical music and summer camp to a university education.

This was around when Sigmund Freud's popularity peaked. In 1909, he came to Clark University in Worcester, Massachusetts, (where I mostly grew up) and gave five lectures at a conference organized by G. Stanley Hall, Clark's president, who was himself a psychology pioneer.[ix] It was Freud's only visit to the United States, and Hall saw him as a guiding light or "the source of it all," as he put it.[x] Both men focused heavily on child development. Together they brought the science of the mind to education and parent-child relations, and once again, caution prevailed. According to Freud and psychoanalytic theory, risk-seeking behavior (especially in the young) was the sign of a diseased mind; it was abnormal for an individual to overcome natural fears, and those who pursued danger were seen to have a death wish.[xi]

The twentieth century began with the leading scientist of the mind telling people more or less the same thing I often heard in upper-middle-class parenting circles, that embracing risk was irrational and might be a sign of mental illness.

I have never been a fan of Freud, or psychology in general. The only time I'd ever seen a therapist (at least before being assigned to cover Iraq) was during my parents' divorce. I was about eight years old when a judge forced me to spend an hour or two with some woman in a musty office who, in a quiet voice, kept probing for signs of damage. I hated the assumption that I had to be seriously messed up because my mother was not around much, having been lost to liquor and drugs. I hated the pity and "aw, poor kid" sympathy I could see in the eyes of adults who thought no motherless child could be "normal." I just felt my normal was different—Dad took care of me, and he did a pretty good job.

Sure, my childhood was confusing and I wished my mother had stayed healthy—she played a half dozen instruments and sang like Stevie Nicks—but I had plenty of love, not just from my father but also my stepmother, my grandmother, my aunts, my teachers, and my coaches. When my mother let me down, as she often did, failing to show up for planned visits or making a scene during family holidays, they were the walls that held me up.

What I failed to realize, however, until I discovered the work of Martin Seligman is that despite my resistance, I'd been surrounded by psychology's influence my entire upbringing. It wasn't just the imprint of Freud that I'd found in court; it was also the way that psychology evolved after World War II in America, shaping my parents' generation and my own.

Seligman opened my eyes with a passage at the start of a chapter called "The Self-Esteem Movement" in his book *The Optimistic Child*:

> We were surprised by what we saw in the public school, though we probably should not have been, because what we saw just reflects the way most American parents of the boomer vintage are now raising their children. Armies of American teachers, along with American parents, are straining to bolster children's self-esteem. That sounds innocuous enough, but the way they do it often erodes children's sense of worth. By emphasizing how a child

feels, at the expense of what the child does—mastery, persistence, overcoming frustration and boredom and meeting challenge—parents and teachers are making this generation of children more vulnerable to depression.[xii]

Sitting in my Sydney home office, I reread the passage. The book was published in 1995. He was describing my own coming of age. Growing up in the '80s and '90s, self-esteem was like perfume: never far away and more intense in some places than others. I remember hearing it discussed by teachers at school. It was always on television—in the news, in sitcoms, in the earnest after-school specials that tried to teach us how to live—and it was one of those powerful forces that parents talked about in hushed tones while drinking coffee or wine.

"I know he's smart but he's been getting in a lot of trouble. I think it's because he has low self-esteem."

I never questioned such statements. I never even noticed that there was anything worth noticing. That's how pervasive self-esteem's influence seemed to be. Or, as Seligman put it, "The self-esteem movement has teeth."[xiii]

After finishing his book, I started exploring its origins. In Mexico, I once pitched a story that would follow the complete path of the cocaine that cost Charlie Sheen his job on the sitcom *Two and a Half Men*. He had just been fired for a wild binge, and I wanted to map the journey to his nose, from the farm where the coca was grown, to the shack where it was processed, to the mules that carried the kilos across the border, to the dealer who handed him the blow. My goal for self-esteem was similar: trace it to the source and beyond.

I reached out to Seligman by email. He's considered one of the most influential psychologists of the past five decades, having discovered the concept of learned helplessness early in his career only to shift toward what's known as positive psychology later on. He's sold millions of books, served as president of the powerful American Psychological Association, and he's been a consultant for everyone from the U.S. military to Geelong Grammar, Australia's most elite high school. I did not expect him to get back to me right away, if at all.

So I burrowed into the reading. One of the first and most surprising things I found was that the so-called father of self-esteem was none other than Nathaniel Branden, a psychotherapist and philosophical dabbler who was an Ayn Rand acolyte and her former lover. Branden's impact on American life deserves far more scrutiny than it has received, but since he wrote and talked about himself quite a bit, it's not hard to piece together a general outline.

He was Canadian, precocious, and tall, with thick hair that he held on to until he died at age eighty-four in 2014.[xiv] In his teen years in Toronto, he considered himself a genius, dropping out of school to teach himself and writing a fan letter to Rand after reading *The Fountainhead*, probably because he saw himself in the novel's hero, the brilliant Howard Roark. She didn't respond at the time, but in 1950 while still studying at the University of California, Los Angeles, he tried again. This time, they connected and started working together immediately. A few years later, they started sleeping together.

"He was 25 years younger than she and, like her, married to someone else," wrote the *New York Times* in its obituary of

Branden, who changed his name from Blumenthal at the request of Rand. "That hardly mattered. Both believed in 'rational self-ishness' and unlimited capitalism, theories Ms. Rand embraced in *The Fountainhead* (1943) and her later blockbuster *Atlas Shrugged*, which was published in 1957 and originally dedicated to both her husband, Frank O'Connor, and Mr. Branden."

As a pair, Rand was the iconoclast and Branden the chief marketer of her ideas. In 1958, he started the Nathaniel Branden Institute, where he helped repackage Rand's objectivism philos-ophy into more digestible lectures, recordings, books, and arti-cles. Over the next decade, the institute spread to cities all over the country and drew in many high-profile fans, including Alan Greenspan, the future chairman of the Federal Reserve.

But not surprisingly for two people who preached about the beauty of selfishness, Branden and Rand eventually split up, romantically and intellectually. In the summer of 1968, Rand announced that their collaboration was over. She claimed that Branden and his wife had taken financial advantage of her (which they denied). As the *Times*'s obituary writer noted, it's also possible that Rand was angry because Branden had recently begun a relationship with a fashion model, Patrecia Scott, who was fifteen years his junior (and would later become his wife).

The very public dispute divided Rand's disciples and pushed Branden in a new direction. A year later, he published a book called *The Psychology of Self-Esteem*, which is considered by many to be one of the first self-help classics.[xv] It drew on the work of Stanley Coopersmith, a young psychology professor at the University of California, Davis, who had devised a test that aimed to measure how good people felt about themselves.

Branden's approach was far more sweeping and would go on to expand with several books that followed. In *Breaking Free* (1970), he wrote about how the hurts and wounds of childhood shape us as adults. In *Honoring the Self* (1980), he wrote about the importance of self-esteem for business and personal relationships.

Branden also wrote books on romantic love, including one written with wife number three, Devers Branden, but his influence—and the influence of self-esteem—reached a high point in the late '80s and early '90s after he wrote a bestseller called *How to Raise Your Self-Esteem*. In that book, published in 1987 with a simple cover of giant purple text and no imagery, he asserted that there was nothing more important than self-regard. Or, as he put it: "How we feel about ourselves crucially affects virtually every aspect of our experience."[xvi]

By that point, he was hardly alone in declaring self-esteem to be the essential element of human existence. A year earlier, a colorful California politician named John "Vasco" Vasconcellos had persuaded the state's Republican governor to sign legislation creating the California Task Force to Promote Self-Esteem and Personal and Social Responsibility, with a budget of $245,000 a year for the next three years.[xvii] He was convinced that low self-esteem led to a wide range of social problems, including unemployment, failure in school, homelessness, and gang warfare. Fix how Americans in particular feel about themselves, the argument went, and you can improve the world.

Vasco and Branden had a lot of support for their beliefs. Near the end of the Cold War, America's obsession with self-worth and individualism had practically become a national religion, presented as the moral and economic antithesis to Soviet Communism. At the same time, the country was struggling with a paroxysm of fear around threats real (crime) and exaggerated (child abduction), all of which led to more interest in the self-esteem movement, which was being presented as the solution for nearly every problem on the horizon.

Americans wanted to feel good about themselves, and they wanted to believe that would make their country better too. Feelings, after all, are a lot easier to fix than, say, systemic racial and economic inequality, which accelerated in the Reagan-Bush-Clinton years. So while hundreds of psychological papers attempted to pin down the impacts of low self-esteem, newspapers, magazines, and television news programs fueled the obsession with headlines such as "Low Self-Esteem Called Major Reason Women Often Pick 'Wrong Man.'" Or "Former Bank Teller Says Low Self-Esteem Led Her to Steal." Or my favorite, from a *Chicago Tribune* advice column: "Body Odor May Be a Sign of Low Self-Esteem."[xviii]

But of all the places where the focus on improving self-esteem blossomed, there was no greenhouse as fertile as child-rearing. Seligman notes that many educators latched on to low self-esteem as a crisis to such a degree that it was common for children to stop being held back a grade if they were failing, lest they be damaged for life with low self-esteem.

Everyone seemed to take part in feel-good interventions. Children in primary school, for example, joined exercises where they'd throw a ball to each other along with a compliment. "I like your shoes" (toss). "You have pretty eyes" (toss). "You're funny" (toss again).[xix] The messaging in classrooms echoed the niceties, and as children moved through the system, grade inflation in the United States began to soar.[xx] Children who used to get Cs got Bs and As.

It was all a bit like the skit from *Saturday Night Live* with Al Franken's life coach, Stuart Smalley—a sad sack trying to be a self-help therapist by declaring, "I'm good enough, I'm smart enough, and doggone it, people like me."[xxi]

The problem with all this feel-good intervention wasn't immediately apparent. Sure it was hokey, but what could be wrong with building people up? The deeper I read into the academic papers and articles of the '80s, the more I also struggled to see why Seligman saw the self-esteem movement as so problematic.

Then I stumbled on an interview with Branden from May 26, 1989, on *Oprah*.[xxii] Oprah was at the peak of her cultural power, and by that point, Branden was Dr. Branden (with a PhD in psychology). He came on at the end of the show, which was usually how Oprah worked. She often started with the dramatic tales of real-life people, then delivered an expert with the insights everyone onstage and the viewers at home had been primed to crave.

What they were discussing that day (as on many other days) were the cycles of negativity, abuse, and cruelty in families. About halfway through, Branden jumped right in to explain that we are all products of our childhoods.

"The real trouble is that we carry on the work of the people who most hurt us long after they're dead and gone," he said. "It's as if we're still saying to the child within that we once were, 'You're stupid, you're unlovable.'"

"Or you're ugly," Oprah chimed in.

"Or you're ugly," he agreed.

And then, he said, we take that experience and turn it outward to others.

"And the next step is that we treat the people we love most in a way that reflects just that lack of internal self-respect. First we do it to ourselves, then we do it to the people we care about most, such as our children."

Not to sound like Oprah, but did you get that? First we do it to ourselves, then we do it to the people we care about most, such as our children.

In other words, when you say or do anything to your children that might hurt their feelings, it's because you don't love yourself, and that's because your own parents hurt you. The lessons are clear: (1) If you don't feel good about yourself, it's probably because someone wronged you when you were a child, not because of anything you did or failed to do along the way to adulthood; and (2) Don't repeat the pattern by saying or doing anything that might make your own kids cry, even if it's a candid, legitimate critique designed to help a child grow into a capable, mature citizen.

The problem with the self-esteem movement, even if the goals were noble or driven by the existential dread that comes with modernity, is that it's always been backward looking, blame dependent, and focused on what is said or felt, not how we behave. Branden and the psychologists of the day believed that if you increased people's self-esteem, they would be more likely to achieve and be bold, self-reliant, strong, and healthy in their work and relationships. They told entire generations that if you feel good about yourself, you'll accomplish all your dreams, and if you don't, that's probably your parents' or teachers' fault, because they didn't give you enough affirmation.

But the gurus of the movement got it backward. A healthy level of self-esteem, as I was starting to see in Nippers and at Baz and Amelia's school, is the *result* of successful action, not the *cause*. As Seligman was trying to say in the passage above, children—and adults—feel good when they *do* well.

The truth is, as any non-American would know, there was never any real crisis of self-esteem in the United States. In fact, later studies showed, most Americans see themselves as above average, a statistical impossibility. Many psychologists now believe that the effort to boost self-esteem has done little more than produce a more bountiful crop of narcissists.[xxiii]

What's increasingly clear is that the massive push to make people feel good about themselves, which continues today, has backfired. Despite Branden and Vasco's odd blur of Randian capitalism and California liberalism—bipartisanship in America seems to work best with the support of selfishness—the most reliable data shows that even as self-esteem levels increased, depression and anxiety rose in the United States, and academic performance declined.[xxiv]

Studies that followed the self-esteem boom, which never really had much empirical evidence anyway, also found that in many cases, repeated praise separated from results actually reduces motivation. As Roy Baumeister, an American psychologist who now teaches at the University of Queensland, explained in a comprehensive review of thousands of self-esteem studies, "If a school program intervenes directly to boost self-esteem regardless of academic performance, then students can enjoy the rewards of self-esteem without making the effort. One major incentive to work hard would thereby be eliminated."[xxv]

Then what happens when the grades come in or the failure becomes too obvious to ignore? Some people crumple into depression, Seligman found. Narcissists tend to get aggressive and violent, according to Baumeister's research. Others hide from future challenges, becoming too afraid to stretch beyond their shrinking comfort zone and test their mettle because it could mean confronting an uncomfortable truth that stings like a betrayal: *Wait, I'm not as great as I've been told?*

That's where Freud and the self-esteem movement start to intersect with risk. When we've bought into the idea that we're entitled to feel good about ourselves and that seeking risk or overcoming fear is unnatural, we're less likely to take on an uncertain challenge and stick with it long enough to reap the rewards. Maybe we're fragile—"easily broken or damaged," as the dictionary defines it—because too many of us let ourselves be guided by a lie: *I'm exceptional and I deserve to feel good and get attention no matter what I do.*

How many of us have also been repeating the pattern with our children?

Seligman emailed me back. With homework. "Required reading first, Damien… *The Hope Circuit*. Then I'd be happy to schedule a conversation."[xxvi]

The Hope Circuit is Seligman's autobiography. Though it's a hefty four hundred pages, I finished it quickly. To call it a coming-of-age tale would be too simple, but the account of his life and research follows a fascinating path from helplessness to agency.

When we spoke by video, he immediately won me over with his vulnerability and curiosity. A professor at the University of Pennsylvania for the past fifty years, Marty—which is what he insists everyone call him—wore a simple golf shirt, and on his round head, he had the closely cropped white hair of a man who never much cared about appearances. He told me he was mostly deaf these days so he preferred video with closed captioning. I laughed like a shy student and tried not to talk too fast; I was conscious of wasting his time, but he asked more questions than I did.

Eventually I got him to elaborate on his ideas about self-esteem. He started off praising Baumeister's work and making an important distinction, noting that any conversation about psychology and society needs to differentiate between those who are dealing with serious mental health issues and the rest of us who are mostly healthy but could be happier.

"Depression is at least partly a disorder of low self-esteem, so if we're concerned about depression in our children and depression in our young people—and there is evidence for an increase in this going on for at least a century—then it's not unreasonable to try to protect their self-esteem," he said. "But if we're dealing with normal, healthy kids and leaders doing well in the world as opposed to a therapeutic society in which we're trying to minimize depression, then I don't think it's a particularly good idea to go out of our way to inflate people's self-esteem artificially."[xxvii]

That last word was the one that mattered. *Artificially*.

Seligman's entire career, from his first experiments in 1967 testing whether dogs that could not control minor electric shocks learned to be helpless, has been focused on exploring measurable actions, not feelings.[xxviii] He was not opposed to self-esteem being raised. He just believed talking about it didn't do much good beyond giving people an artificial sense of their own importance. As he put it, "I'm much more concerned with people's behavior, with what they do. With success, with kindness, with meaning, with accomplishment."

The "touchy-feely" approach to self-esteem, he said, leads to little change in actual behavior, as Baumeister's comprehensive review showed and later studies confirmed. Far from saving America, it has produced more individual fragility and a society that is more socially disconnected and weaker.

"I think courage and bravery really is a major value, and we have to be concerned about building that, particularly since we're often dealing with cultures, nations, and competitors who are braver than we are," Seligman told me. "So that kind of fragility that comes from touchy-feely self-esteem and avoiding risk is a real worry to me."

I asked him what the real costs might be. Isn't fragility, like fine art, a desirable luxury?

"Well, one of the costs of fragility is when things go wrong in your life, when you're forty, you very easily get depressed, you get anxious."

That was me in New York at forty. I'd gone in confident and been shaken.

Seligman added that countries filled with fragile people are also forced to find ever more creative ways to provide the protection and sense of security that the fragile crave. One way it

happens in America is through innovation, whether it's weapons no other nation can match, breakthroughs that help people
live longer lives, or entertainment and technology that distract
us from our fears. But it also happens through specialization.
Organizations and professions that involve higher risks—
emergency management, policing, firefighting, war—select the
already brave and train them into a subculture of their own.

"Our solution is to have a fortress," Seligman said.

He wasn't sure it would work, not forever. I wasn't sure it
worked at all. It reminded me of Hobbes with his sovereign, but
in real life, the fortress requires soldiers, and the soldiers I knew
deeply resented the civilian-military divide; they railed against
people who put "support the troops" bumper stickers on their
cars but rarely sacrificed or struggled. And not all life's challenges
can be solved with innovation or special forces. Sometimes the
people inside the walls (or the school) are the ones who need to
be strong, facing violence, a natural disaster, or a pandemic.

"I'm just wondering," I said, "when a society starts to lose some
of this, some of these values, how do you build them back up?"

"That's the reason why West Point wants to talk to me on
Thursday," he said. Earlier in our conversation, when I was telling him about Nippers and surf lifesaving, he had mentioned
that the elite military academy for the U.S. Army had reached
out to him for guidance on training.

"That's their business, right, to build people like that. But it's
not as if there's a lot of science behind it. You're asking exactly
the questions that we don't know the answer to and that West
Point and the Marines don't know the answer to."

I wondered if he might be hedging, just being a cautious

scientist. In *The Hope Circuit*, he had written about coming to Australia to help Geelong Grammar develop a program around positive psychology and building optimism. He knew that his book sounded touchy-feely too—"I had to tell my publisher not to put a smiley face on the cover," he said—but it seemed like what he had tried do at Geelong was build on the school's own efforts to prioritize the skills and group effort that led to confidence and maybe even bravery.

"That is one of things that I like about Geelong," he said when I brought it up. "The Geelong Grammar model, it is an attempt to build courage."

For ninth grade at Geelong, students leave Melbourne and head to Timbertop, a mountain camp of two thousand acres nestled in a secluded valley of the Australian Alps.[xxix] Students work in small groups, boys and girls, and camp out on their own for around fifty to fifty-five nights while spending their days with a mix of academics and outdoor education. The curriculum, modeled on the Outward Bound program developed in the 1940s by veteran seamen in Britain, concludes with a three-day trek that the students choose and navigate themselves.

In 1966, Prince Charles spent six months at Timbertop.[xxx] A few years later, he described it as the most enjoyable period of his entire education. Many other schools in Australia have emulated the program, adding bush experiences for both boys and girls, while many families embark on six-month driving and camping adventures around Australia. On a sparsely-populated continent filled with deadly snakes where foreign tourists are often found stranded in the wilderness for days after their cars break down, survival skills and adaptability are highly prized, even among urban elites.

"The philosophy seemed to be that if you just challenge the kids and didn't help them, they'll become strong," Seligman said, recalling his time at Geelong in 2007. "If they were cold and wanted to take a hot shower, for example, they had to go out and get firewood."

Seligman said that during his time working with Geelong, he also heard some of the old-timers at a fiftieth reunion tell him that they attributed their success to even harsher treatment—to getting caned by teachers. He couldn't tell how serious they were, but it was clear that part of his job was "to do sort of the opposite, and that is to make the environment much more supportive and positive. What you need is a balance."

Australia seems to have done a good job with that. In schools and with extracurriculars like Nippers, teaching has evolved to be more amiable than it was a generation or two ago, while the influence of the self-esteem movement has been well contained. The cascade of personal injury lawsuits and huge awards for "pain and suffering" that coincided with America's growing concern for feelings hit a barrier here with commonsense caps on damages in New South Wales and other states. There is also scant evidence of grade inflation at the university level or below in Australia, as I discovered when my own kids got their report cards and their teachers had to explain to me that a C (the first I'd seen for either of them) would not doom their prospects forever.[xxxi]

Australia, though, isn't the only country to have found a healthier balance. Across the Tasman Sea, outdoor education is often described as central to the psyche of New Zealanders and an important part of growing up. Kiwis have their own junior lifesaving program along the coast, along with popular courses run through schools and organizations like the YMCA, which offer children and families lessons in bushcraft, river crossing, and emergency response. The country's no-fault compensation scheme for accidents also limits personal injury lawsuits and makes adventure travel more affordable by reducing insurance costs.

Iceland is another nation where the environment has shaped a national character of "versatility, self-reliance, independence and an egalitarian turn of mind," according to Guðmundur Finnbogason, one of the country's most esteemed twentieth-century philosophers.[xxxii] He also wrote that the country is known for "equanimity in emergencies"—an ideal embodied by Iceland's sprawling system of emergency-response volunteers. In the *New Yorker* a few years ago, Nick Paumgarten described its nearly ten thousand members (in a country of three hundred thousand people) as "a peerless kind of national-emergency militia."[xxxiii] Like Australia's lifesavers, the local teams stand apart from government and are well trained in risk and revered by the public, saving lives while bringing together people from all walks of life.

Other countries, many of them small and easily overlooked, have also created a shared skill set for risk with less of a time commitment for participants. In Norway, first aid training has been mandatory since the 1960s. The campaign now involves the entire population, from preschool children to the elderly. As a result, more than 90 percent of Norwegian adults are first aid trained, ready to handle everything from heart attacks to drowning to car accidents.

All these countries, it's worth noting, rank higher than the United States in the OECD Better Life Index for a combination of life satisfaction, community, and civic engagement.[xxxiv]

Not that anyone in Congress will have noticed. For Americans, it seems, training with strangers for that moment when something goes wrong has fallen out of favor. Suburb or city, Republican or Democrat, it's not cool, and it's not common. Volunteer ambulance and firefighting corps, for example, which thrived during my grandparents' time, are in steep decline. Across the country, there are thousands of open paramedic positions, both paid and unpaid. In Pennsylvania, where Benjamin Franklin founded the nation's first volunteer fire company in Philadelphia in 1736, the ranks of volunteer firefighters have fallen to 30,000 from 360,000 in the 1970s even as calls for help have tripled.[xxxv]

Americans are simply not as willing as they once were to expose themselves to risk and help each other out of danger.

Even experts who know the value of pushing people out into our uncertain world have a hard time bucking the trend—especially when it comes to parenting. Seligman told me that in his own life, with seven children, finding equilibrium was often difficult. He was more of the tough-love type while the children's mothers (he was married twice, so there were two of them) favored more of an attachment approach. At Geelong, one of his sons was at the age for Timbertop, but his mother, Mandy Seligman, a developmental psychologist, preferred to keep him at home.

"It's really difficult as a parent because you really don't want your kids to feel bad," Seligman said. He laughed thinking about the years when their children were young. "Mandy has pretty much won most of these battles."

Still, thankfully, Seligman's research points to a way out. The more we talked about his family, the more we both started to see connections to the arc of his career and how it all applied to the ideas of risk and parenting and risk and society. He started out in psychology thinking about helplessness, declaring that the dogs he worked with in his first experiment learned that it was no use trying to jump over a small barrier because nothing they did could stop the pattern of minor electric shocks. More recently, though, he concluded that helplessness was not learned.[xxxvi] It's a default, like risk aversion, or maybe it *is* the risk aversion default with another name.

When we face uncertainties and shocks we cannot fight or flee or when we settle into routines that do not force us out of our comfort zones, we retreat; we lie down. We play it safe, even though backpedaling into a corner with our children is not good for them. Many of us make that mistake. In a 2021 study of 185 parents, a majority of mothers and fathers said they believed that teaching their children the world was dangerous would keep them safe.[xxxvii] In fact, their negativity was found to be correlated with less success for their kids, less job and life satisfaction, worse health, and even increased suicide attempts. Teaching our children to see threats all around them may make us feel better; we can pat ourselves on the back for being prudent parents. For our kids, all it does is make them more likely to struggle than thrive.

But there is a path forward, what some might even call a cure for our fearful, risk-averse errors. It can be found in the actions of the other group of dogs in Seligman's original experiment, the ones that jumped over the barrier once they figured out they could stop the shocks by pushing a panel with their noses. They were the ones that overcame the default of helplessness with action and "learned industriousness."[xxxviii]

They discovered that they could do more than they had thought. Experiencing control with one act (stopping the minor shock) led them to make a second, better decision—to jump out of the area where the shocks were administered.

Seligman, who found the animal research harrowing but extremely valuable in the curbing of depression and human suffering, concluded that's where both psychology and policy needs to focus: on getting people moving, breaking through the inertia of helplessness, negativity, and hesitation, and helping them build competence and confidence.

Hearing him explain it reminded me of what I had also heard from kids who endured outdoor education and what I found reading the testimonials of volunteer rescuers all over the world. There's an energy that they often associate with adrenaline but that in fact goes far beyond a single hormone.

In *The Hope Circuit*, Seligman provides us with a complex technical portrait, explaining that our brains create new circuitry and protein flows after experiences of control, which together reduce passivity later on. There's essentially a circuit in the brain, "the hope circuit," that fires up and propels us forward, telling us that because of our prior achievements, we can accomplish the next task we face. If you get the hope circuit firing often enough (a big if), it builds strength, optimism, and the ability to deal with setbacks—a virtuous cycle that's the opposite of self-esteem's spiral downward into depression, risk aversion, and helplessness. Prioritizing hope and the unknown is especially vital for children. As Seligman wrote, "Early experience with control immunizes us against the ravages of uncontrollability later in life."[xxxix]

The trick, he said, is getting people past their helplessness setting.

"My life's work has really been about agency," he told me.

He defined it as a mix of efficacy, optimism, and imagination. Instead of looking inward or in the mirror, as Nathaniel Branden actually suggested, you have to look outward at the world and imagine a range of possibilities and goals that you believe are attainable through the buildup of skills and effort. To become proficient, you can't stand in place or insist on being protected. You have to believe in the potential for positive improvement. You have to advance.

Diana bought a surfboard, a big blue eight-foot foamie that made her eyes light up like candles. "It was cheap," she said.

I wasn't unhappy, just surprised. For most of our relationship, Diana had stayed dry. She loved the beach for vacations, our honeymoon, but she only ventured into the water if it was bathtub warm, and it was rarely for more than a quick dip.

"I'm Cuban," she'd tell me. "It's my Caribbean blood."

In Sydney, though, she seemed more eager than usual to try new things. She saw the move as an opportunity for reinvention, or at least redirection. Maybe it was spurred on by memories of the past. When she studied here in the '90s, she had only one day of classes each week at UTS in Sydney, and she spent a lot of time traveling and testing her own tolerance for risk. Or maybe it was midlife frustration—why not fight the inertia and make the most of our new home, so far away from our past lives and New York habits?

The board she bought signaled a commitment. It was big and wide, as royal blue and bright as the noon sky, a billboard announcing that she didn't just want to repeat what she did before.

Meanwhile, I didn't know how to stop doing what I'd always done—work hard, ignore everything else. I was waking up before 5:00 a.m., always rushing, editing enterprise stories that came through the bureau, doing events, trying to build a business, hire new people, and mentor others, all while attempting to write a weekly newsletter and "front-page" stories of my own. More than once, I made some dumb mistakes at work while trying to juggle too much.

I was trying to leave that behind, or at least I wanted to try. Australia, I felt, was my last best chance to readjust, to grow into a well-rounded adult, to stop feeling like I was always forgetting something that really mattered. But despite the distance of several thousand miles, my mind was still attached to the old routines. Like Seligman, who wrote about having the wrong tempo at times during his career, I was moving too fast to think. On many occasions, Diana would be talking to me for several minutes and I wouldn't hear a word. It was as if I was still in New York. Absent and wired.

She was more malleable, like clay before the kiln. Her approach to risk was one of the things that always surprised me about her. She'd get nervous about a plane's takeoff but think nothing of changing up where she lives or what she does for work. Maybe it was how she was raised; her parents moved often for her father's job in the pharmaceutical industry, which meant she changed schools and cities more than most. As a family, they often seemed to be anxious with the small stuff, brave with the big.

How else could I explain how she ended up in Iraq with me, leaving independent film to cover war as a video journalist for the *New York Times*?

I loved that confusing spontaneity, that unpredictable taste for adventure, and in Australia, it intensified. She said she was thinking of taking a class called Women on Waves but wondered whether the fortysomething mom who takes up surfing was too much of a cliché. She'd even seen an episode of the TV show *Girls* built entirely around millennials making fun of the idea.

"Just go for it," I told her. I'd decided that even if I was slow to change, I'd encourage others to grab hold of their own agency. It seemed to work for the kids. Why not adults?

I did wonder, though, how Diana was managing in the water. After she showed me the board, I must have looked confused, because the next thing she did was walk me over to a closet and point out another new purchase to go along with the board—a wetsuit to keep her warm.

A few weeks later, I stopped by to check out the place where Diana was taking lessons. The surf shop, named Let's Go Surfing, sat on the road abutting Bondi Beach, a few steps up the hill at the northern end, next to a cafe called Speedos. There were surfboards outside and a lot of coming and going inside. Groups of kids twisted themselves into lime-green rashies. A bunch of instructors pasted zinc on their faces while a group of tourists scanned the boards for rent. Diana, they told me, was in the water. In jeans and boots that made me look like an alien from an office, I walked over to the fence near the beginner lessons with the smallest waves rolling into a corner. I tried to find her in the group of people with the large boards near the shore. She was farther back, where the waves were breaking. I saw her paddling toward an instructor wearing a bright blue rashie. When a wave came, he pushed her into it and she stood up slowly, wobbling for a moment, before moving toward the shore and falling. The next wave was much the same—a struggle with a split second of glory. She didn't seem to mind.

When she finished, she saw me and ran up the sand on her toes. She arrived with a huge smile.

"Hey, you're here," she said, surprised to see me. With her dark hair slicked back, in her new wet suit, she looked ten years younger. "That's Shannon," she said, pointing toward the water. His loud Aussie accent could be heard over the surf. "He's the one who does Women on Waves. I think I'm going to do it."

She was still cold. I could see it on her face and in the way she held her arms close to her sides. But she was surfing anyway. I wondered what an experiment with Seligman's dogs would reveal if they had to jump toward a toy or food they loved. Maybe the fastest way to break through the helpless-and-risk-averse default is with something easy and enjoyable?

Fun, like fear, can be contagious. Seeing Diana cold and smiling, seeing Baz surf—Amelia was still resisting after I pushed her into a wave and the board hit her in the head—they made me want to give it a shot. As Nippers ended, I signed up for a three-lesson package. For the first lesson, I showed up early. With the awkwardness of a new kid at school, I slipped on a rented wet suit struggling with the zipper in the back. I was with four other beginners, and as we walked out to the sand in Bondi's north corner, the ocean sounded like a jet engine.

We found a line of red and blue banana-shaped boards waiting for us where dry sand turned to wet. Our instructor, Nigel, who seemed to be about my age, with a shaved head, a sun-pink nose, and a red rashie over a thick wet suit, pushed up a pile of sand to explain how a wave works. Next, he modeled the motions of a pop-up: arms by the chest, arch back, ass into air, lift back foot to the board, then front. Stand and balance.

The people I could see in the water seemed to do it in one motion. We practiced each step on dry land before getting wet, creaking our way through the process like rusty cranes trying to move steel beams.

"Okay, are we ready?" Nigel asked. "Grab your boards and follow me."

We waded in and stopped where the small waves were breaking. I slid onto my board and lay facedown. I was surprised at how vulnerable that position felt, with my face so close to the water. Nigel stood above and behind me with his hand near my leg. It was like being at the doctor or dentist. I was not in charge of my body. I didn't quite know what was about to happen.

Without warning, Nigel gave me a push. I wobbled as the broken wave carried me forward. I got my hands to my chest, then I fell. The next wave, I managed to get to my knees before toppling off to the side. Over the next hour, I had a few waves where I actually got to my feet but not at any angle close to standing. In the entire lesson, I didn't ride a single wave. Not one. It was the second surf lesson I had ever taken—the first was on vacation in Costa Rica with Diana, and I didn't stand then either.

I left with a sore neck and back along with bruised pride. I felt foolish and old. I was in pain and I probably would have just given up, except that I'd already paid for two more lessons.

My second attempt mirrored the first. During one mild wave, my hand slipped and I slammed my chin into the board. During another, after a fall, I stood up underwater and bounced my head into the board. It was a Marx Brothers experience. I don't think I could have possibly felt less coordinated—I couldn't even sit on the board without falling off. If doing well was required for boosting self-esteem, I still had a long way to go. At the start of my third lesson, when we all shared our goals, I shouted, "I want to stand for two seconds." Success meant staying on a wave long enough to enjoy the view.

But in the water, as waves came and went, I admitted to myself that there was something humbling and thrilling about being terrible at a new task. I could see how I looked to others—it was funny. The humor of failing without any severe consequence felt liberating, silly, and absurd. Even if I didn't yet feel good about myself, I felt like a kid again, eager to learn. Each little improvement became a triumph and the tiniest hope circuit spark. I was happier as a beginner than I would have guessed.

After that, I started borrowing Diana's board when we went to the beach, and I started going once in a while on my own. Two-second waves happened a pinch more often. Then a four-second. Then twenty falls. When Diana bought a new board designed by Mick Fanning—the Australian surfer who punched a shark during a pro competition in 2015—I took it into the waves…and broke it.

Eventually, she decided it was time to get serious. Sick of all my borrowing, she announced we'd be going surfboard shopping. For me. On a rainy Saturday, as we listened to local radio discussing Prince Harry's new American fiancée, we pulled up next to the surf shop that would help me become more Australian. It was small, sign-less spot—a hole in the wall on a side street a few blocks from Manly Beach. Inside, there were boards piled into every corner on a carpet of fake green grass. All I could smell was foam.

"So what are you looking for?"

One of the owners, a tall older man with stringy hair that looked like it was last brushed in 1969, greeted us warmly. Diana explained why we were there, and he did his best to make sure I didn't feel completely stupid as I considered a few entry-level options. We ended up paying around $200 for a green board with black trim that was seven and a half feet long, heavy and full of float. I also bought a cheap wet suit and a leg rope. We put it all in the back of the Subaru, crammed in, and drove home in the drenching rain.

"Are you excited?" Diana asked me.

"I think so."

It took me a few days to put the new board to use. I still didn't think of myself as a surfer. But when I got out there in the north corner of Bondi, with all the other kooks and my green monster, I felt even better than I expected. There was a word for it—one Amelia and I had come up with to describe how she felt before a public speaking assignment at school. *Nervoucited.* Nervous and excited, all twisted up in one.

I paddled out full of energy, the water splashing into my face, waking me up like a cold shower. I sat on my board and looked around. A small wave approached and I paddled forward, popping up, wobbling, then splashing into the surf. Again and again, I tried, making ever so minor progress, but it felt like that was enough. Surfing was a way to expend some energy and engage in what the Australian surfer Dave Rastovich calls "meaningful play."[xl]

One day, when the waves were small and the wind was still, I had a brief moment of bliss. Diana was with me, showing me up as usual. I was sitting a little south from the rocks when I saw a wave that looked decent. I slid into position on my board and started paddling a little late. The wave lifted me up—*damn, it's bigger than I thought*—and I stood, expecting the white water I was used to taking in, but this time, the wave was still green. I could see the sand through what looked like aqua-painted glass as I slid forward and sideways at the same time. The moment was brief, but the sensation stretched out time. Those two seconds of joy felt like ten minutes.

I didn't know what I did right, but I imagined it must have been how Baz and Amelia felt when they rode a wave in or how Jack London felt after he mastered his first wave in Waikiki in 1907, when he called surfing "a royal sport for the natural kings of earth."[xli] It was the feeling of fear rising and falling; I'd harnessed a force beyond my control, briefly, and instead of fleeing or resisting, I found a way to work with the power it produced, to communicate through action in a language without words. Maybe that's how all "risk management" should be defined—connecting with something that could hurt you in a way that creates partnership and awe. It was just enough to make me want more.

THREE

In the Pool

Why I hate swimming; the German vs. American ways of risk; Brock Bastian and the purpose of pain; fish guts and football with Matt Zurbo

Pulling off our wet suits at the car in the Bondi parking lot after a quick surf, Diana posed an unexpected question.

"Why don't you talk to me?"

I looked up, confused.

"In the water. Why do you ignore me?"

I hadn't really noticed that I was staying away, but I also couldn't deny it.

"I don't know," I said. "I guess I just like to be quiet. Do my own thing."

We both appreciated the way surfing placed us in the moment, cut off from our phones and our concerns. We had a new hobby that we shared and we loved, but we were discovering there are different ways to grow into new experiences.

For me, surfing was a solitary and silent challenge. I loved not having to do what I do at work—talk to people. In the waves, I could recover and reenergize with the only voice I heard coming from my own head, telling me which wave to go for and when to paddle. Especially after a few weeks of managing visits from high-profile *Times* colleagues, I was ready for a communication detox.

For Diana, surfing filled a very different void. Job hunting while working on freelance projects and a reader-generated feature for the *Times*, she was toiling mostly alone and found in the waves just enough of a shared experience to draw her into new friendships. She had already made a commitment to go surfing every day, no matter what. When I happened to join her, I usually stayed far enough away to just watch, but I often admired her initiative. She seemed to sniff out all the kind and fun-loving people who were as excited about surfing as she was, moving gradually from seeing people she recognized to saying hello to becoming friends.

Many of them were interesting women of one-syllable names like Em and Sam and Kaye. Some were teachers or therapists; others worked in hospitality; only a few were wealthy enough not to work. One or two were polyamorous.

There were also surf instructors like Shannon, a son of Bondi, quick with a story about the old days, who seemed eager to help Diana whether he was teaching or not, and she had also gotten to know a crop of friendly men, some older, some younger, some Aussie, some not, who waved hello whenever they appeared. On the best days, with smallish waves, light winds, and a warm sun, I could understand their urge to socialize. The rollicking surf produced a need to wait, to take turns. It was a crowded pub without the beer, and while I insisted on just bellying up to the bar by myself, Diana found a way to drink it all in with others.

Our differences also appeared in how we surfed. I finally knew how to identify and use a rip to get out past the break, but my tempo was still rapid-fire: I was the guy who went for too many waves, missed most, fell more, and tired too quickly. Diana was more selective. She chose fewer waves, rarely competing with other surfers for the biggest or best waves. Sometimes she doubted herself and let fear get the best of her, but when she committed, she stood gracefully almost every time. Joining a group within the expanse of infinite nature—in the ocean after a lifetime on land—she'd surf for hours, then come home quicker to smile and laugh.

"I just feel healthy out there," she said.

We both did. Doing well didn't mean the same thing for Diana as it did for me, but the experience led from one new thing to another.

Diana's turning point came in early 2019, when she passed on a job working with the standards department of a major online video company. Watching the way social media was pulling America apart—Trump had pushed the country into a government shutdown at the time, and we both had relatives preferring to shout rather than think—Diana concluded she no longer wanted anything to do with the attention machine of clicks, shares, and impassioned hot takes.

"I don't want to waste my energy trying to change things I can't change," she said one night over dinner. Amelia asked what she wanted to do if she could do anything at all, and Diana surprised us all with her answer: "Write a novel."

It was a risky proposition. Diana had always prioritized work in a company, making money with a path to advancement. But she wanted something else, and even though she wasn't sure if what she wrote would be just for her or the wider world, she moved forward.

She started right away. She wrote at least five hundred words a day for weeks, then months—crafting the cinematic story of a woman struggling with her own sense of risk in the water and in love. She also started developing a post-surf hair conditioner with local ingredients like lemon myrtle. Chemistry was never something she imagined enjoying, but she had always wanted to start a business, so when she noticed that becoming a Bondi regular meant destroying her hair, she created a solution. She happily turned our kitchen into a lab, constantly mixing materials and formulas.

With online video in New York, she was especially good at eliciting a feeling of outrage. The writing and solid bars of conditioner (made in Bronte, named Kendishna) aimed to soothe.

"Dad, over here," Baz said.

We were trying out a new surf spot at Garie Beach in Royal

National Park. The swell was bigger than what I was used to, and I was drifting into a rip. Baz, who had been taking a weekly surf lesson for months now, knew where to go, setting up a few meters farther north. While I headed toward him, he paddled his knife of a pink board into a wave taller than he was, popped up like a spring, and sped across, pumping his legs to gain speed. When he fell near the shore and started back toward me, I could see the energy in his eyes.

"Hey, nice wave," I said when he paddled back out. He smirked and said nothing. Like me, I suppose, he preferred to surf quiet and seemed unable to put his own joy into words.

He still had moments of being afraid in the water. An anxious, orderly boy by nature, he hated days with crowds and messy waves. But as 2019 brought us into a second Australian summer and another season of Nippers, I could see that his relationship with the ocean had matured. He was getting used to managing in the midst of uncertainty. And on that day at Garie Beach, the repetition of risk-taking delivered a milestone. Surfing was suddenly and obviously the first thing that he had gotten better at than his father. When that happened for me, I was a teenager; after a long jog with my father, a lifelong runner, we sprinted home and, for the first time, I beat him to the driveway. I think I was sixteen. Baz had just turned ten.

His openness to the world was expanding. Despite a severe allergy to almonds and other tree nuts, a risk we'd been managing for a few years, he'd suddenly become a less picky eater, leading to a newfound love for Indian food. At the beginning of fifth grade, with Australia just starting to chatter about the upcoming federal election, Baz even shocked us all by announcing that he was joining the debate team. For a boy who often struggled to put his thoughts into words, public arguing was an enormous challenge. At his first debate training, Baz froze and cried. Then he collected himself and finished. I wasn't there, but one of the parents said she was impressed with his willingness to keep going and fight his fears.

Watching my family embrace risk in more areas of life was inspiring. I started a risk journal to keep track of all the new things we were doing, from food to hiking steep cliffs in Tasmania to jumping off the rocky cliffs by the Bronte pool or the harbor. It would be a way, I hoped, to recall the experiences later, when we needed a reminder of our own courage.

Each of us had grown in one way or another. It felt as if managing our worries in the water made us steadier on land. I was looking slightly less often at my phone, especially on weekends. Diana had a new routine for her writing and making the conditioner. Amelia was also bouncing back to her happy self after months of dealing with a bully at school, a challenge resolved in the most Australian of ways: with help from her mates and a physical triumph. In Honolulu, on a layover from our trip to the United States to see family, a young Hawaiian woman in a colorful bikini encouraged Amelia to get on a longboard in Waikiki, cheering as she rode in a few slow curlers with perfect poise (and without any parental involvement).

I could sense that we were building confidence and momentum with our embrace of risk, and so could Baz, who decided to issue a new challenge one Sunday as we were walking home from Nippers. He wanted to know if he would have to do it again next year. He was hoping the answer would be no, but as a new debater, more certain of his ability to persuade, he laid out a proposal: "I'll do Nippers again if you get your Bronze Medallion."

I laughed. I didn't even really know what the Bronze Medallion was, and neither did he. All we'd heard was that it was a challenge, a training program to join the volunteer lifesaving crew that, among other things, kept all those Nippers safe in the water.

A week later, Baz repeated his offer. "You do the Bronze, I do Nippers." By that point, I'd given it more thought. I was open to the idea. I'd written something for our bureau's weekly Australia newsletter praising the managed risk of Nippers, which brought a surprising level of positive feedback from all over the country, including a few readers in Bronte who also suggested I go through the Bronze course to deepen my involvement.[i]

Maybe they were right. Surfing and swimming were complementary. I was feeling stronger in the waves. *Maybe it's time to throw myself in the pool and become a "Bronzie."* I knew there was a test—there was always a test—but an American friend in Bondi had told me it was manageable, a four-hundred-meter swim in something like nine or ten minutes.

On the day of the trial, Diana had to remind me. It was 3:30 p.m. The test was at 4:00.

"You should go," she said. "It will be good for you."

Baz lit up at the possibility of me swimming while he watched.

"I'll go with you," he said. "I'll time you."

Walking down to the surf club, seeing where the ocean met the horizon, I pictured myself in the water with the kids for Nippers. I'd lost some weight, I knew by then how to find the

Bronte Express, the rip that runs along the rocks by the bogey hole, and I was looking forward to learning more.

At the steps of the club, there were a few other people—a stocky woman with tan skin, a tall guy in a green Speedo, a few younger people. It all looked friendlier than I remembered. The sun reflected off the glass, and an Australian flag waved above us.

"Hi, everybody, I'm Kimberly." She was in fitness shorts with tanned skin and a clipboard. "You're all here for the test?"

After a round of affirmatives, I asked if it was okay that I hadn't signed up in advance. I figured they'd want as many volunteers as they could get. She said the Bronze Medallion classes appeared to be full but that I should do the test and we could probably work it out.

"It's four hundred meters in eight minutes, forty-five seconds," she said.

"Any stroke?" I asked.

"No," she said. "It has to be freestyle."

That was news to me.

"I have a friend in Bondi doing it there, and she said you can do any stroke in, like, nine minutes," I replied, guessing that Kimberly had made a mistake. A little bit of breaststroke wouldn't hurt, would it?

She looked at me like a disappointed parent. "Bronte is dangerous," she told me. "We have a duty of care to the people in the water and to you."

I knew from Nippers that she was right. I started to stretch. As we walked down the promenade to the pool, I looked my fellow contestants up and down. Half of them seemed to be older or heavier than me. If they could manage, I figured, so could I.

At the pool's edge, Baz asked to hold my phone and my watch.

"How many of you have timed yourself to see if you'll pass?" Kimberly asked.

A few nodded. Some raised a hand. I did not. No one in the group seemed particularly worried, and when they started jumping in at thirty-second intervals, I could see why. They all moved quickly through the water, regardless of their body shape or age.

Suddenly I was at the front. I dived in after a roundish older woman and the tall guy with the body and bathing suit of an Olympian. I swam as hard and as fast as I ever have. The test required fourteen laps, thirty meters each. The first two were fine. Around lap four, I started to run out of air and confidence. *I don't know if I'm going to be able to do this.* I felt like a rock pulled through concrete. By lap six, I was gasping for air and slowing down. Around lap ten, I thought I might drown. It took everything I had to keep going. When I turned my head out of the water on the last lap to take in as big a breath as possible, I could see I was the last one still swimming.

Baz was in the middle of the group, holding my watch, waiting. Finally, I reached the end and grabbed the edge of the pool. Kimberly looked at me and shook her head.

"Ten minutes, seventeen seconds. It's just fitness," Kimberly said as I climbed out of the pool. "Your stroke seems okay. You're just not there yet."

Yet. She seemed to think I'd be back.

Humiliated and dizzy, saddened by my own arrogance and weakness, I walked back up the hill with Baz beside me, thinking of all my efforts to push him into the water. Failing felt lame.

Maybe I'd been too certain and cruel with him. With the roles reversed, he was quiet and sympathetic. He grabbed and held my arm in his, giving me a squeeze.

"Well," I said, "I guess I need to practice more and do the work."

He smiled. Maybe he thought he had just managed to get out of Nippers. Or maybe he recognized that now I'd be the one going to the pool. He offered to come with me, and in his voice—so much softer than mine—I heard kindness. It reminded me of Amelia asking Diana what she wanted to do with her life. When given a chance, kids can be such empathetic mentors. Closer to the pain of new things, they teach with sympathy and humility.

Baz and I walked into the house through the back door, near the laundry room. Diana rushed around the corner with the expectation of triumph.

"How'd it go?"

I looked down and offered up the only two words I could: "I failed."

I didn't tell anyone else that I tried. I pretended it never happened. I forgot what the people I swam with looked like and I hoped they would forget me as well. But of course, the experience weighed on me. However much it hurt, I knew I couldn't quit.

A few weeks later, I went online to sign up for swim lessons through Mermaid Academy, where the kids took their lessons at Icebergs. I reached the end of the online process, then got stuck before making a payment. A couple of hundred dollars for a package of lessons seemed like a lot. The whole "Mermaid Academy" thing also didn't help; it was a reminder that most people who take swim lessons are knee-high without gray hair. A few days later, I tried again. Still I couldn't do it. I found some excuse to leave the form incomplete. Was I afraid of embarrassing myself? Or did I just hate swimming?

I tried to recall the last time I tried to swim, really swim. Despite my rejection of Freud, something in my attempt to conquer and master the water seemed connected to my childhood. It started with my grandfather. He grew up poor in Brooklyn during the Great Depression but became a world-class swimmer, a specialist in the butterfly and freestyle. He was heading to the Olympic trials when World War II intervened, and he wound up in the South Pacific instead.

In my mind's eye, we're in the pool at a country club outside New York City where he plays golf. I'm miserable, a cranky, stubborn kid recoiling against his instructions. I hate the snobby crowd that Grandpa worked so hard to join. I hate that he wears a forest-green Speedo. Mostly I think I hate that I am not very good at swimming.

Grandpa's not exactly thrilled with my progress either. I'm his first grandchild—the son of his eldest, hippie daughter and that crazy guy she met in Jamaica, the first boy to arrive after his four daughters. He has high hopes for me in every way, and even at eight or nine years old, I know he would love for me to follow his lead and become a serious swimmer.

I can still see him doing his best to teach me. Stretch your arm out like this. Turn your head like that. Keep going. There I am in the middle lane of the pool, far from the diving board where I want to be, as I try, fail, try again, get frustrated. Or maybe I don't try at all, not really. The chlorinated water tastes like a kitchen floor. I can feel my own stiffness as I remember thinking: *This just isn't...me.*

"Fine," he says. "Swim how you want."

That was the last lesson he ever gave me. And the last swim lesson I ever had, from anyone. I wonder why my father never tried to help me swim (or teach me to surf, a sport he loved in his youth). I wonder why I got to a passable level of swimming and stopped. I guess I just didn't want to do it, and after Grandpa understandably gave up on me, no one pushed me on it, and probably with good intentions. I wasn't going to drown, so why make a child of divorce cry in the pool?

But it was also part of that cycle of affirmations, where we're only encouraged to do things that make us feel good, where success comes readily. Even before social media, many of us pursued the "likes" and smiley faces of easy approval. But that's a trap. We train ourselves to think that if we don't have immediate success, we're a failure at something not worth doing, and that's a prison, because it keeps us from trying new things we might learn to love.

Australia offered me another chance. I didn't have to be the intellectual New Yorker or the digital creative or the Gen X cynic. I could also be something else.

I decided that swimming would be my middle-aged attempt at metamorphosis. I had been resisting because I didn't identify as a swimmer. Because I didn't like swimming, as a child or adult. But as the kids and Diana were already showing me, our default setting and our profiles—our identities—can evolve. And once in a while, especially for men like me who don't even notice the ruts that deepen over time, they probably should.

Sometimes embracing risk isn't about starting something new or fun, like surfing. Meaningful risks can also involve trying something again that we left behind, unfinished and unresolved. Something that might also set an example for our kids?

I was forty-four and ready to try again. I went back online and paid for the damn lessons.

Icebergs looked ridiculous in its charm—an L of two pools and clear blue water, built into a cliff by waves rolling to Bondi's shores with enough white paint to evoke the Greek islands. In America, from *The Graduate* (1967) to *The Big Lebowski* (1998) to *The Great Gatsby* (2013), pools are signs of personal wealth and status. [ii] In Australia, they are proving grounds for the wider public.

Diana, eager to try anything in the water, decided to join me for my first swimming lesson, which made it slightly less uncomfortable or maybe more awkward. I couldn't be sure. We stood in our swimsuits, goggles in hand, waiting in the same place we usually stood to drop off our children.

Our instructor showed up a few minutes late—Katie, whom I recognized from lessons with Baz and Amelia. My stomach dropped. *Well, that's humiliating.* With what sounded like a Scottish or Irish accent, she asked about the kids (doing great) and why we were there (I failed the Bronze, Diana just wants to learn). She nodded and smiled, then asked us to jump in and swim a couple of laps so she could assess our skills and needs.

Even though it was early March, the water was colder than

I expected. With a name like Icebergs—the pool got its start in 1929 as a winter swimming club—I shouldn't have been surprised, but I was.[iii] The Pacific in Sydney often looks tropical but feels Canadian.

Goggles on, I pushed off the edge and started swimming, breathing on my right every other stroke, trying to remember what my grandfather used to tell me.

The Icebergs pool is a little longer than Bronte's—fifty meters instead of thirty—and I was already winded by the time I turned and headed back to Katie. When I reached the end after two laps, she stopped me and explained that the lower half of my body was sinking too far under the water, creating drag and slowing me down, which is apparently common for men. My stroke was also a mess. My grandfather used to tell me to stretch out my arms but I was doing it wrong, slapping the water, pulling at the wrong angle, and moving slowly.

"That's what we call the windmill," Katie said.

When I looked in the other lane, I could see Diana gliding through the water, stroke after stroke.

"So for you, we need to work on breathing," Katie told Diana when she stopped. I laughed. I didn't even notice she left that out. "And you"—she pointed to me—"there are a few things."

She grabbed a kickboard, handed it to me, and told me to swim a few more laps. The lesson pushed me back to the very beginning. It was one arm only, through the water, to the board, through the water to the board. I tried and found that I was exhausted even doing that.

"You don't have to go so quickly," Katie said. "Just slow down and focus."

After doing it with both hands, she took the board away.

"Now just do the same thing. Pretend like you still have the board. Hold the catch. Don't move one arm until the other arm reaches it."

We went like that for a while, but I was still moving at a rapid pace. My legs, my arms, I was in a hurry, which led Katie to try a few more drills—including one with a float between my legs to keep my legs quiet and counter my sinking lower half. At the end, Katie told me the main thing I needed to do was slow down, think, and practice. *Sounds like good advice out of the pool as well.*

I left feeling half-frozen but energized, which is not the same as motivated. I should have been swimming two, three times a week. I decided to aim for once, combining it with a run. So late one morning, I headed south toward Coogee along the coast, returned, then took off my sneakers, put on my goggles, and jumped into the Bronte pool. Two laps in, I felt no better than I did the day I failed the test. Probably worse, thanks to the run.

I kept going anyway, trying to focus on everything Katie told me while also talking to myself in my head. *Just keep going. Start with ten laps. That's not bad. You did go running. Do fourteen next time.*

I went again two days later. I swam the full four hundred meters but without contentment. When I learned to surf, the awe came easily—standing on a wave felt superhuman. My swimming experience up to that point was all subterranean struggle. I had to be the most reluctant swimmer in the water, there mostly out of guilt—because I'd let my grandfather down, because I was due for another lesson and didn't want to tell Katie I'd barely done any swimming. Every time I approached the water, I was uncertain, listening for the whisper of skeptics: *Will you dive in? Will you finish the difficult task you'd rather avoid?*

Like everyone else, I had a hard time connecting something I hated doing with the idea of a worthwhile benefit. Swimming, for me, required belief—faith in a certain set of values and in a better future outcome. That's of course what made it a risk. I couldn't know where I would end up: happy or miserable, heroic or helpless. It was the same for Baz and Amelia with Nippers. I wasn't sure whether my pushing would actually do any good in the long run.

One afternoon, on a video call, I asked Lorraine Daston, the historian in Germany, if she had any experience with conflicts over physical risks with uncertain rewards. I knew she was married to Gerd Gigerenzer, a German psychologist who also studies risk. I was looking for a family anecdote I could relate to, something to keep me going, and without hesitation, she told me she often ran into conflicts over how to raise their only child, Thalia.

"Here's an example that still makes my pulse race when I think of it," Daston said. "Our daughter played the cello when she was in school. All German children get to school on their own. This is changing; there has been an Americanization so there are more being driven, but at that time, she bicycled to school, and she bicycled to school with this gigantic instrument on her back, which I thought was just insane. I mean, balancing this instrument on her bicycle in the morning traffic and..."[iv] Her voice trailed off.

"My husband," she continued, "for his entire school career had balanced a much heavier accordion on his back on his bicycle. So he had no problem whatsoever with this."

I could tell from the rise in her voice that this was a fight that had lingered. Her eyes veered right, toward a window.

"In the end," she said, "I think my husband was right. Although unfortunately my daughter did not continue with the cello after high school, her confidence now as a cyclist and her kind of enlarged sense of physical competence is a result of having done that when she was young."

Looking back, she said, Thalia benefited from her parents agreeing to suppress their fears of a traffic accident, embracing a risk rather than a ride with comfort. It wasn't a perfect comparison with swimming and Nippers, but I wondered what Thalia thought.

I sent her an email to see if she took away from the experience. She told me she was only twelve when she started riding to school and never thought about the danger.

"The predominant emotion I remember having was one of extreme embarrassment—I was worried that I looked ridiculous, and possibly somewhat nerdy," Thalia said. "But I do think it was this sense of independence that prepared me somewhat for living in India later on."[v]

After many other challenges and international moves, she's now finishing a PhD in anthropology at Princeton, focusing on changing attitudes about stress in Delhi.

What they had found back then as a family was what I was just learning to accept and what the self-esteem promoters had missed: the positive role of moderate pain, both physical and emotional. The commute to school for Thalia was somewhat dangerous and very uncomfortable, but Daston and Gigerenzer made her do it anyway. Instead of looking down on hardship, they chose the stressful option, trusting that it would lead to strength and an end to childhood fragility. What I found especially interesting was that they had arrived at this conclusion after debating the issue from the perspective of very different national cultures and childhoods.

Daston was born in 1951 in East Lansing, a small Midwestern city of factories and Michigan State University, where her father earned his PhD in psychology. Her upbringing was shaped by a comfortable, suburban postwar America at a time when Dr. Benjamin Spock's brand of parenting was ascendant, arguing for a drenching of affection rather than strict discipline. His parenting guide, *The Common Sense Book of Baby and Child Care*, came out in 1946. It followed Freud's lead and was a precursor to the self-esteem movement. Children were effectively put in charge—what they wanted, they got, from breastfeeding onward.

Even Dr. Spock later admitted that his readers took his nurturing ethos too far. "Parents began to be afraid to impose on the child in any way," he explained in an interview with the *Times* in 1968, after his own children were grown.[vi]

Gigerenzer's experience fell at the opposite end of the spectrum. He was born into a country of ruins. "Munich, Berlin. I mean, these cities were flattened by the final bombing of the last years of World War II," Daston told me. "And these children were just sent out in the early morning and told to come home for dinner. They played in the ruins. There were mines, bombs regularly went off, etc. etc.

"The parents," she surmised, "had a very contracted sense of their own responsibility. Their responsibility was, somehow, to get through the next week, to put food on the table.

"What they did would be considered child neglect by present standards but I must say, the generation of Germans who went through this are among the hardiest can-do people I've ever met."

Gigerenzer, while humble, did not disagree. A lover of jazz and a contrarian with a bald head and a brush mustache, he has spent most of his career trying to prove to the world that human intuition and adaptability are underestimated. *Blink*, Malcolm Gladwell's book about gut feelings, relies heavily on his research. More generally, he's part of a loose network of scholars (including Seligman) who have argued for years that the culture and industry of psychology overemphasizes human weakness, from mental disorders to irrational behavior. They believe we're better off building on our strengths, as individuals and in groups.

To me, they resembled happiness farmers. Arguing that optimism, hard work, and exposure to minor or moderate stress produce a bounty of strength, they tend to be psychologists and neuroscientists who look to evolution for clues about human behavior. Many have studied both animals and humans. Like Daston and Gigerenzer, they often find connections between physical challenges (riding a bike while carrying a cello) and whole-of-self rewards (confidence and mastery). I think of them as farmers because they argue for small acts, repeated over time—almost as if we need to water and weed our own routines—which can combine with calculation and luck to produce a rich and lasting harvest. They also reminded me that anything worth savoring takes at least a season to grow.

They're not sadists. They acknowledge that extreme trauma

and chronic stress can be damaging to our bodies and minds. They also recognize that we often make split-second bad decisions regarding perceived safety or risk based on various biases that should be resisted, whether they involve race, gender, or moments of irrational fear or overconfidence. But unlike a lot of social critics, from the left and the right, they resist jumping to harsh conclusions about human nature. They worry about what Gigerenzer calls a "bias bias"—a tendency to assume that every mental mistake reflects a pattern of unconscious flaws when the cause could be something simpler and less contentious, like a lack of information or a distracted moment or a bad guess.

In some ways, they are asking everyone to view each other the way parents look at their children—as works in progress, often foolish rather than cruel, stupid, or conspiratorial. Their research suggested to me that we should give people the benefit of the doubt more often and not assume there's someone or something systemic to blame when errors emerge.

They are also quick to note—with a similar push for nuance and depathologizing—that not all adversity is the same, nor are our responses universally negative to even the worst traumas of life. Where others emphasize our irrational defects in decision-making, they draw attention to human adaptability, willpower, and the decisions we get right, occasionally with hardship's help. As Friedrich Nietzsche famously said, after a childhood shaped by the deaths of his father and a younger brother, "That which does not kill us makes us stronger."[vii]

No one may have done a better job of explaining and expanding the science behind that particular statement than an Australian—Brock Bastian, a psychology professor at the

University of Melbourne. Through his own studies and his book, *The Other Side of Happiness* (2018), he has become a leading expert in the reevaluation of pain, which he defines broadly to include everything from a hand held in cold water to an awkward social situation to the death of a loved one.

When we met one afternoon, his thick salt-and-pepper hair was a mess and he was wearing a pink business shirt. He didn't look like a masochist or a drill sergeant. He looked like a suburban dad with young children, which is what he is. And yet pain's relationship to joy has fascinated him ever since he was young, growing up outside Melbourne and enjoying the melancholy sounds of Australian warbler Nick Cave.

Bastian's research began with experiments that showed the overpromotion of happiness can lead to its opposite. Being surrounded by messaging about wellness and happiness and forever smiles, like the push to increase self-esteem, can make many of us feel like we're doing something wrong when our moods don't measure up.

"Living in an environment that requires positivity can lead to depression and anxiety if you feel those negative emotional states are not being valued and you're not meant to be experiencing them," he told me.[viii]

His findings about pleasure promotion—which is now often referred to as "toxic positivity"—led him to think more about pain.

"There was a part of me that just felt, hold on, we must be missing something," he said. "Well, what is the value of these negative experiences? What's the upside?"

Looking around, he found there was little work done in

psychology about the positives of negative experience. One exception was Richard Dienstbier, an emeritus professor of psychology at the University of Nebraska who is known as the father of "mental toughness." In one of his most cited papers from 1989, Dienstbier started with the observation that stressful or painful experiences lead to increased physiological arousal—the adrenal glands pump higher amounts of adrenaline, noradrenaline, dopamine, and other hormones into the brain, which intensifies alertness and preparedness for action.[ix]

"It is exactly this process that increases our heart rate and gives us sweaty palms before giving a speech or jumping out of a plane," Bastian explained to me.

In studies of rats, the adrenal glands grew when the animals were exposed to repeated minor stressors, such as a small electric shock, signaling increased capacity for a physiological response.[x] But when faced with a challenge, the rats with the bigger glands and more experience with hardship were calmer, less emotional, and less fearful than the control group. This was counterintuitive. If they could produce more stress-related hormones, why didn't they?

In fact, they maintained lower levels when resting in their cage, but when exposed to a new stressful situation, their bigger adrenal glands found just the right level of intensity, responding more effectively by releasing a calibrated surge of hormones in the moment and then reducing those levels quickly when the stressful situation passed. In short, they were more efficient, better at both relaxing and responding to stress when needed. They were like sports car drivers who knew exactly which gear was needed for every turn and straightaway.

In another experiment, small doses of pain pointed even more clearly to improved performance.[xi] A group of rats were trained for fourteen consecutive days by either swimming in cold water or experiencing electric shocks for short episodes, followed by periods of recovery. The researchers found that when the rats were exposed just once to the electric shock or cold swim, they simply accepted their fate and did nothing in response to a second stressful task, which involved a loud noise followed by a shock. The rats that had experienced more stress prior to the second task, however, became models of problem-solving: they jumped over the barrier holding them in, avoiding the second shock rather than just letting it happen. Their prior experiences with minor stress made them more alert and less afraid, pushing them out of helplessness and producing a better real-life decision during a stressful event.

Bastian said the conclusion was obvious. Pain helps us focus and see difficulties as a challenge we can manage, not a threat to fight or flee. He and others set out to prove it was also true for humans. In a series of experiments at Australian universities, he compared the responses of people who had experienced minor pain, through cold water, standing in an uncomfortable position, or eating hot peppers, with those who experienced no discomfort. First, he found that painful events enhanced the interaction with whatever happened next.[xii] In one study, people who'd held their hand in ice water subsequently reported enjoying a chocolate cookie significantly more than those who had not. In another study, the pain-toughened participants performed better at identifying tastes in solutions flavored to be sweet, sour, salty, and bitter.

Pain with a purpose, he wrote, can be like meditation: it increases a person's engagement with and enjoyment of their sensory experiences. It prompts us to pay close attention in the moment and with whatever comes next.

When we spoke, he added another point of emphasis: the long-term impact on how we view ourselves. Telling someone they are strong and resilient, as Branden and Oprah might, has about as much impact as an advertising jingle. Experiencing struggle and recovery, the doing, that's the actual product. It alters our brains and our sense of self. As Bastian put it, "Once you know what you're capable of, you can transport that to other activities." A study of Norwegian paratroopers, for example, showed that increased adrenaline levels from a parachute jump improved competence in technical writing tasks as well.[xiii]

I told Bastian what I'd seen with Diana and Baz—the way confidence in the water made them more willing to try new things on land.

"That's it exactly," he said. "You just don't know what you're capable of until you're tested and once you know you can keep going."

Risk, he added, is a vital part of the process because that's how we learn about our strength. Children in particular should be exposed to experiences that allow for empowerment—that give them an opportunity to face their fears and hone how they respond. Like Nippers. Like Timbertop at Geelong Grammar. Like a lot of other bush camps that Australian public and private schools include as part of the curriculum, and like a few entirely new schools in Australia, such as Candlebark, which was started in 2006 by educator and writer John Marsden. He built the school on eleven hundred acres in Central Victoria with the explicit goal of prioritizing firsthand experiences over traditional book learning.

Bastian also pointed to a study by Ellen Sandseter, a developmental psychologist in Norway, who has suggested that there may be evolutionary reasons why kids benefit from risky play. In a paper subtitled "The Anti-Phobic Effects of Thrilling Experiences," she wrote that climbing and other dangerous games allow children to experience not only exhilarating positive emotions but also natural fears that, with time, they learn to master.[xiv]

Even injury, she writes, should be seen as part of the process: children who hurt themselves falling from dangerous heights when they were between five and nine years old are less likely to be afraid of heights when they become adults.

"Risk is a very, very important part of a healthy life," Bastian said. "And that does mean that if we find ourselves in an environment where the patterns of life have very little risk, you probably do need to find a way to engage with it in a healthy, productive way."

Swimming was not especially risky, not in the pool, but I could see that the pain of it heightened my senses. Even now, I can still describe the sand patterns on the bottom of the Icebergs pool from my most miserable swim sessions. And the hot shower afterward felt like a dream, not unlike the first meal after a long fast.

Being forced to slow down and think while swimming also made me start to do the same with surfing and with other parts of my life. I walked to work rather than getting a lift with Diana, just to give me a little more time. Simple things I'd usually hurry through, like making dinner, I relished, losing myself in a state of flow that I'd only previously experienced with writing on deadline.

But I also wondered about how we're affected by the pains and dangers we encounter without choosing them. Because that's the thing with risk—whether it's a rogue wave, a sudden illness, or an unexpected windfall, the test of our humanity comes with not knowing and deciding how to respond.

Bastian had done some work on that too, mixing personal experience with research around the 2011 floods in Brisbane. [xv] At the time, he was working at the University of Queensland, which sits just beyond the winding Brisbane River. When the water levels surged to levels not seen in forty years, damaging and destroying the homes and businesses of more than two hundred thousand people, he found himself marveling at the response. Alongside the trauma, there was community. More than fifty thousand people volunteered to help anyone who needed a hand after the water receded. They showed up with cleaning supplies and sandwiches, beer and equipment. They spent hours and days in the muck, creating bonds and friendships that did not exist before the disaster.

"As a sign of the trust that had emerged within the community, people were letting strangers walk into their homes and help them to throw out their damaged furniture or remove the layers of mud that had covered their floors," Bastian said. "People were wandering the streets with brooms and mops looking for something they could do."

This was the beginning of his research on pain as "social glue."[xvi] In the lab, Bastian decided to see if much smaller difficulties would yield the same lean toward generosity. First, the researchers split students into two groups: one would be forced to plunge their hands in ice water for as long as they could while trying to grab small balls in the basin and place them in a submerged container; members of the other would do the same task, but instead of ice, their hands would be placed in room-temperature water for ninety seconds.

Next, members of the ice group would have to do a wall squat (back against the wall, knees bent) while members of the room-temperature group would be asked to balance on one foot. They could switch feet or hold on to something if they wanted. Both groups could see each other throughout. At the end of the study, Bastian asked each individual how much pain had been experienced and how he or she felt about the other study participants. The students who had gone through the icy water and wall squats had not only felt more pain, they also reported a stronger bond with their fellow sufferers. They felt more solidarity and more loyalty, reporting that the experiment had created unity. Those who had participated in the nonpainful version of the experiment felt no such thing.

Additional studies showed that small doses of pain led to greater cooperation and even creativity. Because people felt supported and equal through the experience of adversity and more alert, they were able to produce a larger number of new ideas and more adventurous presentations (as determined by independent judges).

Our comfort zone, in other words, is not our creative zone.

As Bastian concluded in one of his papers, "We need to endure the challenge of sometimes stressful, novel, and potentially threatening environments to foster true originality."[xvii]

The mix of risk, inventiveness, and "social glue" can be found in many environments that help children test their mettle—group hikes into the mountains, teenage rock bands, intense sporting competitions, shared science projects, even something as simple as a rope swing over a pristine lake. It also reminded me of my experience in Iraq. The reporters and photographers Diana and I worked with in Baghdad were strangers whom we lived with. In the big yellow house on the Tigris River that we shared with a half dozen colleagues, we woke up almost every morning to the thunderous boom of car bombs. With gunfire providing a frequent soundtrack at night, our dinner discussions often turned to what we would do if insurgents came over the blast walls protecting our compound.

Those conversations, often dark and humorous in equal measure, helped us all bond over our shared vulnerability. But the doing—the day-to-day mission of journalism in a dangerous place—was what held us most closely together.

I learned a lot alongside my colleagues. Don't stand near windows—they might shatter in an explosion. Walk in other people's footsteps to avoid stepping on a bomb.

Brave photojournalists like João Silva also modeled smart behavior, combining a relentless work ethic with a strategic focus on safety. One scorching desert day in 2007, while I was interviewing someone at a Baghdad music shop for a story about weddings in war, João walked me to the corner of the street and pointed up at all the rooftops and balconies from which I could be shot or not shot, depending on where I stood. He was small, with a round head and a wife and kids at home in South Africa, and he spoke in close, not to scare me but rather to show me that with knowledge and awareness, I could use my surroundings to reduce the risk. A member of South Africa's famous "Bang-Bang Club," he hated nothing more than a reckless journalist who walked into danger with ignorance, arrogance, or both.

He believed, above all, in the acceptance of danger for a cause and in tempered risk. He was one of many who taught Diana and me to follow that creed. Take chances when it matters, with your wits and within your limits. "Everything is okay until it's not" was the phrase we learned to repeat. It was the wartime version of Pascal ("We are something, but we are not all"), and João experienced it firsthand. A few years after we were in Iraq together, he lost his legs after stepping on a land mine in Afghanistan—at some point, probability catches up with you. But he fought hard to recover and still shoots photos for the *New York Times* in Africa on prosthetics that (as he's been known to joke) at least made him taller.

The war—as war often does—pushed everyone it touched toward humility and bravery. It showed us human durability and cruelty, it produced friendships like no others, and for Diana and me, the experience also strengthened our marriage. We'd gone through the shit together, and the experience of risk revealed parts of our personalities we might have otherwise missed. Iraq is where we discovered that I crawl into a mental bubble when overwhelmed, while Diana reaches out for affirmation. We also both found we were more capable than we'd thought.

"If we survive," we used to joke, "this will be the best job we've ever had."

Our team was a finalist that year for the Pulitzer Prize. Everything immediately afterward seemed, as Bastian's research suggested, more meaningful, real, and present. Children, work, family. It was all just easier and so much richer. For the next few years, we relished it all—a glass of cold white wine with condensation on the glass, a bikini that fit just right, a hug that held your breath, the birth of Baz.

"On occasion," Bastian told me, "a person's character can grow and develop as a result of adversity and trauma—they can literally become better people."

But the timing part was murky. How long does it take for struggle to make us better? How long do the impacts last?

Looking back from the vantage point of Australia, I could see that so much of what the war taught us or what we taught each other evaporated over the decade that followed, like a river during a slow and steady drought. I had let myself take the moments that mattered for granted, and worse, I overlooked the steady resolve of my wife and the small joys of fatherhood. Diana had changed too. The stoic confidence that came from doing work that she thought was important and valuable faded, and like me, she often let herself get caught up in worrying too much about office politics and domestic logistics. The values and bonds forged in youth and affliction—they required more maintenance than I'd thought and far more effort than I often managed to contribute.

Even in Australia, my progress toward a healthier and more connected equilibrium was achingly slow. I was swimming but still self-centered and sealed off. Making it all the more obvious, I came across a study of risk from 2002 that pointed to a gender divide: the women surveyed tended to be less adventurous with physical hazards and bolder with social risks, while the men found physical danger easier but avoided scenarios involving other people that might produce shame, embarrassment, or awkwardness.[xviii] Later studies noted that women and men have similar affinities for risk overall as long as researchers included a wide range of scenarios—not just gambling or skydiving, which skew male, but also making a new meal for friends or joining a new group.[xix]

I returned to my definition of risk as anything that scares and thrills as I replayed in my mind the scenes of surfing with Diana. She was going for bigger waves and getting them, clearly pushing herself on the physical side. And me? I was still shrinking from interaction, with Diana's friends, with everyone who might push me in an unforeseen direction.

At home in America, Congress was hurtling toward impeachment—Trump was being accused of threatening to freeze aid to Ukraine unless officials there drummed up a scandal about his future opponent, Joe Biden.[xx] All I could see in Trump's aggression was cowardice, a desire for self-protection. His circle of confidants kept shrinking to those he knew would never challenge him.

Am I like that? Is this what men do as we age? Retreat and hide?

I couldn't really figure out how to do or be the opposite of Trump, so I tried a few things. I stopped arguing on Twitter. I volunteered to work at the Nippers barbecue in Bronte. I agreed to do more at school. I joined a bunch of other dads on a basketball team called the Buzzcocks, in which we lost every game despite our fancy blue-and-gold uniforms. I also, finally, started talking to some of Diana's friends while surfing.

None of these were landmark examples of bravery. They were simply very small acts of discomfort—social pinpricks of risk and pain. But they were hard for me and they felt right, like a slow turn on a long wave.

I also started to change how I worked. Instead of just trying to please my bosses with sheer worth ethic, I looked for stories that would let me participate alongside people, walk in their shoes, as I had done in Iraq with soldiers. That's how I ended up meeting Matt Zurbo. An avid *Times* reader had emailed me to tell me he was the kind of character you could only find in Australia—a larrikin, a boisterous maverick in the bush, writing a children's book every day for a year.

By the time I found him, he had left the mountains of Victoria and landed in Tasmania, where he was working as an oysterman around Eaglehawk Neck, a ribbon of coast east of Hobart. We agreed to meet at a beach parking lot near his house because it was easier to find, and when I arrived, Zurbo was walking out of the frigid water after a swim, shirtless and pale with a thick mess of hair flecked with gray. He was fifty but he looked thirty-five. There was only one other person on the beach, a woman in a thick down jacket walking a small dog.

"We usually go to more remote beaches," Zurbo said as he rifled around in the back of his truck for a shirt. "Sorry if I smell like fish guts."

At his house, a small, green, wood-framed one-story rental from the 1970s (or so said the linoleum), I met his wife, Elena, who was originally from Venezuela, and their two-year-old daughter, Cielo. He had insisted that I stay with them since there was not much else around, and when I asked what I could bring to dinner, he suggested whiskey. I broke out the bottle I bought in Hobart, and he poured us a hefty draught as Elena finished cooking.

Zurbo, I could tell right away, was one of those Charles Bukowski types, someone who preferred a life outside the establishment. His father was an immigrant from Transylvania. His mother was an arts administrator who drifted in and out of the avant-garde theater scene. Though Zurbo started writing in high school and published a rough young adult novel in his twenties that won a few awards, he never bothered with university. Some of his happiest childhood memories involved long trips out to nowhere with his father, and as a somewhat angry young adult, he gravitated to the physical challenges of nature. He worked mostly in the wilderness or in remote national parks along the coast, clearing trails, managing temperate rain forests, planting trees. It was backbreaking, dangerous work usually done with small groups of men who also felt like they belonged far away from society.

Zurbo met Elena during a rare day off in a random pub. She was fleeing a bad marriage and trying to write a novel. He was hitting middle age and, as he put it, "waiting around to die." They connected, married, had a baby, and moved. He liked Tasmania because the place still felt rough, like timber yet to be sanded smooth, without the convenience and increasingly wealthy selfishness of the mainland.

"There's a freedom here that Australia lost thirty years ago," he said over a vegetarian dinner and smaller glasses of whiskey. "People help each other. It's not about money."[xxi]

He was referring to Australia's long boom, which began in the 1990s and continued without a recession for nearly three decades, driving up property prices in major cities and making most of the country richer. Like me, he seemed to be searching for a simpler ideal, separate from somnolence, home renovation stories, and selfies.

The next morning, we woke up at 5:00 a.m. for a day of oystering. Normally I'd carry my notebook and talk to people and observe. This time, I volunteered to work. Zurbo's boss seemed happy enough to have me as we pulled out into the water under a hot-pink sky. I spent the day carrying heavy baskets of oysters from place to place, feeding them into a giant sorting machine, and counting them out by the dozen.

Zurbo worked faster and harder than the rest of us, and he spent every break writing his story for the day. He was on 282 out of 365—he'd asked me about Amelia the night before, and I had a hunch that what he was writing was inspired by something I said. He seemed to be one of those people who only knew how to sprint. I wasn't sure whether to try and keep up or tell him to slow down and breathe.

After we finished, we met up with Elena and Cielo at a community center in town. Opening a creaking door into a room with old curtains, yellowed and covered in flowers, we found a dozen older women sitting around a table knitting. Elena was teaching them Spanish; they were guiding her through sweater making and helping with Cielo, a blond whirlwind of a child who Zurbo grabbed and twirled before she walked us to a corner with toys and books. In another corner, tea and food could be "purchased" for a small donation placed in a mug.

"How great is this country," Zurbo said. "This is all free. Every town has one."

I had to admit, I was impressed. I recorded the community center in my running tally of where Australia's community spirit resided. Sitting in a rocking chair, my muscles sore from hard labor, with Zurbo on the carpet reading to his daughter while his Venezuelan wife laughed with retirees twice her age, I wanted to just take a nap and stay in Tasmania for as long as possible.

But I suspected that an element of anxiety fueled Zurbo's drive, perhaps because I related to it. Although he was clearly a risk-taker and outsider by disposition (many of the children's books he had already published toyed with the feral), it seemed to me that his mania was in some measure a compensation for a lack of confidence in himself as a provider—a husband and a parent—and in the system set up to judge his value as a member of society. I felt the same unease when I arrived in Australia; we both feared failing to meet the standard of safety and economic security that modernity and the Equitable, England's life insurance pioneers, set in motion so many years earlier with the insistence that food, shelter, guidance, and love were not enough to qualify as a good parent.

On the ride back from work, Zurbo had told me oystering didn't pay much. He was putting his 365 stories out there for free, and Elena's architecture credentials didn't transfer to Australia. She and Cielo seemed happy, but he struggled with guilt and wondered: was he putting them at risk by not settling down in some city or suburb? It felt like the pressure to comply with a safe and traditional approach to life had floated, like a mushroom cloud, all the way out to Eaglehawk Neck.

At that point, Zurbo was still refusing to give in. He told me there was one place where he always returned for some mental grounding: the football pitch. He'd been playing amateur Australian Rules football since he was a kid and had the busted body to prove it—he'd broken his back, and his fingers were gnarled from multiple sprains. One of the first things he'd done in Tasmania or "Tassie" was join a team, and tonight was training. So after some food shopping, we hopped in his truck and headed off, speeding down twisted rural roads, windows open, music blaring as loud as possible from a crappy red portable speaker. *This is why he doesn't move to safer locales*, I thought. *There's more life to be found in the lands without streetlights.*

We arrived just as the night turned dark, after an hour's driving. Although surrounded by scrub and dirt, the field felt like it belonged in a giant stadium—the grass was perfect emerald green under the bright lights, and men were yelling out each other's nicknames (Gussy, Griff, Dolly) as they sent the ball sailing back and forth during their warm-up. Zurbo was known as Old Dog. He kicked the ball skyward alongside men half his age and looked happier than I'd seen him at any point since we met.

After a few minutes, he ran over to me at the fence with an idea that I should have seen coming. "Do you want to play?"

I was standing there in black boots and jeans. I never seemed to know how to dress for Australia's physical activities.

"I don't know," I said.

He asked one of the guys if there were any sneakers around that I could use. Then another. They both said no.

"I wonder if there's anyone I can call who could bring some," Zurbo said. "Would you play if I get you some?"

He wandered off, dialing frantically, before I could answer. I already had more than I needed for my article. I was scared about looking foolish and didn't love the pressure he was exerting out in the open with all the other guys, but could I really say no? And—more importantly—was this one of those moments I'd been thinking about, when it was time to say yes?

A few minutes later, Zurbo suddenly appeared carrying a plastic bag with some shorts that smelled like a dead animal, a jersey, and a pair of black Nikes. I changed in the locker room with the other guys, who looked at me like I was some weird old uncle. I didn't match. The sneakers I'd borrowed lacked spikes. I had on a Rip Curl cap. I looked ridiculous.

But I did it anyway. I walked out onto the field wondering what the hell I'd gotten myself into. Old Dog told me how to hold the ball, tip down.

"Don't look at me. Just look at the ball."

My first few kicks were wild, off right. I'd played a couple of years of football in high school but never did much kicking. The Australian Football League ball was bigger and harder than its American equivalent, and I sent Old Dog chasing my errant attempts for a while until I got one just right—the ball flying end over end, straight to where I had aimed. I kicked it again and there it was, soaring. Not very far, but heading in the right direction.

Out of the next ten tries, most of them wobbled, but I felt like I'd gotten somewhere. Watching each kick head up into the white blazing light, time stood still, with the ball gliding in slow motion.

Then it was time for stretching and drills. The guys there were brawny Tassie brawlers, with legs the size of ham hocks. Zurbo, while older, was no slouch. And there I was, the silly American, trying to keep up as the team sprinted and stretched. At one point, to swing our legs, I had to grab Zurbo's shoulder, and then he had to grab mine. It was the closest I'd been to a stranger in a very long time, but at every point, Old Dog was right beside me, whispering what I was supposed to do. He didn't give a damn if other people thought his guest was weird. He'd brought me in. He kept me close. When we started combining sprints with punching the ball, Old Dog chased down my erratic efforts. He offered small tips—tilt the ball this way, aim here—and encouraged each small improvement.

It went on like that for a while. By the time I bowed out, I was sweating, making progress—and deeply grateful. For the first time, I fully understood a game I had only watched. I also saw how quickly nervousness and the pain of embarrassment could be transformed to improvement and fun, especially if there was someone to apprentice with.

On the way home, after a beer at the football club, Zurbo and I were in the car again, blaring music, driving back to his tiny little house and family. He had his unfinished beer between his legs, just the one, and seemed calmer. He thanked me for joining him on the field, for reminding him that there were still strangers out there who would just go for it, humiliation be damned.

"Are you kidding?" I told him. "Pushing me like that, it was a gift."

"It's one of those things," he said. He was banging his hand on the steering wheel with the beat. "People will remember more about you than you will about yourself, so do good. Drop those little bombs." It was the first time I'd ever heard someone refer to small acts of inclusion and kindness as explosive.

FOUR

The Christchurch Attacks

What if we're scared of the wrong threats? How white males distort risk perception; nudges vs. risk savvy; lessons in trust and recovery

The date was March 15, 2019. I'd just picked up the kids at school, and I was holding my phone in front of me, with an email that said: "URGENT—New Zealand."

"What's going on in New Zealand?" Baz asked.

"There was a terrible attack at a mosque," I told him. "Some guy shot and killed a bunch of people while they were praying. He's an asshole."

Even as I was saying it, "asshole" seemed inadequate. I was still trying to absorb the news. The email was the latest in a long chain with my editors, and I'd just found out that the shooting spree at two mosques in Christchurch, which left dozens dead, was livestreamed to Facebook by the shooter. We didn't yet know that he was a white Australian from a small town north of Sydney, but there was no escaping the fact that the shooting was a terrorist attack, the worst in New Zealand's history. We'd already sent a reporter to the scene.

Amelia suddenly appeared, late coming out of class. I tried to be casual, asking about school, but at home, I dispatched a second reporter and started writing. Diana was away with friends for the weekend, and I was trying to let her linger. She was the one who texted me first to see if she needed to come home.

"Let's give it a few hours," I told her.

I wasn't sure I could get to New Zealand. Flights were filling up and being canceled; reporters were asking if the airlines feared a sudden revenge attack from Islamic extremists.

Around dinnertime, Amelia yelled from the living room. "Why are you working so much? You're not hanging out with your kids!"

I stepped away from my desk in our home office and found them watching TV, surrounded by snack wrappers and piles of school stuff they ought to have put away. I tried to explain why I was distracted. In the end, I found myself saying, "It's just that sometimes this is what I have to do. Bad things happen, and I can't always predict when."

Baz and Amelia both nodded, seeming to understand. I wasn't sure I did. Aside from the challenges of how to cover the event and make some sense of it for *Times* readers, how could any of us assimilate such violent hatred into our worldviews? I'd spent the last year or so thinking about manageable risks, hoping that exposure plus a little pain and practice with others would make me and my family stronger. But Christchurch scrambled my thinking, making clear that the biggest challenges in life have nothing to do with whether to choose an adventure. The risks that hurt most are the ones we don't see coming, the unnatural disasters of human cruelty.

In the haze of the moment, I knew there was some connection to the themes I'd been exploring in my own life, but I couldn't see how it fit together. I felt nauseous just thinking about the bloodshed. I wondered if the shooting could have been prevented. I worried that the attack would lead to more violence.

And I had to go. I found a last-minute flight and bought a ticket to Christchurch for the following morning as Diana made plans to rush home.

I landed in Christchurch the day after the shootings. It was gray and damp as I drove my rental car toward Al Noor Mosque, one of two that were attacked. I had to park on a side street because the main road leading to Al Noor had been blocked with yellow police tape. Just in front of the flapping plastic, a memorial to the victims had sprung up with photos, candles, flowers, and handwritten messages. It reminded me of American mass shootings that I'd covered. I snapped a few photos of the notes placed between piles of daisies.

"This is your home and you should have been safe here."

"We understand the tough times you are going through."

"Christchurch, Christchurch, what will we do?"

A small crowd of mourners were walking through the park. I followed them until we all reached a squat brick building where victims' families came to get information, food, and whatever help they could find. Everyone looked exhausted, except for one man in the middle of it all, wearing a gray dishdasha and moving across a patch of grass between grieving men and women with a small entourage that signaled leadership. When I approached him, he told me his name was Lateef Zikrullah Alabi. He asked me to call him Lateef. He was the imam from Linwood, the second mosque that had been attacked. Suddenly he looked familiar: I'd read about him on the plane. He had rushed to the wounded after the shooting, appearing in photos on the local front pages covered in blood.

"Walk with me," he said.

Lateef explained that there was a meeting with government officials at the hospital a few blocks away. Between phone calls, he told me he was originally from Nigeria, that he had been in New Zealand for three years and was finishing a PhD. He said what worried him most was that the Muslim community in New Zealand might never again feel safe.

"It all depends on how it is handled," he said.

When we reached the hospital, I barely noticed the guards out front as I took notes while walking up the stairs and toward a door that said "relatives' room." Lateef stopped there. He shook my hand and said goodbye with a look that seemed to say *don't screw this up*. He stepped into a side room with other Muslim leaders while I walked into what turned out to be a cafeteria with blue and red institutional chairs and about two hundred people crammed together in small groups—the victims' families, grieving, bereft, trying to hold themselves together.

I appeared to be the only reporter there. Lateef must have wanted me to see what was happening—he'd taken a chance and trusted me. I told a huddle of men standing near me that I was a journalist, asking if it would be okay to stay and listen. They nodded. All around us, there were women wiping tears from their eyes and men who looked like they hadn't slept in weeks.

It was clear that most of the families were seeking basic information. New Zealand officials had still not announced the names of the dead or even many of the seriously wounded—an unusual delay that no one in the room could understand. Nearly an hour after I arrived, a police commander finally appeared, standing on a chair to address the crowd's concerns. Women in black headscarves and men who smelled like cigarettes pressed forward.

"Give us the names," someone shouted from the right side by a set of stairs.

The commander was a squat, middle-aged man in a blue sport coat, the kind of guy you can tell is a cop the moment he enters a room. He told the group that everyone was working as hard as they could to identify the dead. No one seemed to believe him. The room erupted with outrage until an imam stood on another chair and tried to calm everyone down.

"It's not a car accident. It's an international crime scene," the imam said. "They have to be careful not to get anything wrong."

Still, the crowd demanded answers, "So we can rest!" shouted one man in a far corner.

His name was Ahad Nabi. His father, Haji Mohemmed Daoud Nabi, a leader in the local Afghan community, was missing and appeared to have been killed at Al Noor.

The man I stood next to, Zuhair Darwish, a taxi driver with gray hairs in his beard and a bright yellow shirt, shook his head. We'd been talking for a while. He was originally from Jordan. His brother had also been at Al Noor.

"This is the best they can do?" he asked.

So many of the survivors were crushed and disappointed, in New Zealand and in the supposed promise of the West. Quite a few of the room's families came from Iraq, Afghanistan, Pakistan, and Syria, places where nearly everyone had learned to live with unpredictability and strife. Here they expected better, starting with safety in a house of worship, but they didn't demand perfection—just clarity, community, and a path to closure.

Amazingly, despite their heartbreak, many of them seemed intent on bringing New Zealand's cautious bureaucracy along. When the authorities said they wanted to release the names all at once but were struggling because some of the dead were hard to recognize due to their wounds, the victims' families did not flinch in horror. They calmly offered suggestions: let us share photos so we can help; let imams identify the dead.

That was the message they kept delivering to the authorities. Don't try to protect our feelings. Just let us do something as a group so that we can get more done.

"This is a test," said Zia Aiyaz, a young engineer originally from Afghanistan, who was standing near Darwish. "God is testing us all."

The conflict between the victims and the mostly white

Western authorities reminded me of Iraq, when parents of the missing used to show up in the Green Zone to ask the American military if they had seen their sons. The Americans never did much with those requests, possibly because they viewed their situation as hopeless, or because of the fortress mentality Seligman talked about—they saw themselves as the experts and omniscient arbiters of what mattered and what was possible in a dangerous situation.

But New Zealand's authorities, stunned by an experience unlike anything they had ever seen, were less haughty and more open to adjusting how they operated. A few minutes after the officials disappeared in a sea of shouting, the police returned with a new announcement. They'd talked it over and agreed to let people send photos to the police and choose imams to identify those they could. The entire room of relatives seemed to exhale. Mothers who had been staring straight ahead started tapping through photos on their phones, looking for images of their sons to share. Something had given way. The cultural chain of command, the cloud of blame. It was the sign of a diverse community leaning into each other.

"The survivors knew this victory would only bring more pain," I wrote in the last line of my story for the *Times* that night. "But at least they were moving toward a resolution, together and alone."

What that "resolution" would look like was hard to see. Covering the Christchurch attacks after spending more than a year trying to embrace more risk in daily life was a jarring experience. I knew that even if we don't acknowledge it, choosing to exist in an open society means accepting some degree of risk—we fly, we drive, we gather at schools and sporting events without passing through metal detectors. Terrorism aims to convince us that our belief in the probability of coexistence—our belief in each other, in the idea that most people did not want to harm us is simply a delusion. Life is always high risk, terrorism tells us, so we might as well pull into a cocoon of distrust.

I didn't want to accept that argument. The argument that said we need to build a fortress and stick with our own. And I didn't want my kids to live like that either. I wanted them to play at life, err toward optimism, believe the best about people, and grow into generous, community adventurers. But would that be possible after serious trauma? When tragedy makes anxiety rational, it gets a lot harder to ask people to push beyond what feels safe. I wondered if it was barbaric to expect that kind of thing in a place like Christchurch after the attacks, or if it was exactly what the traumatized need to heal. Perhaps, I thought, there are lessons to be learned in the aftermath of terrorism that could be applied to life's more minor setbacks.

I decided to look for a family who would let me spend time with them as they tried to recover from the attacks both physically and mentally. Zulfirman Syah seemed like a good place to start. I first discovered hints of his story online, in snippets of news stories. In the long catalogues of the dead and wounded, he was described as an artist from Indonesia and a hero who saved the life of his two-year-old son by diving over him during the attack. He'd been shot several times and seemed to have survived, but the status of his injuries was unclear. Syah had been at Linwood with Lateef, and between the dead and wounded, he found the courage to protect his son. With all my questions about risk and recovery in mind, he was the one I wanted to meet.

I found his wife, Alta Sacra, on Facebook, correcting errors in the news reports. She had a degree from the University of Massachusetts, where many of my friends from home had studied. Guessing she had to be American—possibly the only American touched by the attack, perhaps making her more likely to talk to me—I sent her a message.

"It looks like you're already dealing with some frustrating experiences with media so I apologize for bothering you," I wrote. "But I wanted to run something by you."

I told her I was hoping to follow a single family over the course of a year or more to document their response to the attacks. I was not interested in quick-hit sensationalism; I was just seeking the truth of whatever happened, and I promised to be fair. Her reply came a few minutes later. "Of all the media inquiries I have received, yours is something I would consider."

Later that day, we met at a table in the dark and empty break-fast area of my hotel near a few condemned buildings with large cracks from the 2011 earthquake that killed 185 people in and around Christchurch. Alta had shoulder-length hair, glasses, and a nose ring, and she was indeed American.

She looked spent but asked sharp questions, telling me that her caution with the media came in part from the severity and intimacy of what they were dealing with—bullets had blasted into her husband's back and his scrotum while their son, Roes, was hit with shrapnel that sliced through his diaper, requiring stitches.

I told her I'd go over every word I wrote with them to ensure it was accurate and that they were comfortable with whatever I planned to publish.

"I need to think about it," she said. "And I need to talk to Jul," which is what she called her husband.

The next day, she told me they'd allow me to visit them with a photographer. I picked her up that afternoon to go meet Jul after we stopped by a store to pick up a few items—a tablet so he could watch movies, some toiletries to make him more comfortable. The photographer, Adam Dean, had flown in from Bangkok and was waiting for us at the hospital, but as soon as we reached Jul's floor, a tall, wispy woman from the public relations team suddenly appeared and tried to make us leave. They'd apparently caught a foreign TV reporter sneaking into someone's room after the shooting, but Alta, who had been cheerful up to that point, skipped straight to yelling, rejecting the attempt to protect their privacy.

"I told you they were coming. I want them here, and you have no right to stop us," she said, drawing looks from up and down the hallway. "This is my family. *My* family."

I could see the trauma and anger in the tight muscles of her face. Inside the room, by contrast, Jul, with an unruly goatee and warm brown eyes, was a sea of calm. He welcomed me with a wide smile and told me to grab a seat next to his bed.

"How are you feeling?" I asked.

"I feel very lucky to be alive," he said.

"And your son, I hear he's doing better. I can't believe what you did."

"It was instinct," Jul said. "Anyone would have done the same."

He readjusted his body in the bed, wincing for just a second. He was on his back, tilted slightly forward to reduce pressure on his wounds. Wanting to avoid retraumatizing him, I pulled back to general questions.

He told me that he and Alta met through a Muslim dating app in 2015. She was thirty at the time, with light green eyes, a loud American accent, and no interest in returning to the United States after converting to Islam in Bali. Jul was a few years older, the son of a teacher from Sumatra, who longed to make art and build a family somewhere beyond Yogyakarta, where galleries were selling his abstract paintings as fast as he could produce them. In January 2019, they landed in New Zealand, where Alta had spent some time before. It seemed like a chance worth taking. An investment in a better life. Until the shooting.

Slowly, as I leaned close enough to the bed to smell sweat and iodine, he told me what happened.

"It was only the third time I've taken Roes to mosque," Jul said. "Usually we sit in the back part so it's easy for me to leave if I need to, when prayers start. But this time we were in the middle. He was lying down and I was going to move his body closer to the window but I said to myself, 'Oh, I'll just wait.'

"When we started to pray, he woke up and cried. The crying was like a sign for me," he said. "The other times we went, he didn't cry. So when he did I held him and I was holding him while I prayed."

That was when the gunman arrived. The first shots came from the parking lot.

"One time, two times—it didn't sound dangerous to me," Jul said. Then the shooter entered, in the back, where Jul would usually be right near the door. He started firing in bursts. Gunshots smashed the room.

"All the members…" Jul paused. "They started to lie down."

A nurse suddenly appeared at the door of his hospital room. Jul and I both breathed a small sigh of relief.

"Do you think that pain relief has kicked in?" she asked. "Are you feeling comfortable enough for us to go ahead?"

Jul nodded and rolled onto his side, facing me. With his permission, Adam and I stepped behind him and watched as the nurse pulled off the bandage covering the center of his back, revealing a moist red hole. It measured more than two inches in circumference, big enough to hold a tennis ball. Worst of all, it was deep. I held my breath as she snaked a narrow probe six inches straight into his back, plus another couple of inches to the right. Jul closed his eyes and breathed through it all.

"Well, it looks clean. Is it very sore?" the nurse asked.

"No," Jul said without hesitation.

His answer drew a skeptical glare—he'd apparently developed a reputation for resisting attention and sympathy.

"Have they told you how long you have to be in here?" I asked.

"A few more days," he said. He pointed to a machine that sucked the pus from his wound to prevent infection. "I have to take that with me."

The next time I saw Jul, two weeks later, he was at home in their two-bedroom flat with mostly blank walls and the kind of anonymous furniture that always comes with an affordable furnished apartment. Roes, still traumatized, was watching television and wearing sunglasses that he refused to take off. The window shades were also drawn. And Jul's wound machine was beeping. Something was broken or not working, and Alta was freaking out.

"Fuck, what's wrong with it?" she said as she turned the machine on and off repeatedly.

In the hospital, she'd told me she was afraid of having to be Jul's nurse, of doing something wrong that might hurt or kill him. She was worried about being abandoned.

"They say they're going to take care of us, but what if they don't?"

Compared to some of the other victims I'd met, Jul and his family were indeed more alone. They had only arrived two months before the attack, so while their apartment had a pile of gifts in a corner, mostly from people in New Zealand's Indonesian community, they didn't have many friends to turn to for help. The healthcare network, while working relatively well for Jul's physical injuries, was also struggling under the weight of so many people in need. Jul had regular appointments with doctors to keep him focused on recovery, but Roes and Alta were being left to manage on their own. The government's crisis response was common and obvious: start with the most affected, and ripple out the recovery resources from there if you can. But within a family, trauma blurs the line between individuals—the psychological toll affects everyone.

Alta was trying. Hard. She had created spreadsheets tracking Jul's treatment. She pushed and prodded caseworkers to provide Roes with the therapy he was promised, all while running errands, putting food on the table, and fighting viral lies from extremists. In the worst case, a video from inside the mosque after the shooting was being shared by right-wing conspiracists who accused Jul of being a "crisis actor" because he could be seen on the ground holding his cell phone before passing out. He'd been calling Alta. She reported the video to both American and New Zealand authorities whenever she saw it.

I worried about how sustainable this was. Though Alta's sister had just arrived to assist, it seemed to me that Alta was trying to control too much and sleeping too little. Brock Bastian's studies of the Brisbane floods had shown that people pull together in times of trauma, and that's what I had seen in the "relatives' room" right after the shooting, but what if there were not enough people to help out?

There was at least a little hope in some of the academic papers I'd been reading, which found that post-traumatic stress disorder (PTSD), while widespread, is still the exception rather than the rule.[i] In the wake of a traumatic event, including death, terrorism, and combat, 65 percent of people show few or no symptoms of PTSD. Even among the families of 9/11 victims, one study found, most people did not report long-term psychological issues.[ii] Moreover, another study Bastian turned me on to showed that people who had experienced adverse life events—such as the death of a loved one, cancer, a war, or a natural disaster—were usually emotionally and physically stronger. [iii] Spanning ages and backgrounds, they reported better mental health and well-being than those exposed to high levels of adversity or no adversity at all.

There were a couple of things I took away from the data. First, humans are more resilient than we might have thought. Second, a hardship-free life can leave us just as unhappy and unhealthy as a life filled with endless trauma. What I couldn't figure out was where Alta fell on the spectrum of struggle or how the process worked in the blood, sweat, and tears of real life. What amount of adversity is optimal?

Even before the attacks, Alta's life had not been easy. She'd grown up as the middle child of Christian fundamentalists, "The kind who wouldn't let me wear pants." As I knew from my own experience with close-minded Christianity, not all religion brings solace. The discipline from her father tended to be severe. She married a man she later realized she didn't love, leading to a divorce and "an interim period of mediocrity," which prompted her move to Bali. One of her brothers was in jail. It was if she'd already run a marathon, and the shooting added an extra ten miles. Was she more equipped to handle it? Probably. But she was also sprinting all the time. I could see she was getting tired.

Nevertheless, she didn't stop. And—even more strikingly— she didn't shut herself off. Even though there weren't that many people stretching toward her, she kept reaching out.

Not long after the shooting, for example, Alta decided to take Roes to the public memorial service for the Christchurch victims in the park near Al Noor. She thought it would be good to be with some of the other victims and to show them that Roes had survived. I walked with them from the hospital to a section of the park where there were thousands of people gathered in the early autumn sun. Many of the non-Muslim women around us wore headscarves out of respect while Muslims leaders clustered in groups by a large screen that had been set up so speakers could be seen and heard from the crowd.

There was an area to our left specifically for victims' families, but Alta preferred to try and blend in with everyone else, so we sat together in the middle, on the grass. It was a beautiful day, but she looked anxious. She was mostly worried about Roes.

"Is it the right decision to bring him here?" she said. "I don't know."

Roes had a truck to play with and seemed fine at first, just a usual fidgety toddler. But when the service began with a traditional call to prayer, he grabbed on to Alta. She tried to calm him—"Look at the sky," she said, "look at the sky"—but he began to whine, making it suddenly apparent that he was the only child around.

"I want to go home," he said.

"It's okay, it's okay," she said, patting his back and holding him tight.

"Home, I want to go home."

After a few minutes, Alta picked up Roes and walked quietly back to the car, tears streaming down her face. I accompanied them in silence, unsure of what to say. The walk seemed to last forever. She clearly believed in the value of seeking connection and community, but the pain was still so present, the road ahead so long. And before I could work out where the journey would end, I found myself getting angrier and angrier about how it all started.

Before Christchurch, I'd been focused on how often humans overemphasize prudence and miss out by avoiding risks that make them afraid. Seeing Alta hurt, seeing Roes so broken, I became furious about all the times we choose the wrong fear to obsess about or are not scared enough of legitimate threats. Why do humans get risk wrong so often and what can we do to improve?

In the 1950s and '60s, the study of risk expanded from cold mathematical calculation—what is the probability of X—to a deeper examination of the way that humans perceive those risks and therefore how we prioritize them. Along with, say, trying to gauge the likelihood of a plane crash, we began to investigate why some people fear flying more than others.

A psychology professor at the University of Delaware, Marvin Zuckerman, pioneered the field by trying to analyze people's likelihood to take risks based on the rather Freudian evaluation of "sensation seeking."[iv] In the 1970s, those discussions of personality developed alongside debates over nuclear power. Scientists insisted it was safe to develop and use, but in survey after survey, the public said it didn't trust their assessment. Reams of scientific reports and probability studies as well as proof of strict protocols—not to mention the clear lack of deadly accidents—failed to persuade the skeptics. There was a stark divide in risk perception, and the nuclear industry was at a loss about why or what to do.

For Paul Slovic, a psychologist at the University of Oregon, the tension between expertise and public opinion sounded familiar.[v] At the urging of a geographer he admired, he'd already been trying to work out why, after natural disasters like hurricanes, floods, or earthquakes, people return to the same place to rebuild and face the same risk again. Zuckerman's studies of sensation seeking could not fully explain the behavior. Something in the communication and understanding of risk seemed to be failing with what Slovic called "society's gambles."

Slovic and his colleagues developed a questionnaire that probed how people assess a variety of dangers.[vi] In 1978, he and his team presented test subjects with forty-one different causes of death, including diseases, accidents, homicide, suicide, and natural hazards like flooding. They asked everyone to compare two risks at a time and choose the more likely cause of death and the ratio of greater to lesser frequency—essentially, which one was more deadly and by how much. The results forever changed how we think about human rationality and risk because, again and again, the participants got it wrong.

They said tornadoes were more likely killers than asthma, even though asthma causes twenty times more deaths. They said lung cancer was a more potent killer than stomach cancer (it's not), and they judged accidental death to be far more likely than stroke (nope: strokes cause twice as many deaths as all accidents combined). Overall, most respondents rated diseases and accidental death as roughly equal. In fact, death by disease is eighteen times more likely.

Slovic wasn't quite sure what to make of such egregious errors, so he started looking for patterns. Over time and with additional studies, he worked out a matrix of mental shortcuts and unconscious biases that make us especially sensitive to certain kinds of threats and not others.[vii]

We underestimate the risk of disease, for example, because of our tendency to emphasize the catastrophic rather than the chronic. There are Darwinian reasons for that—the earliest humans survived by clustering together. So even now, a risk that could kill many people at once (and thus wipe out the whole tribe) scares us more than a threat that kills people one by one over time. For a similar evolutionary reason, when kids are at risk, our fears are greater. As Slovic noted, toxins in a workplace don't frighten us as much as toxins in schools.

We also favor hazards we can control, in part because we tend to be overconfident about our own abilities. We're more likely to resist a risk imposed on us (a driver texting in the car next to us) than when we voluntarily expose ourselves (texting while we drive). The harder a risk is to understand, whether it's chemicals, artificial intelligence, or mRNA vaccines, the more frightened we feel, and unanswered questions make that even worse (which helps explain why new technologies scare us more than old; there are more unknowns).

The information we consume and who we trust can also move one risk or another to the top of our priority list or the bottom, where it tends to be ignored. Risk psychologists ascribe this, in part, to what they call a "finite pool of worry"[viii]—another mental tic for coping with risk that means there are only so many fears we can handle at once. We're built to not sweat the small stuff even if we misunderstand what's small and what's not.

"Attention is akin to a spotlight," Slovic told me on one of our many calls and video chats, as he helped me understand how we think about risk.[ix] "It shines on some piece of information, and everything out of the spotlight might not be seen."

When I asked him how to summarize what his work revealed, he said it all boils down to one simple truth about humankind. "We make decisions based on our emotions."

That elemental insight has inspired a number of new models for how our decision-making process works. Daniel Kahneman, the Harvard psychologist who wrote the bestselling *Thinking, Fast and Slow*, often turned to Slovic's work as he and his colleagues developed their own theories about how we evaluate options. So did an entire generation of behavioral economists who for years have been punching holes in the fundamental free market belief that consumers act rationally.

But I had a very different kind of question: why did Australia and New Zealand fail to keep the Christchurch attacks from happening? In my calmer moments, I wondered if the question was even fair. Perhaps it was an almost impossible task to see the threat posed by one man in two countries with a combined population of thirty million people. And yet the authorities in Australia, the United States, and elsewhere often bragged about breaking up future terror plots involving Islamic terrorists. They had no problem writing new laws to broaden their surveillance powers or bolstering budgets for counterterrorism of one particular kind. Governments also fully embrace their responsibility to protect people on the roads with infrastructure, regulation, and policing, which shows that when the authorities want to tackle a risk and reduce an anxiety, they can, and they do. But there is also a lot they miss. Christchurch made that bloody obvious. Why not this terrorist? Why didn't they see or prioritize *this* threat?

The answer, of course, lay in the sort of terrorist he was. Like individuals, societies are imperfect at discerning threats. They rely on emotions, they develop prejudices, they misjudge people and circumstances. In this case, there was too much trust in the shooter because he was just another white guy in white-run countries that still saw terrorism through the lens of 9/11 or perhaps the often-flawed perceptions built up over centuries of colonialism.

Again and again, the killer-to-be was given the benefit of the doubt because he wasn't *perceived* as a risk: in his hometown of Grafton, Australia, where he worked at a gym and was known for being, yes, an asshole; and in New Zealand, where he bought an arsenal of high-powered weapons, often appeared at shooting ranges, and hung out in online groups filled with mind-sick extremists. If he had a different name and different skin color—if he looked like Jul or the bearded young men in the relatives' room—he would never have made it as far as he did. If humans (and especially people with power) were better at seeing the realities of risk, I thought, someone would have stopped him.

Just thinking about that made me angry. Slovic, unsurprisingly, had a term for what I was feeling—hindsight bias.

"Things always look clearer in the rearview mirror," he said when I asked him about the shooting. "It's very hard once you know how it turned out to recover the sense of uncertainty and ambiguity that was there at the time."

He was being generous. But he also agreed that there was another, more embedded form of bias at work and a divide in perception about security that rarely gets noticed. Those who "run the show," as Slovic put it, tend to have a very different view of risk than the public at large.

The 2000 paper "Gender, Race, and Perceived Risk: The 'White Male' Effect" sharpened the point. Slovic and a few other researchers took as their starting point a study from the early

'90s showing that women judged many health risks to be larger and more problematic than men, from nuclear waste to food additives to smoking. Taking a deeper look at the data, though, Slovic and his colleagues noticed that risk perceptions actually tended to be similar between the genders for all but one demographic: educated white men with higher household incomes. These low-risk white males (LRWMs)—who by virtue of their race, gender, education, and wealth were insulated from most of life's dangers—had less concern than anyone else about nearly everything they'd been asked about.[x]

To further explore that demographic divide, the research team conducted a separate survey. Again, LRWMs were less likely to rate a range of hazards as high risk (crime, drugs, pesticides, and blood transfusions, among others). With more questions included, the data also revealed how these men viewed the world: "Compared with the rest of the sample, white males were more sympathetic with hierarchical, individualistic, and anti-egalitarian views."

The survey only covered American households. The hazards list was far from comprehensive (terrorism was not on there), and there was more variation by race and gender than in the first survey. But at the end of the paper, the authors presented a recognizable portrait. White men "see different things at risk than do other citizens." They display an "intolerance of community-based decision and regulation processes." They "stood apart from others."

The problem was obvious. Western society's risk priorities are often set by what this crowd of men fears the most and what they fail to pay attention to. They (or rather, we) are the source of the blind spot for white supremacy and other risks we ignore at our peril. It was time for me to recognize my own place in the risk matrix of modern life. I may have my fears, of rough seas and whatever else, but in my quest to reevaluate risk and adventure, I'd probably been too dismissive of the need for caution and not sensitive enough to the reasons why many people—especially the nonwhite and nonwealthy—might not embrace risk and might not believe that most of the time everything would be all right.

And yet diving into the research also confirmed that regardless of our ethnic background or where we're starting from in terms of class and culture, the fundamental challenge is the same. Risk is real, varied, ever-present. At a time when major dangers often seem to be lined up like planes on a distant runway, we all need to get better with risk assessment and risk management at the family and community level. We all need to fight our biases. We all need to get better at self-correction, at living and making decisions with less emotion—if not for ourselves then certainly for the sake of our kids.

So how do we do it?

Some of those who have zeroed in on our biases see the pace of our decision-making as part of the problem and see hope in anything that slows us down or pushes us toward better choices. They support interventions known as "nudges" that guide people's actions toward what's best for them.[xi] Automatic enrollment in retirement savings plans is a nudge. Placing fruit up front in a cafeteria and sugary snacks behind the counter is also a nudge.

Slovic, whose early research on preference construction contributed to this concept, says the idea is to disrupt quick decisions when we only have a slight inclination for one option or another. But there are a lot of scenarios that don't fit the formula. Slowing down to discourage a bad decision wouldn't have done any good during the Christchurch attacks: Jul made a split-second decision to dive on top of Roes—his instincts saved his son. Even with nuclear power, the hazard that kicked off all the research of risk perception, it's hard to see how thinking slow or being nudged would alter the dynamic. Also, there's something more than a little patronizing in the approach. Effectively, it assumes that we're better off being controlled by wiser heads than our own; it's hierarchical and does *not* have much faith in our abilities to improve our own decision-making.

Gerd Gigerenzer and others have taken a different approach, examining what humans get right. Research shows that's what our minds prefer: we're more likely to change our habits and alter our choices in response to positive messages—appealing to pride works better than a threat.[xii] Asking children to join a reading contest with their friends to raise money for a local cause does more than putting a bookshelf at the front of the classroom or warning kids that they'll regret never reading *Huckleberry Finn*.

And where people have responded well to the most urgent risks—in war, fires, or floods, or even with lifesaving—the most successful responses, the ones showing the human capacity to overcome, also tend to be driven by "pro-social" thinking. Nudging appeals to self-interest; it urges you to eat healthy food for your own good. But better individual decisions in the toughest times are often driven by group connection, altruism, self-sacrifice, and something else: trust.

The more I thought about Christchurch and all the research I'd been digesting, the more I started to see trust as the nucleus around which everything was spinning. Trust (between New Zealanders and immigrants) was what the Christchurch shooter tried (deliberately or blindly) to destroy. And it's what Lateef and many other New Zealanders were trying to rebuild in the aftermath. Even Alta, more than anything else, seemed to be looking for other people she could trust. In Christchurch, in fact, it often felt as if everyone I met simply knew that a communitarian approach would be their only hope for both recovery and preparation for any future tragedy.

Their efforts to rebuild connection looked to me like courageous hard work; they were defying what psychology tells us about just how precarious that belief in another person or an institution can be. Slovic and others have demonstrated that it takes just a single error or failure to destroy trust, while building it takes dozens or hundreds of actions over an extended period of time. That was the struggle I saw with Alta and Roes in the park. They were just getting started in the process of reconstructing their belief in humanity, one interaction at a time. It was slow, a bit like rebuilding after an earthquake. It was scary and exhausting, too, but the act of trying and trying again, the research showed, should yield an edifice of strength and confidence eventually.

The science around how to fight distrust (and fear in general) is remarkably clear: we have to get out there, and continue getting out there, building positive experiences; we have to defy our feelings and *choose* to have faith in the world and in each other again and again. Distrust is stagnant water. It feels safe but fosters the sense of helplessness that leads to depression and fragility. It isolates us, makes us look back not forward, which lets our prejudices fester like bacteria and spread to the next generation.

To grow, to reset, we have to move toward what we fear or loathe or just don't know very well. We have to give more people a chance, even after being hurt. Because without small and repeated acts of courage, we don't have social glue or community, and without community, we can't manage the deadliest risks, overcome the most serious forms of trauma, or raise healthy, happy, resilient children.

Interdependence may not be something we talk much about in America, but it matters. Gigerenzer pointed me a relatively recent example: the famous "miracle on the Hudson" in 2009, when Captain Chesley "Sully" Sullenberger safely landed a full commercial airliner in the river west of Manhattan after geese collided with its engines. In the news stories of the day and in the Hollywood movie, with Tom Hanks playing Sully, it's a story of individual heroism. The good guy saves the day.

In Gigerenzer's version, the version I've come to see as more accurate, it's a triumph of mutual trust, intuition, and years of hard work that preceded the crisis.[xiii] In the three minutes between the bird strike and the river landing, Sully and his copilot ran through an evacuation checklist to safeguard against fires and other dangers, communicated with air traffic control, and decided where to land. Without time to calculate the rate of descent, they relied on instincts that told them they were falling too fast to get back to the airport. And just as importantly, the passengers and many others became partners in the landing. The people on board did not panic, and they complied with instructions. When they opened their emergency exits, they saw a ferry ready to pick them up before the icy water gave them hypothermia. There was no stampede. No one died. No one was hurt.

"It was the combination of teamwork, checklists, and smart rules of thumb that made the miracle possible," Gigerenzer said. "The best way to deal with risk is to take people seriously rather than try to nudge them like sheep."

Taking people seriously means believing in human competence, generosity, and resilience. There's inspiration in that, as Jul proved by saving his son's life in the mosque, but when I left Christchurch after my first month-long reporting trip, I admit that I found it difficult to see human nature in a positive light. On my flight out, I watched a war movie because I thought it would match my mood. As soon as I stepped in the door in Sydney, before I spoke to Diana, I walked upstairs and took a long hot shower, where I found myself crouching, trying to work out the trajectory of the bullets that hit Jul. Based on his wounds, he had to have thrown himself onto the ground with Roes under his right arm. He would have been curled up, facing away from the shooter, putting his entire body between the killer and his boy. That's how one bullet raced up his back and another hit him between the legs. In my bedroom, naked, on the gray carpet, I lay down in the position I imagined for Jul.

"I saw smoke coming from a hole in his diaper," he'd told me with sadness in his eyes, describing his last memories of the shooting, between bouts of unconsciousness. "I couldn't care for him," Jul said. "I couldn't help."

Despite his bravery, he felt guilty. He saw his actions as

inadequate. And holding myself in a fetal position and trying not to move, I also felt wretched—journalism did not seem up to the task of making their pain meaningful. I could feel in myself the familiar mix I'd felt after covering violence and death elsewhere: profound sadness and unfathomable anger, like a thunderstorm trapped inside my chest, forceful but unheard. Usually the intensity faded; this time, I hoped there was a way to make it useful beyond just an article.

That night, whether for myself or them, I talked to Baz and Amelia about my trip. Lying together on Amelia's big bed, I could sense that I had calmed down but still felt close to tears. The process of digesting an intense experience was working through me as it had before, after Iraq, after earthquakes, after the mass shootings I had covered in America. I knew the pattern. But I was bringing it to my children for the first time.

Wondering how much of what I was feeling could be seen on my face, I explained to them that I was fine but sad because, as well as great beauty, there was enormous horror in the world. I told them I met people who were broken with grief and that I also met people like Alta, Roes, and Jul, who were kind, calm, and brave.

Amelia, not yet nine years old, in pink pajamas, gave me a hug. She tried to work out what it meant for the rest of us. "Sometimes guns can be okay, like, the police have them," she said. "But sometimes not."

Baz, now ten, was more interested in the details. "Did you see any bullets at the mosque?" he asked. I could tell from his serious tone that he was asking out of fear, not video-game voyeurism.

"No," I told him. "The police were still investigating so I couldn't go inside. But I did see what the bullets did to Jul."

I described the wound in general terms, figuring they needed to know what bullets do in real life rather than in video games or movies. I told them he was going to recover, and I explained exactly how he saved his son, showing them on my own back where the bullet entered. Amelia touched me as if looking for a scar.

"You know how we talk a lot about kindness," I told them. "This is why it matters. The world can be ugly. We have to make it more beautiful."

It was a line that came out fast, just like the asshole comment, and it felt just as clarifying. It was borrowed from *Miss Rumphius*, a picture book I read to them often when they were younger, featuring a woman who traveled the world and returned to her coastal home seeking a way to make life more beautiful. She found it by planting lupins in the wild, a small act made meaningful in part because it was perennial and shared with others—every summer, the flowers would bloom for everyone to see and smell.

Recalling that rhythm with my children, I felt like I could breathe a little easier. Plants that seem to die quietly return and bring joy. Humans can follow the same pattern. If we choose. If we push toward the sun.

Over a glass or two of wine downstairs, I told Diana about Alta and Jul and about my talk with the kids. Safe at home in Sydney recounting the experience, the research around trust, the small acts of goodwill, I could hear my voice getting louder. We needed to keep going, I told Diana, keep cultivating our own garden. She needed to press ahead with her conditioner and her novel and with our new Australian friends. We needed to do more for others and ourselves, buy as many surfboards as we want, and never take for granted every day we have together as a healthy family. I could feel that appreciation for life that I'd felt after Iraq coming back again. But it was more than that.

For the first time since we arrived in Australia two years earlier, and maybe ever, I could also sense a closing of mental distance, a connection between what I'd covered as a journalist and the way I wanted to exist in the world outside my work. My perspective had changed.

I was sick of prioritizing language alone, sick of a culture that obsesses over what is said online or off as if it matters as much as what is done. All the devices and apps and articles and streaming services too—there was too much communication dividing us from each other, too much sharing of sanctimony and outrage, telling us who to hate or rally around without any of us recognizing that we are not really living. We're just arguing.

"Fuck it," I said. "I just want to *live*."

Two days later, I packed myself a towel and headed to Icebergs for another lesson with Katie. Swimming was not something I enjoyed; maybe I never would. But fun was not the point. I was swimming not for pleasure but rather to pass a test to join a group that aimed to help other people. If I endured, if I qualified for and then passed the Bronze training program, my children and I would share the experience of learning to save lives.

Walking along the coast to get to the pool, I knew something so small and insignificant could only do so much. There was a chance I'd spend years as a lifesaver without a single rescue, never called on to be anywhere near as brave as Jul.

But in my own community, I had a chance to do something. To reach outward, to become trustworthy. So I decided I would. After Christchurch, I no longer saw my time in the pool as just a response to embarrassment or an attempt to teach my kids a lesson. It became an attempt to get to a place where I could contribute more to life than words.

Engagement with real life seemed to be part of what the Christchurch shooter lacked. He was radicalized online, with few friends in Australia or New Zealand. What I might once have seen as a violent extension of Australian clubbiness, with its rejection of outsiders, started to look more like a downward spiral into narcissism, fueled by internet strangers, made evil with weapons, and ignored by low-risk white male authorities who failed to see the threat because he looked like they did.

In the locker room, I changed quickly, leaving my work bag, trusting that no one would steal my computer. Determined to put as much distance as possible between myself and the shooter, I jumped into the pool right away to warm up. And I was still awful. I swam like a rock, not a fish. As Katie walked along the side, I struggled as much as ever. The bottom half of my body still seemed designed to sink. I got water up my nose every time I breathed on my right side. It took me fifty strokes to go fifty meters, making me a marvel of inefficiency.

Katie knew I was aiming for the Bronze, so about halfway through the lesson, she timed me for one hundred meters. I came in at 2:15, which meant I was too slow to pass even if

I could keep up the pace, which we both knew would be impossible.

Over the next few weeks, I finally committed to doing the work. I pushed my head farther down (another suggestion from Katie) and kept practicing. I bought a waterproof watch and started timing myself. I did a few more lessons. I even started watching videos on YouTube about how to improve my stroke. None of this made swimming enjoyable. Every time I went to Icebergs, I felt like I was doing manual labor, breaking my back for a result somewhere far off in the distance. But as was the case when I actually did do manual labor, in high school and college, I learned to tolerate the discomfort and enjoy the characters and culture all around me.

Icebergs is the kind of thing Australians are especially good at sustaining—a private club with a public ethos. As Donald Horne wrote in the 1960s about another one of Sydney's small-d democratic clubs in *The Lucky Country*, his iconic exploration of the Australian psyche, "The club represents the Australian version of the old ideals of equality and the pursuit of happiness: that everyone has the right to a good time."[xiv] A swim at Icebergs costs just a few dollars. It's just twenty-five dollars to become a social member, which earns you discounts at the pub-like bar and restaurant that offers the same stunning views as the more expensive fancy restaurant on the building's top floor. The pool is the main draw, of course, but the pub (and a café) pretty much guarantees a crowd loyal to what Horne called "the ideology of fraternalism."

It took me about thirty icy swims to earn my way into the brotherhood. One chilly Friday in June, I had a milestone moment when I found myself getting dressed in the men's locker room after a swim next to two thirtysomethings, an older man in a Speedo speaking to a friend in a thick foreign accent, and a bulky bloke putting on work boots who looked just a little younger than my father.

"Water's pretty warm still, isn't it?" he said. It was early winter, the wind carried an Antarctic chill, and I'd checked the board at the entrance; the water was under eighteen degrees Celsius, around sixty-four Fahrenheit. "Usually it's a lot colder by this time of year. Still really nice."

"Yeah, absolutely," I said, failing to tell him that my toes were numb. He must have known anyway (their shade of blue?), because he pointed to a sauna down the hall.

"It's good for after a swim—after you get your core temperature down, it takes a while to get it back up again. Lot of people come just for that, sorry to say."

He shook his head with disappointment, giving me a look of mutual understanding. And that was when the thought arose: *he thinks I'm like him, tough enough to enjoy a frigid swim!*

A half hour later, my fingers were tingling toward warmth. I wiggled my toes and wondered if his assessment was correct. I was a few months into my swimming regimen, and no matter the weather or water temperature, all I wore were board shorts, goggles, and a swim cap. I'd given up on warmth in a wet suit. The pain of the cold water—even if it wasn't a Bastian experiment— became something I chose to endure in solidarity with everyone else in the water. I'd also started to notice that when eventually I did warm up, I felt freakishly calm (a response supported, turns out, by science).

Icebergs encourages its own brand of cold conformity. Every Sunday from May through September (the coldest months in Australia, when morning temps linger in the 40s across Sydney), the club hosts competitions. Swimmers must compete in three out of four Sundays a month for five years before officially becoming a "mighty Iceberg." That, for many, is the pool's reason for being—an act of shared and moderate pain in winter that leads to well-being and community year-round. It made me think of Bastian's pain studies, Slovic's research on building trust, and maybe just a touch of Jul's stoicism.

"It still feels warm, maybe from the inside." Jul lifted up his shirt to show his scar. It was a warm spring day six months after the attacks, and the indelible mark on his back ran the length and width of a pen. "When I move," he said, "it's a little tight."

Compared to what I'd seen in March, it was a miraculous example of human healing. He looked good, sitting near Alta on the black couch in their apartment. With the shades finally open, she looked better too, with a new shorter haircut and a bit more bounce in her voice. I knew they'd been in a pretty dark place in July, when Jul was having flashbacks at night, Alta wasn't sleeping, and Roes would fly off the handle anytime his father or mother lay down, convinced that meant another shooting.

"What's changed?" I asked.

Alta laughed and said there was a lot going on.

First, she said she had gotten help. She was seeing a psychologist twice a week. It cost more than the rent, but she was hoping to be reimbursed by the U.S. government since she'd been formally classified as a terrorism victim, making her and her family eligible for additional benefits beyond what New Zealand provided.

She was still angry about her family's care, but she also told me that she was starting to have more trust in the New Zealand government. A few days earlier, they finally received notice that they were granted permanent residency under a program that provided fast-track approval for Christchurch victims. Living cheap, they had enough money from government aid and charities to keep them secure for a year.

"We're looking for a new place," she said. "Somewhere with more room so Jul can paint."

As usual, they were advancing. Alta was starting to make friends while looking for work, and Jul was already picking up his brushes. He walked me over to a spare room where he was halfway through an abstract canvas bursting with color. The room was cramped but bright with morning sun.

He and Roes had also started to reconnect. It started with Jul keeping a bag of candy in his bedroom to draw in the boy, who could not even look his father in the eye right after the attack. Then he started reading to Roes again. One book, *Say Please, Little Bear*, about a father and his cub, often sparked a game of tag and hugs.

Physical connection with people and with nature seemed to be especially helpful. As a family, they had started going to the beach, where the air seemed lighter. Roes had found a playground he especially liked, where he was starting to become a normal, playful kid again, and Jul told me he had recently started hiking too, climbing slowly up the mountains near Christchurch to gain the views that seemed to help him keep everything in perspective.

"It's really hard," he said, laughing. "When I get up there, I can barely breathe."

Standing in their narrow kitchen, making a cheese sandwich for Roes, he told me he had also just received good news from his urologist: everything down there seemed to be working. Early on, he and Alta had resigned themselves to a marriage that would no longer include sex. Alta rationalized it, declaring she didn't want a second child anyway. But now, or at some point in the future, sex was back in the realm of possibility.

"There's scar tissue there," Jul said. "But yeah. That's my new normal."

He finished the sandwich and disappeared into the bedroom. A few minutes later, he returned with dark jeans and a designer shirt—it was Friday, nearly time to go to the mosque for weekly prayer. He had agreed to bring me along so I could see how the community was healing. The mosque was an obvious trigger, and it was still touch and go for many. Alta couldn't bring herself to walk over the threshold.

But Jul found that he missed the community. He returned to Linwood once or twice, happily reuniting with a man he thought had died right beside him on March 15. (He took a bullet that might have killed Jul or Roes; it was another example of overlooked interdependence.) Later, Jul switched to Al Noor, where forty-two of the fifty-one victims were killed, because it had more Indonesians and felt like a better way to start over.

"It was the first mosque I went to when I got here," he said. "It's like going back to an earlier time."

On the bus, we sat together near the door. Jul put on his aviator sunglasses as we snaked through the city, which, despite it all, he told me he had grown to love. The mountains, the sea. Despite the cooler climate, it reminded him of Indonesia.

The bus pulled over and let us off near an intersection that looked familiar. We were near the spot where Alta went for the public memorial and where I'd seen the notes and flowers by the police tape. The final walk to the mosque was just a few hundred meters, but Jul tensed up. A car whizzed by, then another.

"When he drove by here," he said, referring to the gunman, "he was shooting out the window."

This time, I recognized the process. Rebuilding trust and comfort with risk takes time and hundreds of actions.

At the entrance to Al Noor, I could see a handful of guards in neon vests and police officers in blue uniforms. I stiffened at the thought of another incident. But Jul told me they'd been coming for a while, and it looked like friendly banter had become the Friday norm. A female officer warmly greeted a woman dressed in gray whom I recognized—she'd been in the relatives' room. Jul walked over to a tall officer with broad shoulders.

"How's Alta?" the officer asked.

"Good, good," Jul said. "We finally got our visas."

The officer smiled. "That's great. Really great."

Inside, the paint was new and cameras pointed toward the main worship area. To my right, I saw a man in a wheelchair, another with a walker—shooting victims. There were a lot of them, in various stages of recovery. The mosque was filled to capacity. Women stood in an area behind us, and dozens of men lined up in neat rows on the carpet, some clearly from the Middle East, others from Africa and Asia, along with a few white faces as well. I sat in the back on a bench with a few others and tried to blend in.

"As-salaam alaikum," said a man in a plaid shirt as he sat beside me. *Peace be upon you.*

"Wa-alaikum as-salaam," I replied. *And peace be upon you.*

Jul, kneeling on the left in the center row, looked straight ahead and listened as prayers began. An older man handed out candies to the boys who were pint-size (and some who were not), then the imam rose to speak. He was young and trim, with a tightly cropped beard and a pristine white dishdasha. His message focused on "excellence of character." He praised the value and strength that comes with caring for family, for community. He called for a morality not of revenge but rather altruism, connection, and a steely form of outreach that defied trauma and fear.

"Islam is about relationships," he said.

The men nodded. I nodded along with them.

FIVE

The Bronze, Part 1

A short history of surf lifesaving; grit, the growth mind-set, and the power of modeling, with Angela Duckworth; training for the Bronze Medallion is really hard

I only started researching the Bronze Medallion when I believed I could earn one, at which point I was thrilled to discover the appearance of a fellow journalist. There were two founders of what is now the Royal Life Saving Society in England, which began in 1891 and offered the Bronze a year later. One was a reporter named Archibald Sinclair.[i] A sports fanatic, he and his friend William Henry, a dedicated ocean swimmer, wrote the manual for the course, which usually ran for eight to ten weeks and focused on group competence in rescue and resuscitation.

The initial aim was simply to spread swimming skills across the population for sport and so more people would be equipped to rescue others if needed. But the course was serious. Efficiency was the official goal, and as such, drills were to be carried out according to the British Army's Infantry Drill Book. Something about the mix of military rigor, joint training, and the thrill of the ocean seemed to have a broad appeal: the first year it ran, in 1892, eighty-six Bronze Medallions were awarded; the year after that, the first ten women earned the Bronze along with 197 men, and by 1897, they handed out nearly twelve hundred.

Around the same time, volunteers were gathering to keep people safe on beaches in Rhode Island, Massachusetts, and New York City.[ii] Wilbert E. Longfellow, another former journalist, even enlisted the Red Cross for a national lifeguard training program that he called "the water-proofing of America."[iii] But in the United States, the volunteer services faded. The Jacksonville Beach volunteer corps, in Florida, claims be the last of its kind.[iv]

Australia's story proved to be quite different. The Bronze was the first and most important lifesaving qualification in the English-speaking world (the Silver and Gold were even harder to obtain), and it did not take long for it to catch on and become an important part of Australian identity. Our little suburb of Bronte actually played a pivotal role as one of the earliest adopters when, on April 14, 1894, Sergeant Major John Bond, a veteran of the Boer War, put on a practical demonstration of resuscitation at the Bronte pool with a squad from his "Life-saving Society."[v]

Swimming clubs and volunteer lifesaving clubs were springing

up all over Sydney at the time, not just in Bronte but also in Bondi
and in Manly, the two larger and more popular beaches farther
north.[vi] Each group claimed to have been the first, and the dispute
is still a source of relentless banter among those who care about
such things. What I found more revealing was that they were all
trying to get their arms around a surge of interest in the ocean that
far outpaced actual skill or savvy. The beach was booming like a
fad. Daytime "bathing" was still illegal, mainly because it was an
activity done "in a state of undress." And it didn't matter. The cold,
crisp salt water was believed to have therapeutic benefits, and with
more people living near the coast, young and old splashed right in.

Newspaper archives from the day are filled with dramatic
accounts of both drownings and citizen rescues. Along with the
danger, there was community spirit. Volunteers saving children
grabbed headlines. The public wanted more of everything that
Australia's coastline could offer.

By the end of 1903, Sydney's coastal councils essentially
gave up on the legal restrictions against daylight swimming.
Some historians have argued that the grassroots movement to
manage the ocean had an impact far beyond the sand. The early
surf clubs, as Sean Brawley of Macquarie University wrote in an
essay a few years ago, "built social capital not only in providing
a benefit to the community but also in educating a cohort of
beachside communities in practical democracy."[vii] Lifesavers, he
found, were overrepresented in the early roles of Australian local
government in part because they were trusted and admired but
also because they'd gained experience in governance. By setting
up their surf clubs, they learned how to work together to solve
problems, organize groups, and stay calm in moments of crisis.

In its early years, lifesaving was also noticeably more inclusive than other organizations of its time. Sinclair and Henry encouraged both men and women to become proficient in an era when women still couldn't vote in most of the world's democracies. Australia's first lifesavers essentially started out as rebels in need of recruits. Volunteer lifesaving was entrepreneurial civil service—it was what startups looked like 125 years ago. Clubs like the one in Bronte were born and grew in opposition to official policy. Volunteers took the community's fate into their own hands without waiting for government.

Many of these early adopters learned to manage and enjoy the ocean the same way Jack London did—from Pacific Islanders willing to share their knowledge and passion. Hawaii's Duke Kahanamoku brought surfing to Sydney. Alick Wickham, the boy who made the crawl famous, came from the Solomons; Tommy Tana, named after his birthplace in New Hebrides (now Vanuatu), introduced bodysurfing to crowds in Manly, teaching lifesavers and fans how to ride the waves with their heads out of the water.[viii] He called it "wave shooting."

These men, some of the country's first sea and swim instructors, were real-life evangelists for the life-affirming power of embracing risk. In their eyes, safety and community could be found through a mix of fun and confronting danger. Major Bond's swimming carnival included not just demonstrations of resuscitation but also "fancy swimming" and high diving off the rocks. Even Wickham grew up to be an adrenaline seeker—he set a world diving record in 1918 when he performed a sixty-two-meter swan dive into a river in the city of Melbourne.[ix]

In Bronte and all over Australia, service and satisfaction

came with adventure. The people performing for a rush and applause were the same ones who could also drag a drowning girl out of the deep—and the culture of winking fun plus competence has lingered. Australian culture today is many things in many places, from outback cattle stations and remote Aboriginal communities to inner-city neighborhoods, but in all of them, I've seen an embrace of nature and physicality; a social dynamic defined by shared experiences more than words or purchases; and a sense of playfulness. Lest there's any doubt, consider this: When Sydney hosted the Olympics in 2000, a phalanx of volunteer lifesavers wearing tight swimsuits carried the pop star Kylie Minogue into the stadium for the closing ceremony on a giant flip-flop, which Australian call a thong.

I wasn't at the point yet where I felt comfortable in a Speedo or could do any "fancy swimming" or lifesaving, though maybe I was getting close. With a few weeks to go before my second attempt to get into the Bronze Medallion course, I changed my swim technique. I turned my head every third stroke and added the occasional flip turn. My cheap Casio watch showed that I was speeding up, but in the days just before the test, my times were consistent and still just a little too slow.

Underwater, on the day before the test, my mind wandered to the idea of performance-enhancing drugs. *Is there something I could take to get faster?* When I was done, out of the pool's slow lane and in the Icebergs shower, I could hardly believe my own thoughts. *Steroids? Protein shakes?* But the following morning, I was still trying to think of what I could do to make sure I passed.

Then it hit me—what do swimmers do to make themselves glide more quickly through the water? *They shave.*

I dug around under the sink in our upstairs bathroom and found the clippers I'd bought a while back to trim Baz's hair. Without a moment's hesitation, I threw on a number 2 and manscaped my unruly mane from belly button to neck, moving with surgical care around my nipples. Looking in the mirror, I could suddenly see that I was thinner, with more muscle definition in my chest and arms. I nodded with satisfaction. Very *Queer Eye. Maybe I should manscape more often.* Then I looked at my legs. *Would anyone notice if I went for my whole body?* I listened at the door to make sure Diana was downstairs and ran the blades over my legs, up and down. The hair on my head was already short, so I finished with my arms.

It was an odd and intimate sensation. I'd never shaved my body before, and the pile of curly hair on the floor looked disgusting. But as I cleaned it up, I dreamed only of swimming success. *As long as it works, it's worth it.*

On the day of the test, I woke up feeling ready. That morning, the kids had their own Nippers proficiency swims for the new season that was just starting. In the car, on the way there, I asked them how they were feeling.

"I'm annoyed," said Baz.

"I'm worried," said Amelia.

They'd both grown, Amelia more than her brother. Their accents were American with the occasional Aussie rise at the end of a sentence.

At the pool, I walked up the stairs with just a little less dread than usual. The swim test was now a mid-September ritual. I saw a few friendly faces, and I counted a dozen children swimming through the water like penguins in tight, bright bathing suits, with goggles securely on heads that popped out for perfect breaths.

Baz pushed his face into my stomach; he was crying and trying to hide it. Like a lot of boys his age (ten and a half), he was unsure of how to handle or even talk about emotion.

"Are you worried about being embarrassed if you fail?" I asked.

"Yes," he said.

I gave him a hug.

"I feel the same way."

We were still foreigners—not fish out of the water but buffa-loes at sea. We'd found the right swim caps and terry cloth swim ponchos, but our fears of failure, of the water, had only faded, not disappeared. Once again, I hadn't told anyone I was going to try out for the Bronze for the same reason Baz was trying to hide. But as I looked around, I thought of Diana's father. He came to the United States from Cuba in 1960 at Baz's age with little more than a suitcase as his own parents fled a divided and violent country. Maybe some difficult moments are best ignored. To grow, to improve our lot in life, maybe we just have to get used to living with more fear of failure in our heads and more nausea in our guts.

Baz suddenly let go. "Okay, I'll do it now."

He wiped his eyes and grabbed his goggles. I walked him over to his Nippers instructors where Guy, wiry thin with a chin as square as a cigarette box, checked off his name.

"You got this, Baz," he said. "It's eight laps. No problem."

Baz jumped in. He had five minutes to complete two

hundred meters, a moderate pace for a regular swimmer his age, and as he moved back and forth, he seemed to be staying calm.

Guy returned to telling Al a story about surfing in Indonesia. "The waves were double, triple overheads," he said. "Every morning, you're scared but you just have to go." He laughed. "There was no turning, just getting down."

He told Al that was how he got injured—dragged along a reef, ripping his arm to shreds. I could see pink scars in a patchwork. He showed us a photo of what it looked like after it happened. "They had to use hydrogen peroxide and a clean toothbrush to scrub it all out," he said.

I caught myself grimacing. *No wonder Baz and I are nervous. These people are crazy.*

Amelia's turn came up in a lane to the right. She pushed off the end without hesitating.

"She looks great," Diana said.

"They both do," I added as Baz headed toward us for his final lap. "Almost like they're Australian!"

Almost. The kid swimming behind Baz caught up and passed him. After a couple of laps, the girl in Amelia's lane did the same—then Amelia stopped unexpectedly. Baz suddenly finished and was heading our way, but all I could do was stare at his sister. She got out too. I squinted to read her lips. "I can't do it."

She walked toward us on the verge of tears. Baz stood beside us in new tight Bronte bathers. He'd passed but was shivering.

"I kind of want to hug her but I kind of don't because she's wet and cold," he said.

Amelia collapsed into my arms.

"I can't do it," she said. "I can't do it."

Some of the research papers I'd read said that if we see a stressful moment as a challenge we think we can overcome, the hormone mix in our bodies pushes us to the goal; if we conclude it is a threat where we'll fail, our bodies and minds rush to quit and flee. Amelia had just experienced the latter.

"It's okay. You just haven't been swimming very much," I told her. "We'll just practice and I'll do it with you, then you'll be fine."

Diana tried to persuade her to try again.

"Can we just go home?" Amelia said. I hated seeing her broken, that bright light suddenly dimmed. I worried that her lack of confidence in the pool had something to do with her unsettled social dynamic at school, with groups of girls forming, dividing, and subdividing. I decided not to push too hard this time, to slow down and see what she could discover on her own. We walked down the stairs and toward the car. I held her close.

"I just feel so bad," she said. "You want me to do it, and I can't."

After lunch, I asked Amelia to come with me to Icebergs for my swimming trial. I wanted her to see me do something that was hard, a challenge I was still trying to overcome. Under a warm spring sun, we walked from Bronte along the coastal walk, looking for whales and dolphins in the dark blue water. The view from the rocky path over the Pacific calmed us both as Amelia returned to her normal chatty self, talking about her favorite dogs (corgis) and YouTube stars (Georgia Productions) and asking if we could get ice cream on the way home.

We arrived at Icebergs about twenty minutes early. We stood on the highest step above the pool, looking out at the water.

"Are you scared?" she asked. It would normally be such a jarring thing to hear from your tiny daughter. But I was impressed that she noticed.

"Yeah, a little bit."

I didn't bother to tell her that I had tried to give myself an edge by streamlining with clippers. I rubbed my hand over the stubble, less sure it would make enough of a difference.

Kimberly—the same Kimberly who saw me fail seven months ago—gathered a dozen of us together. She and Garry, an older man with a calming voice and long limbs, explained the plan: eight laps, four hundred meters, in 8:45. It's a requirement for Bronte lifesaving, Kimberly said, but it's also a way to see where we're all at so they know who will need more help once training starts.

She asked if any of us had timed ourselves, and this time, I nodded with the majority. Figuring I'd be on the later side of things, I stayed quiet as people volunteered their times.

"Around 6:30," said a fifteen-year-old with braces.

"About 7:00," added an older woman in a bright swimsuit. It went on like that for a while. No one said a time longer than eight minutes. When they were done, I mentioned my own fastest time: a Phelps-like 8:30.

We went down to the pool, and the first five started at thirty-second intervals. The teenager in braces, Will, finished in 6:08. I didn't even know that was possible. Everyone clapped as he jumped out of the pool. I was standing farther back, quiet, as each swimmer came in. They all passed as well.

Our group went next. I was third in line, after a guy my age who said he did it in eight minutes, and a young woman—maybe in her twenties—who just showed up and decided to give it a try. The sun had shifted so we were swimming in the shade. When I jumped in, the water was chilly but not ice-cold. Kimberly held up her stopwatch.

"Five, four, three, two, one—GO!"

I pushed off the wall, reminding myself not to try too hard, not to go too fast. The first lap felt good, but I could tell I was nervous and moving on instinct, windmilling my way forward. Once I flipped and headed back, I slowed down and remembered: *hold the catch, high elbow, push up my torso and rear glide.*

Halfway though, I was more tired than I should have been, and I worried that what I'd hoped would be a challenge might soon become a threat. The pool was murky, with sand on the bottom, and I found myself staring at the odd little ripples caused by water going back and forth. *Stress creates patterns. Movement produces surprises.* I wished I could just sit there like the sand, letting the forces of life wash over me.

But I moved and kept moving. Somewhere around lap six, I passed the guy in the black top. My chest was heaving as I forced out a half dozen strokes at the end of the final lap without turning to breathe. I touched the wall and picked up my head, looking up at Kimberly, half expecting a frown and nine minutes.

"7:43," she said. "Well, that was a big improvement." She smiled. "Have you been training?"

I tried to answer but I was too out of breath. I climbed out of the pool and leaned over to try and suck in as much oxygen as possible.

"Daddy!"

Amelia rushed over to congratulate me. I was a little dizzy, with a feeling I haven't had since playing high school football. *I think I might vomit.* I was not proud of that—it's a brief swim, not four hours of sprints and tackling. But I was also not fifteen anymore. Not even close. Nor were most of the other people swimming. At least three of them failed to make it, including the guy in the black rashie who I had passed. He'd been the one reminding us earlier of the local motto—"If you can swim in Bronte, you can swim anywhere." He'd have to try again in March.

Eventually, I felt okay enough to ask what happens next.

"There will be an email with the details," Kimberly said, adding that I needed to sign up for board training and should start swimming more.

That was when I realized: *I'm actually doing this. I have to do this.* As I walked home with Amelia, who was as bubbly as ever, I felt like I was right there with her. Fully alive. Full of questions. Eager for ice cream.

At home, I started writing in my risk journal, reflecting on the concept of a growth mindset, the idea in child psychology—developed by Carol Dweck at Stanford University—that says kids need to learn they're not inherently smart or talented but rather that they can excel at things like math or public speaking (or athletics) through practice.

At Amelia's school, a summary of the growth mindset sat in a laminated sheet on her desk, explaining that intelligence shouldn't be viewed as fixed but rather as an ability that expands with effort. The growth mindset and risk, in my mind, were linked; it's easier to take on a scary, thrilling challenge if you think you can grow into it, and it's much harder if you think you'll never master it because who you are is fixed. So at some point,

I'd given Amelia a sixteen-question test (the Dweck Mindset Instrument) to gauge where she fell on the growth-fixed spectrum. I watched in parental horror as she used a purple pencil to mark "agree" beside statements like, "You can learn new things but you can't really change your basic level of talent," and "To be honest, you can't really change how intelligent you are."

I so badly wanted to get her to the other side—to see that you could build your capabilities through risk, effort, and overcoming. I wanted her to see *all* the possibilities, to break the cycle of *that just isn't me*. But I didn't want to lecture her or force her into training; I wasn't at all sure my aggressive into-the-deep-end approach had worked with Baz, and I could see she was more rebellious. If I tried telling her what I'd read online—"find your inner saboteur...talk back to it with a growth mindset voice"— she'd roll her eyes and reject me.

Instead, as I journaled about my swim test, I was betting there was more power in showing than telling, in trying to live out those values in a way she could see. I didn't really know if it would work. I did wonder, though, why don't we talk more about the growth mindset for adults? Why does parenting advice focus so much on how to speak to our children, not how to learn and grow along with them?

Part of me was inspired by Alta and Jul showing Roes how to engage with the world again. I'd also started to lament what's lost when so many parents, once we hit thirty or thirty-five or forty, accept that we're fixed in place when really we might just be lazy or stuck and tired.

An hour later, as I sat at my desk and finished writing, Amelia came in and announced she had given more thought to her proficiency test. She plopped down on the sofa in our home office next to a picture of Diana and me at a muddy outpost in Iraq.

"When there are time limits, I just get so nervous," she said.

"That's understandable," I told her. "I felt the same way with my swim test. I was really nervous—you saw me. But you don't have to win. You just have to do well enough to pass."

I asked her when swimming started again at school for Friday sport.

"Next term," she said, tugging at her hair. "And actually when I did swimming in first term, I was one of the best. I could dive, and I swam pretty fast."

I nodded but stayed silent. In her dark brown eyes, I could almost see her mindset shifting and her hope circuit firing.

"I can do it," she said. "I just haven't done it in a while. I'm strong but I'm not as strong as I used to be because I haven't been practicing. I need to practice."

The power of modeling—with children mimicking what they learn from adults—is one of the most well-established ideas in psychology thanks largely to Albert Bandura, a Canadian-born American psychologist at Stanford. His social learning theory proved that children learn from what they see in adults, and they learn very quickly.[xi]

It's not just the basics, like how to avoid the hot stove. In the 1960s, Bandura's most groundbreaking experiments showed that children who watch adults beat a toy doll are more likely to mimic such aggression even without any verbal cues.[xii]

More recently, researchers have found that the sons and daughters of mothers who are anxious during pregnancy and in the first few years of a child's life have twice the risk of displaying hyperactivity symptoms at age sixteen.[xiii] Parents who are physically active when their children are young also tend to pass on that habit to their kids as they grow up.[xiv]

But what's especially interesting in the context of risk is what children can learn from adults about failure.

When Angela Duckworth was writing *Grit*, her bestselling book about passion and perseverance, she struggled more than anyone might have expected. It was the summer of 2015. She was a rapidly rising star of the psychology world. She'd been mentored by Seligman. She'd won the MacArthur Genius Grant in 2013 at the age of forty-three. And yet she couldn't get past her own idea of who she was and was not.

"I don't know how to write," she told herself. "I mean, I could write, but I'm not a writer."

On top of her book deadline and the classes she needed to prepare to teach at the University of Pennsylvania, she was facing the added pressure of a family vacation in a town of regal Victorian homes and wide-open sandy beaches on the New Jersey shore that bills itself as "America's oldest seaside resort." Wasn't she supposed to be enjoying a break with her husband and two daughters while somehow also writing a book? It all became too much.

She started lashing out at her husband, Jason, a real estate developer and urban designer. He was the one who thought the book was a good idea.

"I can't do it," she yelled at him again and again. "I hate you and I hate this book."

In many ways, it was an out-of-character outburst. When Duckworth told me the story, she was sitting in her Philadelphia office, an open space with frosted glass and modern blond wood furniture. It was a clean and elegant work area that signaled the efficient achievement that has been a mark of her entire career. Seligman singled her out in his memoir as a marvel of energy and insight, and she spoke in bursts, like a detective putting together clues at the end of a mystery novel. She seemed to relish the recollection of her flawed, messy struggle because it wasn't something she was usually asked about.

"There was a moment in time during that vacation where I very literally nearly threw my laptop into the Atlantic Ocean," Duckworth told me.[xv] "And my husband pointed out, very usefully, that it actually wasn't my property, it was the property of the University of Pennsylvania and that there were lots of other things on the laptop, other than my book, that, you know, I'd probably want."

The reason we were talking about her breakdown—Duckworth's word, not mine—was because I had asked her about her own experience with modeling, the idea that parents and other adults can teach their children more through what they practice than what they preach. She noted that her daughters, who were twelve and fourteen that summer in Cape May, watched the entire drama play out just as they also saw her find a way to get back to work. The saw her lose and regain motivation and then succeed. When *Grit* came out in 2016, it rocketed to the *New York Times* bestseller list and stayed there for twenty-one weeks.

What they took away from that experience, she suspected, was not just the value of hard work. That was something they had already come to know and comment on in the ways that only children can. The Mother's Day cards they gave Duckworth over the years often included hand-drawn portraits of their mom behind a laptop with messages like "hope you get a lot done" ("Because they knew that's what would make me happy," she said).

What the book process showed instead was something that many of us try to hide from our children: vulnerability, self-doubt, sadness, anger, and weakness. She had taken a risk with the project, and that produced a need for resilience. The latter and the former go together: grit grows from managing what we aren't sure we can handle; when we treat risk as an important part of life—as Brock Bastian had pointed out—we're better able to recognize our own resilience and show it to others.

"My recommendation for parents and what I think I accidentally did right is I modeled imperfection but also a noble struggle to put my head up again," Duckworth said. Her kids, she added, "saw a very imperfect person struggling."

I could see how she and Seligman got along. They both valued and lived a life of hard work, and they both emphasized empirical examples of behavioral change over talking cures. If there is a counterweight to our era's focus on human flaws, it's come through the work of those who have built a psychology less oriented around feelings and dysfunction than the lived experience of character.

In that context, the act of witnessing failure and recovery can be especially powerful. There are dozens of studies revealing the sophisticated way that children interpret and mimic the adults around them, but the most interesting work to emerge over the past decade or two involves children observing how adults fail and improving on their efforts. One enterprising psychologist, Andrew Meltzoff at the University of Washington, a pioneer in the study of infant learning, has been especially insatiable in his curiosity.[xvi] Reading his research papers, I often felt like I was overhearing a playful free association of questions and aha moments in a bar. At one point, he became obsessed with whether babies who were too young to speak could still understand adult failures and intentions.

"At what age do babies begin to read what we 'mean to do' even if we don't successfully do it?" he asked. "When can they begin to understand the intentions lying behind our bumbling behavior?"

Seeking answers to those questions, he created an experiment with eighteen-month-old babies where they were shown a series of unsuccessful acts. An adult tried to put something together, but then the adult's hand slipped. Or the adult overshot or undershot the goal. The infants revealed their interpretation by what they imitated. Most of them reenacted what the adult meant to do, not what was actually done.

When Meltzoff created a device to make the same mistakes, the children were just as riveted by the process of failure but not as good at solving the simple puzzle. Those who had watched the adult fail were six times as likely to produce a finished product. The conclusion? Humans matter most when it comes to learning, and babies are quick to discern intent.

"This intention reading is an essential baby step toward the development of a theory of mind," Meltzoff wrote in a 1999 summary of his findings. "The idea that other humans do not just behave but have internal thoughts, emotions, and desires."

As children get older, more recent studies show, their interpretations of failure and how to respond to it become even more sophisticated. One study, highlighted by Duckworth in her weekly characterlab.org blog and led by her collaborator Julia Leonard, focused on preschoolers.[xvii]

Researchers examined how the persistence of 520 four- and five-year-olds was affected by their observations of adults struggling to open a complicated contraption. In some cases, adults put in a lot of effort and succeeded, and in others, they put in a little effort and failed. For some of the children, the adults set expectations before the task began. For example, they told the children, "This will be hard," or they encouraged them by saying something like, "You can do this," or "Trying hard is important." There was also a scenario in which adults did not say anything about children's expectations. Persistence was measured by how hard the children worked on the same task attempted by the adults, which was difficult and new to the children.

The study found that kids cared less about the contraption than they did about the adults. The human to human connection provided a spark—they tried harder after they saw adults succeed. Their persistence was highest when adults exerted a lot of effort, accomplished the task, and talked about the value of the time and work they put into the challenge.

"Our study suggests that children are rational learners—they pay attention first and foremost to whether adults succeed at their goals," said Laura Schulz, a professor of cognitive science at the Massachusetts Institute of Technology, who coauthored the study. "But when adults succeed, children are also watching how hard adults try and what adults say about the value of effort."

Duckworth described the ideal scenario as one in which adults, especially parents, practice what they preach and preach what they practice. She said she spoke to her children at length about her struggles with the book (among other struggles), creating a hybrid of modeling that mixed showing and telling.

"I wonder if one means more than the other," I said.

"I think the practicing matters more, that would be my guess," she replied. "I think the point of that study was to show—and I see sports coaches do this all the time—that explanation can help. But it's definitely the frosting, not the cake."

An emphasis on modeling felt to me like something of a relief. It meant my talking and pushing mattered less than my doing. It confirmed my sense, after Christchurch, that speech is like meringue, seemingly solid but lacking the substance needed to produce lasting change.

Returning to Duckworth for additional examples, she told me that even though she's a daughter of Chinese immigrants, her parenting style did not fit the stereotype of the relentless "tiger mom." Both her daughters are now students at top universities, but they were mostly free-range kids who came home to lists of things they needed to finish before Mom and Dad returned from work. Generally they followed their parents' lead—putting in a lot of effort on their own while seeking out their passions.

"They forged my signature on pretty much everything growing up because I didn't want to take time out of my day to look at what they wanted me to sign," Duckworth told me.

What they did do as a family, however, was commit to the hard thing rule. In *Grit*, she explained that it means everyone in the family has to choose something that requires daily deliberate practice. That's part one. Part two of the rule states that you can't quit until a natural stopping point has arrived (the end of the year, the season, the tuition), and finally, the hard thing rule requires that you get to pick your hard thing.

The idea, she said, is to encourage grit without obliterating a child's independence.

When I first read about the idea, I realized that Diana and I had already been applying the rule without knowing it had a name. At the beginning of each school term, we sat down with the kids and talked through a plan for what they wanted to do and what we would be doing as well. What I only realized after talking to Duckworth, though, was what the hard thing rule assumed, what it was built on.

The concept only works if you maintain a belief in Seligman's ideas of learned optimism, along with what Duckworth exhibited and often writes about—the power of persistence. It is, in short, a test and experiment built on the bedrock of the growth mindset.

Like many others, Duckworth is a fan of Dweck and her idea of mindsets as signals for achievement. A peer of Seligman, Dweck has been studying how children learn and how self-perception affects their progress since the 1970s. If Seligman is a king of the anti-self-esteem movement, she is a queen. Together they (and their intellectual progeny, including Duckworth) have sought to teach children and adults about the negative voices in our heads and how to push past what they tell us.

In one of Dweck's best-known experiments, she gave ten-year-olds problems that she knew were too hard for them to see how they handled a situation beyond their capacity.[xviii] Like the mindset questionnaire I'd used on Amelia (and Baz, who scored closer to the growth side of the spectrum), it was a way to gauge how children viewed their own potential.

She found that some of the kids offered responses like "I love a challenge" or "I was hoping this would be informative." They were the ones with a mindset making room for growth. Other children saw their failure as absolute or fixed, and they were devastated when they failed, like Amelia right after her swim test. They used phrases like "I can't," and they often struggled to keep going because they thought their flaws were permanent and irreversible. Future studies even showed that when confronted again with problems beyond their capabilities, the fixed-mindset students were more likely to spiral downward; they said they would cheat or find some who did worse and focus on that to feel better.

The children who believed their intelligence could change and grow did change and improve. Some experienced what Amelia did—they eventually recognized the value of practice— and they ended up with higher grades and better outcomes later in life.

"Difficulty means not yet," Dweck often says in her lectures. "Basic human ability can be grown."

In our brains, we now know, that growth happens literally: with practice, neural networks grow new connections and strengthen existing ones. Like any other muscle, our minds can get stronger.

Dweck's book *Mindset: The New Psychology of Success*, which has been published and republished multiple times, lays out strategies for building those new connections, many of them mental activities similar to what Seligman also suggested in books like *The Optimistic Child*.[xix] Educators have been the idea's biggest proponents, with school districts in the United States spending millions of dollars on mindset intervention programs despite a lack of conclusive evidence that mental exercises alone can work.

I asked Duckworth if she thinks adults are doing enough to apply the growth mindset to their own lives and to actually model it through action. She said she wasn't sure but that she certainly heard the message fed back to her in the corporate world where *Mindset* has become part of the executive canon.

"I'm not exaggerating. I've never met a CEO or coach who doesn't already have that book, like literally ever. I usually ask, 'Do you have *Mindset*?' and they say, 'Oh, sure, we hand it out like candy.'" She added that many business books—such as *Hit Refresh* by Satya Nadella, the CEO of Microsoft—are based on Dweck's approach, applied to an office setting.

At which point I realized that what had been bothering me about the growth mindset was not just that it was rarely applied by adults but rather that it was almost always deployed in the same way. Especially in America, matters of mindset usually focus on achievement and work—how to make money, if we're honest. It's the same problem with popular efforts to build confidence and even grit; from our youth, our college choices, and on through family life, we're aiming for optimization and riches.

Many of us who grew up in America don't even notice that we look at personal growth through a very particular lens. Maybe it's easier to think of it as a capitalist telescope. Our gaze is locked in place on people like Elon Musk, Jeff Bezos, Sheryl Sandberg, and Warren Buffett, as if running an investment fund or tech company is the only kind of risk-taking, bravery, and betterment worth studying.

Even Australians have bought into this myopic view. Whenever I mention risk, they jump immediately to markets— talking, often with a cringe, about how Australians are too risk averse and seem to prefer cautious corporate rules, about how the four national banks are protected from competitors, about the lack of verve and innovation in Australian tech, arts, and media. What they do not see quite so clearly are their own bold business leaders (like Andrew "Twiggy" Forrest, the eccentric mining and renewable energy magnate), nor do they lavish enough praise on the benefits of free-market caution.

I've often found myself reminding Australians of the trade-offs: think of the lower levels of inequality, of the local butcher shops I noticed when I first arrived or the independent book-stores that define intellectual life in Australia's cities and small towns. America's risky disrupter-techno-libertarian way of working has little use for such things. Are you sure that's a model worth emulating?

Why not celebrate Australia's more moderate and sensible hybrid of economic risk skepticism (aversion is too strong a word) fused to personal and community risk seeking, outside work, aiming for enrichment of another kind?

Maybe we all need to widen our scope. Australia *should* do more to encourage creative and professional risk-taking (with philanthropy and nonprofits too). But America's deployment of the growth mindset combined with its narrow approach to physical and social risk amounts to psychology as prosperity gospel, ignoring what can be learned by applying those princi-ples to life more broadly. Self-improvement in the United States is often just career improvement, which can easily be co-opted by executives and human resource departments who are mainly interested in for-profit productivity rather than authentic well-being.

And does it always have to be about the self? How often does anyone in the companies that Americans admire, including those with dog-eared copies of *Mindset*, have time or make time for an especially difficult task—a risk, a "not yet"—that's tied to their community, their children, new friends, or the natural world, to something other than individual achievement? America's divides and dysfunctions cannot be solved by capitalism and productivity alone.

Australians, in contrast, have often amazed me with their willingness to take a crack at something new that makes no sense, that they are absolutely terrible at, and that other people can see. When I joined the mighty Buzzcocks, I imagined that everyone would be like me—previously experienced with basketball, but a while ago. I was wrong. In their own version of my attempts to swim and surf, there were quite a few fathers who had never played basketball. At all. Ever. They had no problem competing in something for the first time in their forties. In fact, they enjoyed it, and much to my own surprise, so did I. I admired their pluck and their effort. Each one of them found a way to make peace with their inexperience and contribute, usually by playing basketball as if it were rugby.

Even Duckworth laughed when I told her about the team. She also immediately recognized the cultural differences.

"If that were America, it would be some cross-fertilization plan to get to my destination even faster," she said. "And for Australians, it's not a means to an end."

Duckworth and I went on to discuss the Schwartz theory of basic values, which holds that there are a handful of universal values across cultures (achievement, benevolence, security, conformity, power, etc.) and that we define ourselves by how we would rank them in order of importance.[xx] It may be, she said, that Americans value achievement higher than Australians without recognizing that other values like benevolence need more attention.

But of course, the order of our priorities can shift. There was something she had said earlier that stuck with me because I'd already seen it play out in one scenario after another—about how exposure therapy is always the best way to overcome fear and inertia. As Duckworth put it, "Do hard things, realize that you don't die, that you or the other person is fine, and then it basically extinguishes your response.

"Which is why I think part of childhood is actually doing progressively harder things and then extinguishing that natural fear response," she added. "It's the foundation of courage."

Maybe that's the mistake we make in growing up as individuals and as nations—thinking of ourselves as "grown," as completed and done learning. We stop exposing ourselves to risk because we think we no longer need courage. Instead of adding to who we are, we become museum pieces.

Later on, Duckworth emailed me a presentation she was still developing for a course she's teaching called Grit Lab. It was her most ambitious effort yet to put her ideas into practice, beyond the written form, with actual students. It leaned heavily on not just trying to moderate the voices in our heads but also emphasizing the power of physical experience and collaborative effort. Reading the deck as she continued to flesh it out felt in many ways like a private glimpse of her thought process in action.

She started with a very general title, "How to teach anything," and a simple question: "What is a subject/skill you'd like to see taught better to teenagers or young adults?"

The next slide asked, "What's an idea for teaching that you're really excited about right now?" Those questions were for her own contemplation. The goal, which the following slides explored, was to "use psychological science to teach psychological science." In short, she was searching for educational models that included elements reflecting the deeper truths that have emerged in recent psychology—her studies of grit, Seligman's learned industriousness, Meltzoff's insights on failure, and so on.

She identified and studied a half dozen examples from all over the world, probing for lessons that might improve her university course. The one she focused most heavily on was Outward Bound—the arduous outdoor education experience that informed Geelong Grammar's program and has spread to thirty other countries. The elder sailors who founded it in 1941 had been worried that young men were dying at sea because they lacked tenacity and experience with natural hardship. They were not interested in nudging the weak. To build safety and strength, they focused on "physical fitness, enterprise, tenacity, and compassion."[xxi]

In rough note form, Duckworth identified the characteristics that worked for Outward Bound and other successful programs that aimed to build passion and perseverance and that she planned to prioritize for her students:

- completed as part of a team (rather than as an individual)
- feels personalized (as opposed to generic)
- includes person-to-person interaction (with peers, role models)
- elevates metacognition
- is experiential

Iceland's local rescue teams fit the description. So do international nonprofits like ZAKA, which is based in Jerusalem and has trained and equipped emergency response teams in Israel, Mexico, Argentina, Russia, Ukraine, England, and France. Surf lifesaving in Bronte also meets all Duckworth's criteria.

My first experience with lifesaver training began with boards, two weeks after I passed the swim test. It was the last Sunday in September 2019 and yet another one of those spring days that leads Australians to proclaim, "How good is this?"

I was still more American. The training started at 4:00 p.m., and like a fool, despite knowing better, because let's face it, change is hard and laziness is easy, I delayed my departure to arrive just on time so I could avoid the inevitable awkward socializing that precedes anything new. When I arrived at the surf club, I immediately regretted my decision. A bunch of yellow rescue boards sat out on the sand as a small crowd gathered in front of instructors in orange water safety rashies.

Shit, I must be late.

I rushed down there, trying to put on my wet suit as quickly as possible, when I realized I was missing something—one of those pink Lycra tank tops that say Bronte on the back. They look ridiculous, like a parody waiting to be performed, but everyone had one, marking themselves as newbies. Except for me. Letting go of whatever urban cool I used to carry, I ran into the office and asked if I could grab one out of the box near the door.

"Can't help ya," said the same woman I'd met when I signed the kids up for Nippers. "Ya gotta talk to Kimberly."

"I can't just take one of these?"

"I have nothing to do with it," she said without throwing me so much as a glance.

I found Kimberly outside.

"Do you have a board?" she asked.

Grabbing a rashie from the box, she walked me, quickly, to the back of the surf club, which felt like a damp storage locker, musty, dark, and filled with things that float. On the right, I could see a gym without windows and two shirtless young men whose bodies were as hard as the weights they were lifting. On the left was a long line of rescue boards reaching near the three-meter ceiling.

Kimberly grabbed one and handed it to me, rushing me out to the beach. By the time I arrived, everyone had moved down to the water. Feeling like a new kid at school, clueless and embarrassed, I put on my pink rashie, backward at first, as the board trainer, Dave, told us we'd be paddling past the shore break as fast as we could, out toward the large ship in the distance.

I suddenly realized I didn't know much about what I'd be doing. It felt like another one of those annoying instances when knowledge was assumed to have been passed down from a friend. All I had was a warning from another Nippers parent who told me the Bronze experience was much harder than he had expected.

"Physically? Mentally?"

"Both," he said. "There's a lot to study and a lot to do."

The first hard part, I knew, would be getting past the waves—the waves I'd seen crash my kids onto shore. A skinny guy to my left without a rashie and with what sounded like an American accent asked, "Is anyone starting their Bronze?" I was one of the few to raise a hand; apparently the others were club regulars out for a refresher. He introduced himself as Ruk. He would be the main trainer when our eight-week course officially started in a few days, with "dry skills" classes on Monday nights and "wet skills" on Saturdays.

"Nice to meet you," he said. "Did you hear what you're supposed to do?"

He walked me through where to put my body on the board, which was longer and narrower than a surfboard, making it harder to manage. He suggested putting my legs outside the edges to keep from tipping over.

The first group set off, with five or six people on boards moving through the break without much of a problem. When it was my turn, I walked in and realized we'd be heading out with help from the Bronte Express, the rip that has tugged many a swimmer into trouble. I didn't have time to work out how I felt about that.

I jumped on the board after a set of larger waves came through, and immediately I could feel that the rescue board was *not* a surfboard. It was as if I was paddling on a thin round log. It was wobbly, slim, and hard to balance—made for speed to reach a drowning swimmer.

Eventually, I found my way and paddled toward the larger waves. A few splashes in the face later as the nose of the board sliced through the peaking surf, I was past the break and catching up to the group ahead of me. Fear of embarrassment—a potent force for growth?—propelled me. *Just don't fall behind. Just don't be last.*

Finally I made it out there, into the still water beyond the breaking waves, past where the Bronte pool juts into the ocean. I sat on my board, and for the first time, I looked around. I could see all the way to North Bondi on one side, where a burst of white water rose like fireworks from the rocks at the northern point known as Ben Buckler. Looking the other way, I could see Waverley Cemetery, with its colonial-era graves.

The view was unlike anything I had ever seen. I had never gone so far out. The bottom had to be one hundred meters below. I'd seen whales breaching right near where I was floating, but looking back at the land, instead of fear, I felt exhilaration and awe. The ocean takes up 72 percent of the earth's surface, and even NASA calls it "the great unknown" because so much of the deep remains unexplored.[xxii] Sitting out there, I felt like both a speck and colossus in equal measure.

Dave pointed to Bondi. "We're not going to go all the way there, but that's the direction I want you to head," he said.

We paddled north. The wind was blowing, the water was cold, and my arms burned and ached as I counted strokes: sixty-six, sixty-seven, sixty-eight. The sweat from my forehead dripped down my nose. When we stopped, Dave showed us how to sit back on our boards, turn them in a circle, and Eskimo roll, flipping the board under the water by holding on to the side straps, then spinning again until each of us was back into position on top.

A bit older than me, with dark hair and freckles on his arms, he had an easygoing teacher vibe to him that I liked right away. Later on, I learned that nine years earlier, soon after his kids started the 2010 Nippers season, he was diagnosed with skin cancer and his doctor told him his chance of survival was 50 percent. He became the Nippers director the following year in part, he told me, so his kids would understand the need to volunteer their skills and time and so they would have a community to rely on in case he died. Before Bettsy took over, Dave pushed the program to be less obsessed with the handful of kids who wanted to win at competitions and more focused on raising surf competency for all the children.

He was doing the same with us. Or trying to. In my case, every attempt at something new revealed that I was wholly incompetent. I fell off the board just as often as I did when I started surfing. I looked foolish, but I was one of many out there slipping and sliding and giggling like a child. The line between fear and laughter is razor thin.

Once we headed back to Bronte, I thought about the point of all that play. We needed to have total command of the board because at some point, we'd be expected to paddle out, save a drowning swimmer, and return to shore. A few years earlier, a surfer died after crashing into the craggy outcrop we were just then paddling past. Matthew Richell, a forty-one-year-old father of two, was the chief executive of a publishing company, Hachette

Australia.[xxiii] He died on a Wednesday afternoon in 2014 when the swell pushed him into the sharp rocks known as "the Twins."

Dave stopped us just past there and just short of where the rolling swell was breaking. The waves rose and fell, with sets coming in every few seconds. We each took two turns paddling in toward the beach with the surge of the surf thrusting us forward. On my first try, I slid back on my board and rode forward without a problem. On my second try, I toppled off the side. Compared with my kids, I was even more of a sloppy mess, tumbling in the churn of sea and sand.

When my feet hit the sand, I stood, shook my head, and walked away unhurt. *I need to practice.* Luckily, like the Nippers kids, I also had support. Up at the surf club when we finished, I saw Anthony "Harries" Carroll, the *Bondi Rescue* lifeguard the kids knew from watching on TV, standing near the brick steps.

"Seeing everyone come in, wow," Harries said. He smiled, waving his arms through the air as if he were paddling, shouting to the group, "You all looked like little ducklings! Everyone looked great!"

All I could do was shake my head. Ducklings? But I wanted to say thank you. It felt intoxicating to paddle out there, fail, and survive. The ocean seemed to have suddenly opened up its gates, offering me an enchanted and immersive garden, beckoning to be explored.

"The sea, once it casts its spell, holds one in its net of wonder forever," said Jacques Cousteau,[xxiv] the famous French oceanographer. I was still a new student in its magic, but I knew enough to admire expertise, and I found myself looking up to those who quietly put in more time studying the ocean than I did. Walking home after a rinse under a hose at the club, I stared again at the enormous Pacific and saw Dave still out there, past the break deep in the sea, alone this time, his orange rashie magnified by the setting sun.

SIX

The Bronze, Part 2

*Finding the I in team; the Yolngu and the
ancient history of social safety; Sebastian
Junger on war, risk, and training*

I walked down to my first dry skills class at the surf club with
the same contemplative pace Baz and Amelia used to get to
Nippers. It was a Monday night in October, a couple of weeks
after my first experience with rescue boards, and I kept thinking
of something Diana had told me a few days earlier: just remember why you're doing it.

Why was I doing it? I tried to think of what I would say to

the kids. *I'm doing it to be a better father and a better person. Why do I push you into Nippers, why do I push you to take risks, to fail and try again, and why am I pushing myself to do the same? Because I want to be the kind of father who helps make you stronger and helps you see how strong you are. Not just for yourself but with and for the world.*

I sat down at a picnic table on the hill overlooking the beach. The waves were stomping in under darkening skies, producing that great wide sound the poet Rainer Maria Rilke so enjoyed. The intensity of my own emotions surprised me. Maybe that's what new and frightening challenges always do—rev our minds, make us more present. That might also explain why I'd been all over the kids lately, prodding Amelia with homework and Baz with the mumbled "thank-yous" that needed to become clear and vocal.

Even with Diana, I kept trying to find ways to get her more time for her book and conditioner business.

I guess what I really wanted was for them to look back some day when I'm gone and say, "He was there. He put in the effort. It was hard sometimes, but there was wisdom in his toughness and kindness in his heart."

I looked at my watch. *Right on time.*

Inside the surf club's main room, a handful of people were milling around, filling out forms at stand-up tables. In the center of the damp gray carpet, fifteen white plastic chairs were arranged in a circle. It reminded me of group therapy.

One of the trainers—Ruk, from the board class, which had preceded the actual course's start—waved me over to grab a textbook, a rashie, and other equipment, including an orange cap. His smile was as wide as the beach.

"Write your name on everything," he said.

I knew what the Australians would want to call me—Damo, the universal fate of all Damiens. But I wasn't sure about that one. I wrote Cave on my bag and left the cap blank in case I got up the nerve to become Damo.

"Okay, let's have a seat and get started," Ruk said.

He sat down with his back to the surf, barefoot and in a Bronte sweatshirt. Two other trainers sat to his right. Farther around the circle, I could see three teenagers, their ages marked by braces—and one of them was Will, with the superfast time at the proficiency swim. Before sitting down, they had picked up the chairs and moved them farther back. *Smart.*

Next to them were three women, in their twenties or thirties maybe, followed by five graying dad-type guys, which was where I planted myself.

"For the next eight weeks, this is going to be your family," Ruk said. He'd already created a WhatsApp group for all of us. "It's going to be fun. It's going to be hard."

He told us that he moved to Australia from Canada two years ago, that his parents were originally from Sri Lanka, and that joining surf lifesaving was the best thing he'd ever done. The community, the physical challenge, getting to know the ocean. He loved it all.

The next trainer—bald, lanky, also barefoot—introduced himself as Andy, and the third was Jen, a Brit whose nickname was Penguin. With two out of three instructors inducting us into the most Australian of institutions identified as recent immigrants, I began to feel a little more reassured that lifesaving might be more a matter of learning than birthright.

The first thing they did was treat us to a tour. Jen took the lead, walking us down the stairs to a dark hallway, pointing out women's and men's changing areas, the windowless weights room, and an area near the front where narrow boats and boards lined the walls.

"This will all be coming down in the next twelve to eighteen months," Andy said. Plans for a new or renovated surf club were just starting to come together. "It doesn't fit the purpose anymore."

I could see what he meant when they showed us a medical bed that sat behind a rusty storage cabinet to create some semblance of privacy.

"When was the club built?" I asked.

"Around 1970," Jen said. "It's a very seventies vibe. Put it this way, there were no women in the club when it was built. They had to add a women's changing room later."

As we walked back up the stairs, a white plaque identified four former club members who died in World War I and another five who died in World War II. Upstairs, high on a wall near the bar, I stopped in front of a black-and-white photo of someone in the baggy pants of an earlier military era—Sergeant Major John Bond. I nodded my respect to the founder.

He looked a little like my grandfather, broad of shoulder with a stance that suggested command and tradition. Those were the kinds of thing I used to reject; when I studied for a year at Oxford University's oldest college, I proudly told my tutors I didn't care about its medieval history. As an American, I argued for the novel and the new. But in Bronte twenty-odd years later, eyeing Sergeant Major Bond made me more resolute—I'd found something old to believe in.

"Think of a word that starts with the same first letter as your name and is also an action," Ruk said once we all returned to our seats. "I'm Resuscitation Ruk." He did three compressions with his hands pushing down on an imaginary patient.

"Anaphylactic Andrew." Andy modeled shoving an EpiPen into his leg.

I managed to contain the groan in my head but not my squirming in the chair. *Remember why you're here.* Jumping Jenny. Waxing Will. Winking Will. Air Guitar Annabelle. Octopus Olivia. Jogging John. Crash Cam. Physio Phil, or was it Physio Fred?

Eventually the inevitable moment. "Dancing Damien." I snapped my fingers and swayed. *Loser.* Cringing Cave. The eye roll from Amelia would have been epic.

I was saved by the need to press on. We had two classes a week for the next eight weeks and a lot to get through, starting with radios and personal safety. We'd all had to do a few online quizzes before arriving so I had a broad idea of what was coming—beach education, first aid, then practical rescue training—but as usual, I had underestimated the challenge. I didn't quite realize the dangers of the course itself until Ruk explained that while teaching another class, he yanked his chest muscles so far out of whack that he needed physiotherapy for six months. Andy also mentioned stitches from an errant rescue board.

"Know your limitations," Andy said. "Raise your hand if you need help." He waved his hand above his head to show us how to signal for help in the water. "Use it generously."

Over the next hour, we were given some basic ground rules for risk and responsibility, starting with what was *not* required of us. We were told we don't have a formal "duty of care" for swimmers—if we see someone in trouble in the water, we are not required to rush in and try to save the person. We can and we should if we feel able, but always with equipment like a rescue tube and only after making a smart assessment about the best course of action. There were already too many lifesavers who died trying to help other people—people like Ross Powell and his son, Andrew, longtime members of the Port Campbell Surf Lifesaving Club, who had drowned just a few months earlier while trying to save a tourist caught in rough seas near the Twelve Apostles on Victoria's southern coast.

Responsibility, they emphasized, has to be balanced with a sense of collective awareness. Maybe there are others who might be better positioned to help (Harries of *Bondi Rescue* did often appear out of nowhere to save lives in Bronte). Or maybe you should wait for another rescuer to join you before acting. The safest and fastest rescues involved lifesavers working closely together—along the lines of what worked for Chesley Sullenberger on the Hudson.

The advice seemed designed to strip us all of individual hero syndrome. Humility was required, echoing something a colleague told me right before I went to Iraq to cover the war.

"Remember with every decision you make," he said, "you're not just taking yourself to war, you're taking everyone who loves you as well."

When the class ended, I walked home with a deeper appreciation for Bronte. I knew we were fortunate, privileged really, but not in the way that I'd thought about that word in America. We lived a short walk away from risk and natural beauty in a global city with a social safety net and a culture of work that allowed for giving back, where trying to do well at difficult things was part of the community culture. We trusted our neighbors and friends to watch out for our kids and to push them to overcome challenges, try hard, fail, and build their abilities.

It was not something to take for granted, even in Australia. Two weeks earlier, I'd been up in the state of Queensland doing some reporting on climate change when I stopped in at a surf club in Mackay, a coastal city of around 120,000 people, with a very different story. The first clue was a sign out front recruiting for Nippers. Inside a breezy open club that felt far more welcoming than our brick box in Bronte, a few of the veteran members told me their membership tally had been dwindling.

In Bronte, our club had more than seven hundred kids doing Nippers, outnumbering full-member adults and at times taking over the entire beach in a way that impressed some beachgoers and angered others; Mackay had around one hundred Nippers, down from three hundred a few years earlier, and just thirty patrollers. They longed for more commitment but felt unsupported. There were fewer schools doing swim lessons for students. Surf lifesaving champions who used to be household names had been replaced as role models by athletes in other sports or celebrity influencers. Parents were busier, less connected to each other, and without as much pushing, children were less willing to persevere.

"Kids today, if they don't get it the first time, they quit," said Geoff Renehan, a member of a surf club nearby who had come to Mackay to help. "And if you're looking for volunteers, go look in the cemetery—that's where they all are."

Renehan saw the decline as a product of generational change

and increased work demands, but coming from New South Wales, where most surf clubs were thriving up and down the coast and the income ladder, I interpreted Mackay's struggle as a broader warning: the strengths of any community institution are mutable and need nurturing to survive. Cohesion, whether at the local or national level, is not a fix-it-and-forget-it proposition. Without reinforcement and multiple entry points for newcomers, the entire thing will collapse.

Bronte used to be struggling too. Kimberly told me that when she started working at the club part-time in 2012, the culture was pretty typical: blokey and local, a bit stuck.

"We all have those ebbs and flows," Kimberly said. "So I think when I started at the club itself, it was in an ebb, definitely."

Some of the lifers had told me that too—they joked that the guys overseeing annual proficiency tests for patrollers were usually smoking cigarettes and barely paying attention.

To solve the problem, Kimberly and the management board decided to do something that felt counterintuitive but that fit well within what Seligman's research had shown and what worked for programs like Outward Bound: they added more organization and more rigor and tightened the recruitment standards with the hope that by demanding more, people would become more invested and committed. The qualifying swim for the Bronze, which went beyond the national lifesaving standard, was a good example.

As expectations for volunteers increased, Kimberly also no longer felt like she could just watch. She needed to model the change, to be in the mix, throwing her arms around the reluctant, not just communicating strategy.

It didn't come as naturally as it seemed. Kimberly had grown up on a farm at the western edge of Sydney and learned to love the ocean in tough times—through a divorce and postpartum complications that led to a hysterectomy. Like me, though, she didn't initially have the confidence to consider herself an ocean swimmer, never mind a lifesaving leader. She told me it took years of 6:00 a.m. swims with a group led by Bronte's standard-bearer, a soft-spoken former executive named Garry, to bring her around. It took a lot of practice to help her help others see why overcoming insecurity—alongside total strangers—would eventually pay off: individually, collectively, as parents, physically, and in terms of how we all view the world.

"The ocean is such a leveler," she said. "The tiniest person or the biggest person can be amazing in the water. It just teaches you not to judge."

At the first Wednesday morning swim that I managed to get to with Garry, Kimberly was there early, before 6:00 a.m., full of energy, ready to go. It was mid-October. I had a flight to catch a few hours later, and winter had not yet loosened its grip. The sun was still crouching behind the horizon when I reached the North Bondi surf club, where I found around twenty Bronte swimmers. Old and young, they were chatting and bouncing on their toes for warmth. I recognized a few people from my Bronze class: Octopus Olivia, Air Guitar Annabelle, Jogging Jon, Physio Phil.

Garry appeared wearing a swim wet suit and limping a bit. Smiling, he welcomed our group to the morning and handed out neon green caps to make us easier to see in the water. (The orange caps we had received earlier were for Saturdays.) I tried to make small talk with Phil, who was the only one there without a wet suit. Everyone seemed to be both impressed and worried for him. The pavement we were standing on barefoot felt a degree from frozen. The sand, as we walked toward the surf, was even colder.

Garry went through a quick summary of the plan. "We'll start with a few ins and outs," he said. "Swim past the waves, gather out there together, and then swim back."

To make sure we all knew the basics, he told us to dive under the waves that were breaking and to keep swimming even if we get pushed back. We also went through the two signals we needed to know for the swim: waving our hand in the air to ask for help and a hand straight up, which means return to the beach.

"Okay, let's go."

The teenagers—Waxing Will and Winking Will—dived right in as if it was a sunny Saturday afternoon, their legs and arms tossed to and fro as if they were playing in the surf. I tried to imagine myself getting up at 5:30 a.m. for a swim when I was sixteen and failed.

The rest of us moved more deliberately. No one said what they were feeling, but in people's eyes, I saw nervousness and an eagerness to just get going. It reminded me of my first surfing experiences but with a faster heartbeat. Maybe the beginning of training for anything makes people rush—to get over being a novice. I put on my goggles. *I wonder if I'll ever think this is fun.*

The thought didn't linger. Without a surfboard, pushing through the water took more energy than I had expected. I wasn't scared, just winded as I swam out, finally, past the breakers. We all rested about two hundred meters from the shore, and it felt great—to take a breath, to bob and float in waves rising tall, lifting me skyward (inhale) and softly back down (exhale). There, out in the deep, the ocean felt more alive, friendly, and inviting. All the waves seemed to want was for me to be present and surrender, and so I did. I could see the appeal. Clustered with others, with a little extra float from my wet suit, I felt perfectly placed. Balanced.

"Everyone ready?" Garry asked. Reward over, it was time to head for the shore. He reminded us to keep looking back for waves, to ride them in and avoid getting smashed. I swam at my usual pace and ended up being the last one to arrive on the frigid sand, where we had to run fifty meters up to the promenade and back down. By the end, we were all huffing and puffing. Then in we went again. This time, I focused on my timing, trying to work with, not against, the ocean's rhythm. I dolphin dived and grabbed the sand. I slowed down and moved faster, heading out to Garry, who seemed to swim like an eel. We rested briefly, then returned. On the sand back at our starting point, I looked up at the clock on the North Bondi surf club. It was 6:45, a decent showing for my first time.

"I need to run," I told Garry.

At home, as I rushed to make my flight, Diana asked me how it went.

"Hard," I told her. "But great."

When the new season of Nippers came around after our Bronze course started, I felt more empathy for the kids. I understood the force of the waves. I knew how scary the water could be and the peculiar fear of a group challenge—*what if everyone else can do it and I cannot?*

Many of the other dads in the group also expressed a new-found respect for their children along with an urge to share what they were learning. I smiled to myself one Sunday when I saw Jon, a Brit with a salty sense of humor, telling his daughter, who had just started Nippers, about how water moved at the beach. She was five years old and standing at the edge of the rocks near the bogey hole, right near the Bronte Express.

"You feel how strong that is," Jon said. "That's the rip."

He introduced me to his family and I told him about my kids, who were playing nearby. We commiserated about our Bronze class ("it's hard, harder than I expected!") but also laughed at the strange joy of starting something we were asking our children to do as well.

A wave suddenly knocked into our ankles. We both looked up to see what else was coming. By that point, a few weeks in, we were well versed in the various kinds of waves and the dangers they posed. Dumping or plunging waves on the shore lead to spinal injuries. Spilling waves are safer, unless they're huge like the double-overhead monsters Jon and I were happy to avoid on our first wet skills training Saturday. Those waves had traveled for hundreds of miles from a low-pressure system out in the Pacific, and the storm that formed them could be read not just by height. The swell period, the time between the largest waves, was also important. The longer the wait between sets, the stronger those waves would be. The lull hinted at the force of what would follow. Similarly, a rip current, whether fixed or sudden, is simply part of a natural rhythm, providing a way for water, energy, and the ocean to return to equilibrium.

The next time I saw Jon, we were putting our knowledge to

good use, surfing the middle sandbank in Bondi. Watching him grab a nice left on a windless Friday, I could see the ocean as a metaphor for how risk researchers think about life: uncontrollable, uncertain, with patterns that can be divined but that are always changing. Periods of calm are moments to prepare. One big challenge will be followed by others.

"Time for a run-swim-run." Ruk's smile looked a little brighter than usual.

We were near the halfway point in the course, doing our wet skills training on a warm Saturday in November, and he'd been posting a lot of inspirational messages on Instagram. I didn't know him well enough to ask why he seemed especially happy, nor did I have time.

"Go!" he shouted.

We all set off at a light jog for a two-hundred-meter run on the sand, followed by a two-hundred-meter swim and another two-hundred-meter run. We would need to complete all three in eight minutes for our Bronze assessment, and as always, my mission was clear: *Don't get injured. Don't be last.*

In the water, I caught a kick in the ear from one of the women swimming past me. Heading back in, I slipped toward the rip and realized I wasn't moving forward. With every stroke, I just held in place staring at the same strands of waving seagrass, which, like me, seemed to move in slow motion. I might have panicked except that Garry had forced us through the rip on our last Wednesday swim, so I knew it was possible, and with a few stronger strokes, I made progress. I sprinted the final two hundred meters and found that I was not as far back as I feared, landing well within the happy middle.

After that, we shifted to basic lifesaving, pulling people in with our arms or a rescue tube placed under their chest. I worked mostly with Jon and Phil. Then we did boards. I had to save Jen, which meant pulling her up as she pretended to be unconscious, placing her headfirst near the front of the board, on her stomach, and paddling her in, with my chin just above her butt and the rest of me farther back. We did that repeatedly, and each time, Jen and I tried to ignore our awkward positioning. It was a whole lot different from sitting next to people in chairs, doing the theory. Watching everyone else do the same nearby, laughing and trying not to drown, the sense of family that Ruk had mentioned started to feel real.

The Bronze demanded a reduction of personal space along with habit-forming repetition. Our Monday night dry skills class always started with practicing our signals for communication—go farther out to sea (two arms up), return to shore (one arm up), submerged swimmer (make an X over your head with your arms). There are more than a dozen of these, and I loved that they felt so analogue, universal, and timeless.

From there, we moved into practicing first aid or going over other problems that might emerge as a lifesaver. Gerd Gigerenzer talked a lot about checklists as a way to improve how institutions and groups deal with risk; they also come up a lot in medicine, as Atul Gawande explained in his book, *The Checklist Manifesto*, and lifesaving fully embraced the concept.[i] We studied, memorized, and role-played checklists for hypothermia, asthma, allergies, heart attacks, and a host of other problems. Many of the first aid responses relied on acronyms. FAST, for example, referred to the test for a stroke: facial weakness, arm weakness, speech problems, and time to act—if the person has any of the first three, call an ambulance.

The most important checklist, and the one we trained repeatedly to master, was DRSABCD (pronounced "doctors ABCD"). In the textbook we studied from, it took up a whole page with large lettering that made it look like a poster. The D at the start stands for danger. The first thing any lifesaver must do is check for danger to yourself, the patient, and bystanders—a person who looks threatening, a rip current to be avoided, a needle next to an unconscious patient. R refers to response, with a brief script directed at the patient. "Can you hear me? Open your eyes. What's your name? Squeeze my hands."

If there's no response, we move to S—send for help—and resuscitation. Check the airway (A), test if the patient is breathing (B), then start CPR (C) with thirty chest compressions and two rescue breaths, followed by defibrillation (D)—every surf club is equipped with several of the easy-to-use machines.

Some of the training felt familiar. Before Iraq, the *Times* sent me to a three-day program with former British special forces soldiers, which included workshopping first aid, CPR, and how to treat gunshot wounds. I remember my hands getting sticky with fake blood as I worked on a colleague heading to Russia.

For the Bronze, the teams were bigger, the training less frantic. We broke off into groups of four to six, and with every practice round, our strengths and weaknesses surfaced for all to see. The teenagers, so strong in the water, often struggled to take command of a rescue situation. Their voices stayed quiet. Cam, one of the dads, tended to fill the void. He came alive as a first responder, working at maximum volume and efficiency. Mostly, though, the process was an equalizer. We were all good at some things, bad at others. (In the wise words of Kimberly, "It teaches you not to judge.")

My most painful moments came when I had to get in close under the watchful eyes of others. One Saturday, having missed the previous week for a reporting trip to Christchurch, I arrived in a mental mess. We were on the cusp of summer, and I was sweating as soon as I put on my wet suit. Instead of beginning with a run-swim-run, Ruk told us we'd start with spinal injuries. I had to go first with my group, and I failed my first two attempts at getting Waxing Will, the speedy swimmer, safely into position on the yellow spinal board. I couldn't get the head hold right. I was distracted, embarrassed, too aware of everyone watching me manhandle one of my teammates.

Jen and Andrew corrected me, or tried to, then they figured it might help if we switched roles.

"You be the patient," Andrew said.

I switched positions with Will. He became the lead lifesaver for our group. There was no longer any denying that I needed help or that I was nervous.

"You'll just have to deal with my sweaty head," I joked.

Will led our team through the scenario without incident. I could feel my head secured when he laid me down, despite the sweat, at which point I realized he was close enough to smell what I had eaten for breakfast. There were people I'd known for twenty years I'd never been that physically close to. And that was my problem. I was getting the head hold wrong because, despite everything I'd learned, I was still keeping people at arm's length.

To become a lifesaver—to get better at risk, especially as an American—I needed to fully let go of my need for space, my self-regard, my ego. I needed to practice suppressing all the idealized I've-got-this individualism that I'd been surrounded by in the United States. Maybe I even needed a radically different worldview that puts interdependence at the center of everything.

In the Yolngu clans of Australia's far north, I discovered a powerful alternative that pulled from premodern culture and yet spoke to the moment. The people who live in the Miwatj or northeast Arnhem Land region have their own clear conception of the individual. In their language, the character trait Westerners would call "self-centered" is referred to as "gurru-tumiriw," which means "kin-lacking"—acting as if one had no kin.[ii] It's a very particular label and a wounding insult, because there is nothing more valued among the Yolngu than kin and a connection to others.

Witiyana Marika, a Yolngu elder, singer, and film producer—and also a founding member of Yothu Yindi, the famous 1980s rock group—told me the bonding begins in the womb: "You're in kinship with her and her family before you're born."

Babies, from the moment they sit up, are taught to identify every person they see through clan relations. Whenever a person comes into the infant's view, in a home or outside, someone will repeatedly tell the child who the person is using the appropriate kin terminology—"bäpurru" refers to the father's side, "ngändi" to the mother's, and there are additional terms denoting extended relatives, from aunts to grandfathers.

As children grow, the pro-social education continues. They learn from their relatives who are all around, and when they begin to speak, any attempt to use a kin term guarantees extravagant praise from adults. By the time Yolngu toddlers are conversing, they can explain who they are in relation to others and how all the people in their social universe are linked. Songs, stories, and rituals add another layer of repetition and lyricism, fusing kin structures to nature and ancestral relatives.

"Everyone is joined," Marika said. "When we meet anyone, it's through our lines, mother earth, father sky.

"From this soil, we have developed this system," he added, describing his own upbringing as "the perfect way" just outside Yirrkala, with an intermarried clan of about forty people living entirely off the land and sea. "We think as a group, not as just ourselves."

It's not just the Yolngu of course. Aboriginal cultures have existed continuously in Australia for between thirty-five thousand and sixty-five thousand years, making this the home of earth's oldest uninterrupted civilization. By the time the first European settlers arrived, hundreds of Indigenous groups had spread out across the continent, each with their own language and identity.[iii]

But despite those differences, there were striking similarities—kin, clan, and country were generally prioritized. And there was sharing. The story Bruce Pascoe tells in *Dark Emu*, drawing on early settler accounts, points to a consistent and sustainable stewardship of the land where people took no more than they needed and left enough for others.[iv] Some Aboriginal groups even built complex fishing traps that allowed enough water and fish to pass through so that groups downriver would have a catch of their own.

"What happened in Australia was a real high point in human development," Pascoe told me when I visited his farm in Victoria. "We need to get back to it."

At the time, we were standing near a garden of murnong, a yam commonly eaten before Europeans arrived. Pascoe was trying to spur a revival of Indigenous food and human interaction.

"I believe this system was designed to embrace everybody," he said. "The highly skilled, the less skilled, the intelligent, the less intelligent. It was designed so that everybody could be included."

Pascoe's vision sounded a touch romantic—he's spent a lifetime reconnecting with his own distant Aboriginal roots and is as much a poet as a scholar. But the inclusive paradigm he described matched Marika's account and the portrait that has emerged through decades of independent research with Yolngu groups. Among all Australia's Indigenous groups, their interdependent ways are especially well understood, in part because they've gone further than others in sharing their lives and culture with outsiders.

Nicolas Peterson is one of those outsiders. A silver-haired emeritus professor at the Australian National University who has been described as a master anthropologist, he was one of the first researchers to do extensive fieldwork in the bush during the 1960s and '70s, when many Aboriginal groups obtained legal rights to their land again, leading them away from neocolonial settlements and back to the routines and rituals of country. It was a time when many Australians wanted to know more about authentic Aboriginal life, and Peterson often acted as a guide for both the Australian government and the public.

I called him one day to learn more about a phrase he used in an old interview: "densely social."[v] It sounded to me like the perfect distillation of what Marika had described, and to my American ear, it was how Australia felt more generally. All that closeness required for lifesaving training, all the expectations of our neighbors, all the data showing that Australians spend more time than Americans joining clubs and talking to friends and family—what was it if not densely social?

Peterson told me that he first encountered the concept in 1967. As a young researcher, a wide-eyed loner working toward his PhD, he spent nearly a year living with a group of around thirty Yolngu near a swamp in the tropical bush of remote northern Australia, not far from where Marika grew up. Peterson chose that group because they were almost entirely self-sufficient, living without modern assistance. The swamp also represented a source of food security—he could survive on his own if he needed to by fishing.

Living in the camp, he said he quickly learned that for Yolngu men and women, no one was ever really alone or viewed as independent. Along with the web of clan reaching back generations, the design of the Yolngu camp kept people physically close together. Public space in the center could be seen by everyone, and every activity—hunting, fishing, cooking, and eating— involved someone else to an extent that surprised Peterson. He said the "densely social" nature of the group meant constant huddling and conversation.

"What was your reaction to that?" I asked.

"That's a very good question," he said. "It's actually very demanding, especially if you're the sort of a middle-class male who's used to doing quite a lot of studying, which you do alone."

He said the challenge emerged most clearly when he relied on his Western sensibility and got lost "trying to find a place to take a crap."

One day around sunset, he trekked away by himself to do his business with a beautiful spot in mind—a hilly outcrop near the water. "I was a bit muddled as to where that was," he said. "You don't realize how quickly you walk. There was no sun, it was cloudy, and so I couldn't work out the direction of north and south or east and west."

He wandered around for nearly an hour before returning to the camp, sweaty and embarrassed. That was when he discovered that the group was quite worried about him. He saw himself as an individual, someone who was expected to deal with life, nature (and his body) on his own. They saw him, almost right away, as part of their country and clan to whom they owed a responsibility of protection.

"Most men go off together, even to the lavatory," Peterson explained. "It's not a private activity in the way we treat it, and that's probably why they worried about me."

In their own culture, the choice to be alone raised suspicions. It was a denial of kin.

"People going off by themselves are thought to be up to no good—either trying to meet up with a woman or some other illicit relationship or practicing sorcery," Peterson said.

He emphasized that it was hardly the utopian socialism that

some fans of the premodern age would want it to be. When resources were scarce, sharing diminished and conflicts intensified. Because elders often took multiple wives, women were in high demand, and marriages were arranged sometimes even before birth.

Generally, though, the Yolngu way worked with a rhythm that, even now, puts kin, natural knowledge, and physical competence at the heart of everything. Marika, who is fifty-nine with a long white beard that makes him look older and wiser, gave me an example. He said that in his family, his father and his five uncles had a boat or two that they shared, usually to hunt for dugong, a sea cow similar to a manatee, or various kinds of turtle. Everything they caught was then divvied up according to a form of mathematics from the distant past. Turtle markings showed which portions of the catch went to one extension of kin or another.

"It was already in the system, in the song cycle," Marika said, "and with the meat, what we caught followed that cycle."

Peterson observed that conversations were often cryptic and filled with body language in part because there was so much the Yolngu shared and understood as a group. He tried to explain with a modern anecdote.

"Suppose your wife doesn't like yellow at all and thinks yellow dresses are ridiculous, and somebody goes by in a yellow dress, you might just raise your eyebrow instead of saying, 'Look at that dress. I know you don't like it.' That raising the eyebrow summarizes the whole history of your relationship."

Coded communication, he said, is the mark of a community where "everybody has a high level of knowledge about everybody else." It means that in times of need or risk, group responses tend to be quicker and quieter, like reflexes or some kind of shared intuition.

I tried to think of similar environments with people deeply connected to each other and the past: newsrooms back in the day, surf clubs, theater groups, musical ensembles, rescue teams. But the experience that conjured up the closest connection to what Peterson and Marika described was war.

Warriors are modern culture's most extreme example of kinship. The risks of the job create a self-plus-others dynamic that civilians rarely experience and yet admire. In the United States, Australia, and many other countries, the military is the most trusted public institution. Despite war's horrors, there's something we respect in those who volunteer and maybe even crave for our own lives—the selflessness, the discipline, and, perhaps most of all, the camaraderie. It took talking to Peterson for me to see that. To fully recognize that the best way to get our individualism to a healthy level involves immersion in a "densely social" culture. It could be a team, a band, a community group. For me, before lifesaving, it was war.

Even for those of us who have walked with soldiers only briefly, the impacts can be profound not just because of what we learn about the best and worst of human nature, but also because the risk and danger push us out of our individualism bubble and back to a form of primal collectivism that, in some cases, helps us perform at a higher level.

Australians seem to grasp that elemental truth. Their

reverence for the losses and bravery of Aussie soldiers in World War I, which plays out not just on holidays but year-round with "lest we forget" calls for remembrance, points to the culture's high regard for shared bravery and sacrifice.

With all that history in mind, I started to look again at my time in Iraq through a more ancient and Australian lens. Searching for the inspiration that I hoped would help me keep pushing in closer with lifesaving, I found that some of my memories resembled Peterson's. When I was embedded with American troops in Iraq, I often slept in a large tent without interior walls where everyone could see and hear everyone. On foot patrols, I watched and listened carefully to decode an argot of knowing glances, acronyms, and slang, which changed with location and military branch. I had to ask more questions than usual. I didn't get lost going to take a crap, but I often felt dumb, exhausted by the mental labor, and completely out of place.

War altered the reporter-source arrangement. I was an outsider who could write about whatever I witnessed, but with risk all around, the soldiers felt compelled to keep me alive, and I worked hard not to be a burden. The politics of war did not matter. Our fates intertwined, especially in combat.

One of the strongest examples I can recall—an experience my mind kept returning to after learning about Yolngu ways, a day that exemplified the values I want for my children, despite the gruesome details—occurred south of Baghdad in May 2007. It was in a place called "the triangle of death," where river deltas turn the beige of Baghdad green with date palms and long, thick grass.

I was with a photographer named Mike, and Diana was there

too. She'd come to shoot video for a story we were doing about the search for three missing soldiers who were grabbed from an outpost by insurgents. Mike and I were with one platoon; Diana and another reporter were with another.

We all got up at 2:00 a.m. for a long drive followed by foot patrols deep in the hinterland that started just before dawn. Mike and I walked near the front, but within a few minutes of leaving our Humvees, the ground exploded. Dust, dirt, blood, and military equipment filled the air, clearing after several seconds to reveal a frenzied scene of horror.

Where a young soldier had just been standing about fifty yards behind me, there was a crater five feet wide and three feet deep. His body lay nearby in two parts. Three or four wounded men were scattered around him.

Mike and I rushed to the scene. "It was Ski," someone said, using the nickname for the soldier who had just been killed—Sergeant Justin Wisniewski, twenty-two, a practical joker who had already won awards for valor. To my right, a young officer was on the radio, shouting an update. In front of us, the unit's medic, Sgt. Joshua Delgado, was already bandaging the most seriously wounded soldier, who lay with shrapnel wounds to the face, arm, and side. Two other Americans and an Iraqi were also hurt.

One of the injured infantrymen, Staff Sergeant Robert Simonovich, knelt nearby. He had taken his body armor off, and with just a T-shirt on, it was clear he had not walked far enough yet to sweat. His hands rested on his knees. Eyes closed, he said he couldn't see.

"It's not one of our guys, is it?" No one had the heart to answer.

The platoon commander called for a medevac helicopter, and all of us tried to figure out how to help. Mike put his camera down and worked with Delgado, who stayed remarkably calm. I stayed with Simonovich and checked him for wounds that he might be in too much shock to feel. My heart was beating fast. I couldn't offer much comfort, so I just tried to narrate for him what was going on.

Almost immediately, the bonds that he and the rest of the infantrymen had forged started to become visible in their actions. They knew just where they needed to be, protecting the perimeter, managing wounds, moving Iraqi soldiers they were working with out of danger. There were no solo heroes, just a unit. And amid the anger and the sorrow, I heard one phrase more than any other: "I love you, man." I heard it spoken aloud as they worked. When there was a lull as we waited for the helicopter, the men hugged, tears streaming down their faces—and "I love you" was what they said repeatedly, blurting it out as if it was something they wished they had told their friend Ski and each other far more often.

Hearing that simple phrase made me well up with emotion too. I'd seen soldiers go through impossible circumstances more than once by then, but it was rare for their feelings to be expressed without adornment or concealment. In the moment, we were surrounded by unspeakable sadness. To cope, they were bringing to the surface a kinship that preceded the tragedy. The group had been fighting together for ten months, through the most violent year of the war. They found strength in their relationships. They called on their training, a sense of shared commitment, a desire to make everyone feel whole.

Of all the sounds from that day, it's the "I love you, man" that I can still hear most clearly. And perhaps surprisingly, when I think of what's especially indelible in my memories, it's that phrase and a small, simple act that followed. It was after the helicopter took off into the morning haze. We all had to walk back to the road to meet the unit commander, and suddenly, after forgetting the danger, we realized there could be more improvised explosive devices all around us. The path out could be as dangerous as the path in.

No one panicked. To minimize the threat, we adopted a simple method that can only be described as densely social: we walked single file, slowly, stepping into each other's footsteps across the scrub. That's what I remember and can still almost feel—there were many of us but only one shared track of risk and boot prints.

When it was time for the mission to continue, Mike and I were given the option of returning to the base to avoid further danger and process what had just happened. But watching the men getting their gear ready, thinking about Diana, who was already out there, I knew I couldn't flee. Shared responsibility tugged at me—it didn't seem fair that we could leave while they could not.

"We'll go with you," I told the army captain in charge.

He led the way. Once again, the soldiers walked in each other's tracks, and I followed. I can still see the drab, brown dirt and the tall, dusty grass scratching at my pants as I pressed my foot into a spot where the boots of the men ahead of me had been. One step, no explosion, then another. Stay balanced. Stay calm. Stay together.

I'm not the only one, or even the first, to make a connection between ancient living and contemporary soldiering. In a short book from 2016 called *Tribe*, Sebastian Junger laid out his own case for why men fight in wars and what societies lose when they drift too far from collectivism, risk, and physical challenges.

He discussed in great detail the differences between the isolation of modern society and the shared and social way life works in hunter-gatherer societies. In one section that deeply resonated with my experience, he said the reason soldiers have a hard time when they return to Boston or Sydney or London is because "home" is more alienating and transactional than war. The soldiers I met in Baghdad, like those Junger met in Sarajevo and Kabul, struggled because they go "from the kind of close-knit group that humans evolved for, back into a society where most people work outside the home, children are educated by strangers, families are isolated from wider communities, and personal gain almost completely eclipses collective good."[vi]

His main point, made with a mix of personal anecdote, history, and science, was that rather than trying to socialize soldiers to fit back into our civilian world, we need to bring their ancient, cooperative, egalitarian values out of war and into our urban and suburban routines. It's what comfortable Westerners in particular need, he argued, citing a global survey by the World Health Organization showing that wealthy countries suffer depression rates that are eight times higher than poor countries.[vii]

"The mechanism seems simple," he wrote. "Poor people are forced to share their time and resources more than wealthy people are, and as a result they live in closer communities... A wealthy person who has never had to rely on help and resources from his community is leading a privileged life that falls way outside more than a million years of human experience."[viii]

Seligman, viewing the problem from a slightly different angle, sometimes explains the surge of depression among Americans in terms of "spiritual furniture."[ix] Our families and close friends, along with the institutions we rely on, are like a couch or comfortable chair; they're what we retreat to when we need help. But over time, more and more people have let their support systems fall apart, leaving them with less of the help they need to manage life's risks and setbacks.

Junger has spent most of his career writing about small groups facing impossible odds. He first became well known with a book called *The Perfect Storm*, about a fishing boat called the *Andrea Gail* that disappeared off the coast of a fishing town north of Boston. He followed that up with accounts of infantrymen in war.

Talking to academics about risk, I often felt like a student. Talking to Junger felt like talking to an editor after a big news event. We had both grown up in Massachusetts, though more than a decade apart, and were both trying to work out what to take away from far too many notebooks and memories. I suppose we were part of our own tribe—former conflict reporters, airport junkies—and our instincts were global. When I asked about the relationship between mental illness and wealth and between risk and wealth—which we'd both found fascinating—we landed on how people from different countries look at what life will likely hold for their futures.

Perhaps it's not just that people in poorer nations are more comfortable with risk and have lower rates of PTSD because trauma and depression are mitigated by the collectivism that difficult circumstances require. Maybe, he said, "it's because there's no expectation that life is either pleasant or safe.

"So when people are traumatized, it's still within their expectation, there's no violation of their understanding of life, right, whereas 9/11 in New York City—that was a huge violation of what we thought life was supposed to be. And so it was enormously traumatizing for New Yorkers while Afghans wouldn't have fucking blinked. Only three thousand people? Wow. You guys got off lucky!"[x]

Expecting that life will be hard, with risk and pain, means you're more likely to manage adversity and be pleasantly surprised when things go right, building happiness over time. Expecting a life of safety and ease means setting yourself up for disappointment, making unexpected setbacks more difficult to handle. So in the relatives' room in Christchurch, according to Junger's logic, New Zealand authorities (and maybe even Alta) were struggling because they never imagined the possibility of violence, while those who had grown up in violent countries, who accepted tragedy as a fact of life, were less rattled and better able to cope.

His argument seemed to resemble what I'd found in my many years as a foreign correspondent—that although we wouldn't wish danger on anyone, there is wisdom to be gleaned from communities and countries that do not take total safety as a given. And yet the people who define most wealthy Western countries' relationship to peril are typically *not* those with humble expectations or a global perspective. If low-risk white males are the ones deciding which risks to prioritize at the societal level, it's frequently high-risk white parents—the cautious high earners who feel especially entitled to control and harmfree living—setting the agenda at home and in our communities.

Junger pointed to American universities as an example of a place where elites are scrubbing away all discomfort to go along with luxury-priced tuition. Personally, I thought of the white parents who resist racial integration in New York City schools out of unspoken fear for their children's academic future without scrutinizing their own defective risk perceptions, not to mention all the shaming I'd seen in online parenting groups in Miami and Brooklyn for letting kids as old as twelve walk to school or use certain plastic toys or video games. Or what about the mothers and fathers in a handful of American states who had been reported to the police for leaving children at home or in the park when they were eight, nine, or ten years old?

The protectionists seizing the moral high ground—the intellectual descendants of the Equitable, the strivers and elites who believe that pathological prudence makes them better parents and people—are not only in the United States anymore either; the pressure to restrict children's movements and bubblewrap their lives has spread to Australia, England, and many other developed countries. Even in risk-friendly Norway, anxious parents are pressuring child-care centers to eliminate danger—getting them to remove rope swings and ban tree climbing—despite a robust body of research showing that unsupervised, risky play is what children need to build confidence, learn to assess risks, and thrive.

Perhaps it's a function of the global decline in birth

rates—we live in a world of older parents having fewer oh-so-precious children. Or it may be related to loss aversion. As societies have become wealthier, more people are insisting on an anxious approach to life, one that defies probability. Could it be because they have more to lose and—as various psychological studies show—the pain of losing is more powerful than the pleasure of gaining?[xi] I've often wondered if there's a way to scientifically study whether the increased comfort that many of us enjoy actually distorts our thinking and weakens our ability to make logical long-term choices, especially for our kids.

Whatever it is, there's a pomposity to the approach that parents in more precarious circumstances do not often share. Among the bourgeoisie, Junger and I seemed to agree—along with writers like Lenore Skenazy, the author of *Free-Range Kids*, and John Marsden, founder of Candlebark School—children have been gradually infantilized for decades. American children have slipped more than most. In 1969, 89 percent of children in kindergarten through eighth grade who lived within a mile of their primary school walked or biked to class; in 2009, only 35 percent of those who lived that close made their way to school on foot or by bike.[xii] And those numbers have continued to decline[xiii] even further over the past few years as public anxiety and distrust have increased, despite reams of research showing that kids who get to school on their own are healthier and more engaged with learning.[xiv]

That's why, to me, our experience in Australia stands out. My kids started walking to school on their own in Sydney before they were ten because that's what everyone else their age did. In bush camps and in Nippers, they learned to foster a belief in their own agency, focusing on what they could gain by facing fear, not what they might lose if something went wrong. And when trouble did arise, other Australians helped—when Baz broke his arm skateboarding in the city one day, his friends called me and a first-aid-trained father with two toddlers who happened to walk by stayed with Baz, keeping all the boys calm until I arrived.

What saddens me is not just that many of America's agenda setters seem to have lost touch with such simple acts of civility and goodwill, overlooking the value of developing a braver, more collective approach. It's that they also do not see that intense safety seeking, like extreme recklessness, can be cruel and self-centered, giving little thought to the value of independence or the impact on other parents and children who would rather not (or could not) manage every hazard to the satisfaction of wealthy suburban standards. To me, there's something selfish and out of touch about it—demanding that society cater to those with the most extreme fears.

Junger told me he has a question for such people: "Why are you assuming that a feeling of safety is good? What is it about safety that you are assuming is a positive value?"

He argued that while protection from death or unnecessary physical pain is obviously worthwhile, the demand for a *feeling* of safety for all as a prerequisite for debate or action goes too far because it elevates the emotional comfort of the individual over the needs of the group. Whether it's in a university classroom or on the playground, he said, "I just don't think safety is an unmitigated unexamined good."

I wasn't sure I entirely agreed. Creating an environment of emotional security can lead to more openness from people who might otherwise stay silent. Studies have also shown that a collective sense of safety can lead to greater creativity and more productive collaboration. Is that not a goal worth seeking, at least with sensitive subjects such as race and gender, in which the boundaries of acceptable conversation have often been defined by one (i.e., the most privileged) group at the expense of others?

The more important question may be whether *feeling* safe—a subjective determination, shaped by personality, experience, and mental biases—deserves to be so dominant and all-consuming in America. It's a matter of perspective. Has feeling safe as an individual become too much of a focal point for society's spotlight of attention? Have too many of us in America gone too far in what level of comfort we think we have a right to expect?

Many of the psychologists I'd been studying and interviewing stressed that overindulging any natural urge, including the desire for safety, can lead to unexpected harm. Martin Seligman argued that catering to risk avoidance leads to fragility and depression. Angela Duckworth noted that without persistent challenges, the development of resilience would be stunted. Gerd Gigerenzer said too much safety seeking creates what he calls "an illusion of certainty"—the idea that risk, danger, and the unpredictable can actually be erased from life. And should be.

"The idea of zero risk is a fiction," he told me. "Parents should expose their children to risks so they can learn to handle them. Otherwise, they are inept as adults.

"A high need for certainty can be a dangerous thing," he added. "It prevents us from learning to face the uncertainty pervading our lives, and it makes life mind-numbingly dull."

Americans already lead shorter, lonelier and less healthy

lives than people in other developed countries.[xv] Our children are spiraling into mental illness at rates we've never seen before. [xvi] Clearly it's time to look elsewhere for better ways to live, and with the context of ancient societies in mind, it's possible to see what we're missing and where more energy needs to go. Toward community, for one, and the kinds of mission-driven challenges that break down barriers of class, race, politics, and background and help us grow with others, producing confidence, empathy, and sharper decision-making in a crisis. Empathy is something we often encourage in our children, but how often do we also seek it out and practice it for ourselves?

Democracy scholars often focus on the power of "cross-cutting exposure." Spending time with people and opinions we might disagree with helps reduce political polarization[xvii]—a major cause of so many problems in America today. But on a simpler level, maybe investing in experiences with a bit of risk and the need to work in close proximity with strangers can make us better parents and better humans. Maybe we can start to get over what ails us by diving into hard things together, and trying not for perfection, but proficiency.

"What is shock?"

"When your organs start to shut down because—"

"Fail. It's when there is not enough blood circulation."

We were at our Bronze Medallion mock assessment, sitting on the carpet inside the surf club with a trainer from somewhere else, who decided to start with basic questions about first aid. Which we got wrong. Almost all of them.

We were about five weeks into the course. We had all been training, we had read the thick textbook, but when faced with an immediate need for answers, we struggled. The circulatory system? Hypothermia? Anaphylaxis? Fail, fail, fail.

Shifting to radios, we tried to keep our cool. Everyone was given a hypothetical scenario to report back to our patrol captain. Each imagined event reminded us that we must make peace with the unexpected in life and lifesaving, but whatever the situation, we knew there was an easy checklist to help us prioritize the information: position, problem, people, progress. First, report where we are and the problem that requires assistance; then explain how many people are involved or in trouble; and finally, outline the status of the situation—is it getting better or worse? Seemed easy. But we also had to remember how to use the radios, including radio etiquette.

Sally found herself dealing with the case of a lost kayaker. She mixed up the location—she said he was heading to Bronte, not Bondi, which would have sent rescuers in the wrong direction. Max was given a scenario about a four-year-old with autism last seen in Bronte Park fifteen minutes earlier. He couldn't recall the timing and left the location vague.

Sitting back and watching, I wanted to help. Eager to prove myself, to show soldier-style commitment, I wanted to blurt out what they missed. But then it was my turn, and I screwed up too. Dealing with a plane crash, I reported rushing to the scene to deal with around fifty casualties (people, problem), but I failed to explain whether any progress had been made with rescuing passengers. I also didn't identify myself and I failed to say "copy" or "out," leading to cross talk and confusion.

The assessor, a muscular lifesaver with dark, accusatory eyes, did not look pleased.

"You know your pro terms, right?"

I guessed that meant "over and out" and all the rest.

"You need to use them. You have to be formal. That's how it works in the military. That's how it works here."

I wanted to tell him that in actual life-and-death emergencies—in real war and genuinely occurring natural disasters—I stayed calm and helped solve problems. But I knew that would make me sound like what Baz calls a Richard, ten-year-old speak for a dick. So I quietly accepted the critique. After all, the assessor was right. I'd blundered.

In just the first half hour of the mock assessment, we could all see what kind of emergency workers and lifesavers each of us was likely to be: the introvert who gets nervous (Max), the prepared student who just needs an extra minute (Sally), the jaded joker who knows more than it seems (Jon).

The way I was getting to know these people was, for me, entirely new. Where we lived, voters usually favored center-right conservatives, but I had no idea what any of them thought about politics or careers. I didn't even know what most of them did for work. But I did know what made them laugh and what made them nervous. I knew what they liked to do for fun (especially after I ran into Phil and Cam at a U2 concert) and I knew, most of all, that they were good and generous and could be relied on in a crisis.

Jon and I seemed to be most in sync. I liked that he was a Brit with one of those accents that didn't scream Oxford. He'd come to Australia more than a decade ago and stayed, working in various jobs before starting his own executive recruiting business. His wife was American, and he had two younger kids in Nippers. Like me, he was mainly doing the Bronze to help his children in the water. And like me, he wasn't a natural joiner. We had to be the group's most ambivalent students, the ones who would have preferred to sit in the back of the class. But we were also slimming down and stepping up.

On the beach during our wet skills training the previous Saturday, Jon confessed he couldn't believe how much effort he was putting in to get the Bronze. Two, three days of training, hours and hours of reading. He'd surprised himself with how much he cared about doing well.

"It's like, wait a minute," he said. "We're volunteers, right? Volunteers! We're doing this for free. D'ya know what I mean?"

I laughed. Even *I* had forgotten that all this work was for something that would take time out of our lives without compensation.

"It's crazy. I don't even know these people," he said. "But I don't want to let them down."

After our early screwups, it was time to move on to CPR, the part of the assessment that really mattered. If we couldn't keep someone alive, there was no point to the whole ordeal.

Breaking up into teams of five, with one person playing the patient, each of us had to go through the DRSABCD process in different roles—as the first responder or the person in charge of CPR, oxygen, or the defibrillator. In our group, there was lots of yelling the first time through and lots of frantic effort. The stress felt surprisingly real. We were convinced we'd pass or fail as a unit.

When it was my turn to take charge as first responder, I felt ready but struggled with the details. Still uncomfortable handling the patient's head, I kept switching my grip. Then our drowning victim started vomiting, and I quickly rolled him to his side. Too quickly.

"When you roll the person, turn the head with the body. Don't lead with the head," the assessor warned.

This is of course how training is supposed to work. You do something again and again until it becomes second nature. You make mistakes in mock-ups so you perform correctly when it counts. Over time and through failure, you build strength, competence, and just the right level of intensity; your mental tics and biases are rewired for proficiency. Along the way, you spend a lot of time feeling like a buffoon, which hurts, but maybe it's all part of building toward what Junger had described as the "sweet spot" when people are scared but well trained and prepared. In nature, growth includes imperfection: when a seed splits, when a calf learns to walk. We know how much children learn from watching adults fail. Why should we be any different?

After we finished, our assessor sat us down in a circle and gave us feedback.

"If this was the actual assessment," he said, "you would not have passed."

We all dipped our heads in shame. We'd already internalized the collective guilt—each of us felt we'd let the group down. But he did not yell. Like a true believer in the growth mindset, he was convinced we'd improve.

"You have to find the right pacing," he said, echoing Katie's guidance for me with swimming. "There was a lot of panic. I think you really need to slow things down."

He asked us to remember how emergency medical teams approach crisis situations. They usually move out of ambulances without running, with neither haste nor waste. Even if the problem is urgent and the risks are grave, rushing and injecting fear into the situation will only make things worse, because humans really are such social creatures; everyone nearby will catch that anxiety like a virus in the air.

Clearly, our Bronze squad had a ways to go. We all stayed quiet as we put away the equipment at the end of the night.

"I don't know what happens. I just forget everything," Sally said, pushing a CPR mannequin into the closet.

"We all do," I said.

As soon as I got home, I went straight to the office to review the lifesaving textbook with all its red and yellow on the pages to match the lifesaving uniforms we were hoping to obtain. I tried to remind myself of what I had forgotten. I took notes in the margins.

Amelia came in a few minutes later with some homework. It was "paragraph work," a free-writing assignment that she had used to craft a tale about a bonfire, an orchard, and a bus as fast as a lightning bolt. I let out a loud sigh.

"What's wrong, Daddy?"

I told her that we did our mock assessment and that I had pretty much failed, especially with the CPR and the breathing.

"It's hard not to be good at something you want to be good at," I told her. "Do you know what that's like?"

I looked at my kin, my savvy little peanut, as I'd called her since she was an infant.

"Yeah," she said. "For me, it's dancing. I wish I was better."

"I guess we just need to practice," I said.

She nodded. I gave her a long, strong hug, close enough to smell Diana's conditioner in her hair. Doing the Bronze wasn't just about me teaching my children about strength; it was about them and everyone in the class helping me get stronger too.

"You can practice on one of my dolls if you want," Amelia said. "I don't play with them anymore. Use the one with the bright red hair."

SEVEN

The Final Test in Bronte

*From wet spinals to dolphins;
a foreign family learns to belong*

With the final assessment for the Bronze less than a month away, life got busy. It was only November, far before the peak heat of summer, but bad bushfires to the north were also already bearing down on thousands of Australians, sending clouds of terra-cotta smoke over Sydney and dropping black ash on our beaches. On November 9, I wrote about three deaths and seventy fires burning in New South Wales;[i] two days later, I wrote about eighty-five fires, and most of the experts I interviewed seemed to think the worst wouldn't arrive until January.[ii]

Diana and the kids were also running every which way. With the end of school approaching, there were dance recitals for Amelia, soccer comps for Baz, birthday parties, and of course, Thanksgiving, one of the few very American things we held on to wherever we moved. We even planned to have people over—a new development—so that we could share what we were grateful for and pay back some of the past dinner invites from our always social neighbors.

There were moments when it all started to feel like too much. I was swimming in the ocean more, beginning to marvel, not flinch, at the sight of stingrays beneath me. But between that, work, and studying for the Bronze, I was often trapped in my head again. Racing to keep up with work and lifesaving, I couldn't tell if I was doing well or I was one bad night's sleep away from disaster. It felt as if I was in a car with no brakes, sliding down a hill, going faster and faster but unsure whether I'd crash at the end or just slow down.

One day, Diana called me out. We'd been surfing, and I'd cut her off on a wave.

"It's just that it's always all about you," she said. "I'm supposed to just adjust."

"I don't think that's fair," I said. I had tried to give her room, on the wave and in our lives. Later on, though, I apologized. She'd hit an impasse with her novel and Kendishna; neither seemed to be heading for rapid, runaway success like we'd hoped. I could see she was still trying to work out how to overcome her own setbacks when the games of both work and waves still felt rigged to benefit men like me.

She also wasn't entirely wrong; rushing did seem to revive my selfishness. I apologized. I went home, wrote in my risk journal, and tried to open myself up to those around me—starting with Diana. Upon closer inspection, I could see that she'd started adopting new local habits. There were more coffees, more favors done for friends. She had even started taking the time to send thank-you texts or emails after every social gathering, even just a few drinks. We never did that in New York.

She had also recently kicked off a personal experiment on the roads by driving less defensively in an effort to manifest kindness. When someone needed to turn in front of her, she waved them through; when someone cut her off, she forced herself to imagine that they had a good reason to rush and smiled rather than swore. She described it as an effort to conserve energy for more rewarding tasks while ensuring that she wasn't adding rancor to the roads.

Her new Zen vibe certainly made driving more pleasant for more people. It also pointed to an important footnote in Australian risk management: road fatalities per capita here are less than half what they are in the United States; strict enforcement with cameras and fines encourages careful driving, reducing the danger of most families' deadliest daily task.[iii]

Even without having such statistics handy, I followed Diana's anti-road-rage lead by driving the kids to more activities, more calmly, which immediately paid off. I learned more about Baz's internal life on the way to soccer than I ever did at the dinner table. In the car one day, after pulling myself away from the computer, we also had an interesting discussion about the concept of a "nanny state" after he told me about a story he'd read in the *Sydney Morning Herald* advocating for the removal of monkey bars from playgrounds because they were supposedly too dangerous.[iv] He found the idea utterly ridiculous.

My driving duties also included bringing Amelia to one of her newest hard things—singing. She'd started taking lessons with a woman named Jodi, who taught out of her apartment in Randwick, a few miles away. I'd only ever seen kids coming and going when I dropped Amelia off, but when we gathered for a recital at a local Catholic school, Jodi announced that there would be a mix of children and adults and that—like Amelia— many of them would be singing in public for the first time.

Jodi had told Amelia she didn't have to do it if she didn't want to, but without any pushing from me, she decided to give it a try. On the day of the performance, not surprisingly, she was nervous.

"I'm so scared," she said, starting to panic in the hallway to the school theater. "I'm trying to do warm-ups, and I just can't." Her jaw moved up and down. She was biting her tongue, trying to stimulate enough saliva to sing.

I reminded her about the Shawn Mendes concert we happened to have seen the night before. During one of the big ballads, Amelia noticed that his voice had cracked.

"Even pros aren't perfect," I said. "You're going to be fine. You did the work. This is just the last part of the process."

Jodi appeared onstage first, bathed in the blue stage light, wearing a dark dress. She waved an unruly curl from her face and explained the program, preparing the audience for a few anxious newcomers.

"I'm not going to tell you who they are because you don't really need to know, but what I've been telling everyone is that this is the best crowd to sing in front of for the first time because everyone here wants you to do well."

I clapped along with a few others.

"Today, this is just a way to sing for your family."

The performances seemed to alternate between under sixteen and over thirty-five. A mom in tall velvet boots sang Dido's "All You Want." A teenaged girl sang "Mean" by Taylor Swift. A young man in tight white jeans found his way through "Always Remember Us This Way" by Lady Gaga.

Then Amelia stepped up to the stage. She was in her favorite floral dress, with a high ponytail and her new sneakers—a pair of white Adidas with silver stripes. She'd just had a growth spurt after turning nine a few months earlier, which showed up in stretched-out legs and those shoes that looked too big, but onstage, she looked smaller and so alone. It was just her, right there in the middle, singing Grace VanderWaal's "Moonlight." I leaned forward and felt my stomach muscles tighten. I was so proud—what an act of courage, to get out there and sing for strangers—and so scared for her that I wanted to close my eyes.

She bounced her way through with only one pause at the start and a hint of forgetfulness for a lyric later on. She didn't sound stellar, but she didn't sound awful. I clapped and hollered with unbridled zeal. I wanted to make sure she heard me.

Jodi came onstage to finish the show. I didn't recognize the song, but it was a beautiful looping performance, part show tune, part pop showstopper. Afterward, in the lobby, we thanked her for her encouragement of Amelia and praised her singing.

"I just figure if I'm going to make them overcome their fears, then I should do the same," she said. "Right before, I was back there biting my tongue just like everyone else."

I wanted to give her a hug. Her own personal risk-taking was inspiring, and it brought me some relief. It confirmed that no matter what I did with surf lifesaving, there would always be someone in Australia showing my children how to "have a go" at life.

Diana asked Amelia how she was feeling. "Are you glad you did it?"

She nodded and smiled.

Two weeks later, it was finally time for my final Bronze assessment. With fears of the run-swim-run and rescues in Bronte's troubling surf in mind, I woke up early. I was tired, and my back hurt. Maybe it would be okay if I failed. Then I wouldn't have to do the patrols, wouldn't have to keep up with the admin and the WhatsApp bulletins, wouldn't have to worry about letting people down. We'd moved to the other side of the world, for God's sake, and I was choking on bushfire smoke—it wasn't like I wasn't taking risks! Who were we fooling with the volunteer lifesaving anyway? At our beach, there were usually a couple of professional lifeguards nearby, waiting to do their actual job.

Then again, I didn't have much further to go. To get the Bronze, everyone has to pass two high-pressure exams. One is in the classroom—a dry skills assessment, which focuses on signals, first aid, and CPR. Our group had managed to get through that just a few days earlier, with the most nerve-racking moments occurring at the start, with signals. If any one of us got any one of them wrong, we all would have failed. But we didn't, and that set the tone for the rest of the evening—not perfect but certainly proficient.

Now we needed to pass our second test. We had to prove that we could perform in the water and on the sand, where it really counted. And I really didn't want to go. I was still scared of failing and dreading the social pressure.

I looked at my watch: 6:45 a.m. We were due at the beach in an hour. I threw open the blinds to discover a gray spring day. Based on my sliver of ocean view, it didn't look windy.

Amelia rushed into our room.

"Yesterday, Ollie said we could do board training at 7:30. Can I go?"

She was rarely so energetic so early, but she had grown to really love those Nippers boards. The chance to go out and do something with her friends was becoming her preferred choice, even (once in a while) over screens.

"Sure," I said. "Do you want me to—"

She was already gone and, with her, whatever chance I had of calling out sick. If she was there, I had to be there too.

At the beach, the seas were rougher than I expected. Our group straggled in, smiling with the demeanor of college students approaching a final exam. Some arrived with coffee, some with Gatorade. Cam carried the latter. It was his wedding anniversary the night before, and he might have had a little too much shiraz, but he seemed upbeat. We had all been warned—Ruk had sent us all a message suggesting we take it easy on the drinks. Olivia had replied saying she was drinking a gin and tonic. Sally reported a single beer.

Our assessor was a guy named Ryan. He had the square jaw of an actor and appeared to be in good shape. We'd heard that wet suits were only allowed for assessments if the water is below eighteen degrees. Uncertain of the temperature but assuming it was a little above, Jon asked if there might be room for wetties.

"You can wear them," Ryan said.

I was holding my spring suit, with short sleeves and thin, knee-length neoprene. My full-body suit was thicker and at home; it would have given more flotation and streamlining in the water. But a shorty was better than nothing. At least I'd moved beyond jeans and boots.

Ryan laid out the course for the run-swim-run: jog down the beach, around the rip current sign near the southern end, back to where we started, then into the water. We'd swim out to a lifesaver on a board and in through the flags before running the same route again, down around the sign and back to the starting point.

"Anyone have any objection to the course?"

A few of us murmured that the run seemed longer than the required two hundred meters. He assured us his math was right, declaring that our previous run-swim-runs in training had been too short. And with that, we were off: "Go!"

It was midtide, and the sand was soft and steeply inclined, even by the water. I stayed in the middle of the pack for the opening run. At the water's edge, I tried to catch my breath while I fixed my goggles. I couldn't tell where the rip would push me, out or to the side, but then it pulled me in. The ground disappeared beneath my feet, and I had to swim. The sand looked tropical beneath the teal water. It was an amazingly clear day, charming—if you didn't have to race out and back in a couple of minutes.

The waves called for concentration. A few strokes in, I picked up my head just in time to see one heading straight for me. Diving fast and deep, I stayed close to the sand as a heavy plunger crashed above me, pressing down with the weight of a small car.

Eventually I got out past the break, around the bobbing life-saver who waved his encouragement, and came back into what was clearly a strong rip current. I stroked and stroked but didn't seem to be going anywhere. I tried to stay calm like Jack London had suggested when dealing with monstrous surf in Hawaii: "Never be rigid. Relax."[v] Instead of the windmill, I slowed down and tried to focus on each stroke. *High elbow. Hold the catch. Breathe.* I could feel my heart rate steady. And then there was sand under my feet.

In the final run, I sprinted. My chest burned, my legs wobbled, and I began to think that I might not make the required time. I could see someone ahead of me—Sally—and kept running to catch her, still striving not to be last. Sally kept her lead, though, and I collapsed over the line and onto the sand. I looked at my watch: six minutes, fifty-five seconds. A minute faster than required. I wasn't last either—three or four others were just coming in. I cheered and applauded as they reached us. *We all passed!*

Well, we passed phase one. Next it was tube rescues, spinal injuries, and board rescues leading into CPR. The serious stuff of lifesaving. The first few rounds went well. Ruk had switched us up after our miserable mock assessments; for the real thing, I was with Phil, Fred, Sally, Olivia, and Annabelle. We'd passed the dry skills test together, and in the sand, we moved at a healthy pace, alert, not anxious, nudging each other with tips ("Move your hand down," "Roll slowly"). We worked like team members who had known each other for years. We nailed the dry spinal injuries portion without paralyzing anyone.

Wet spinals, as they are known, would be our final and hardest test. One of us would play the patient, incapacitated by injury and stuck where the biggest waves were breaking. This kind of injury is relatively common at Sydney's beaches, where large swells and narrow coves of sand create big shore-breaking waves that damage spines and leave people in sloshing, churning water.

Annabelle volunteered to play patient. One of our group's best swimmers and most dedicated students, she was also the lightest among us and wanted to set us up for success. She wandered out into the waves and pretended to go limp, as Nicolette, our second assessor, told us to get out there and save her. We rushed into a set of dumping waves and quickly put her on the board. With the water chest high, we tried to move her toward the shore, but then a wave above our heads surged forward and crashed into us all. Phil seemed to land face-first. Hit square in the back, I also found myself underwater, sucking for air, under the board, with Annabelle, our patient, flopping in the sea.

We'd come far enough to know that this was the reality of risk and the ocean: they're both unpredictable, and there's no use complaining about it or assigning blame. All you can do is keep doing. Embarrassed but flush with adrenaline, we moved Annabelle back onto the board and managed to get to the beach.

Out of the water, we carried her up the steep mound, past the high-water mark, and carefully placed her on dry sand.

Reconfiguring to the roles from our dry skills assessment, we shifted gears into CPR while keeping her neck carefully secured. Sally took the lead. I was the second responder in charge of keeping the heart pumping: thirty compressions, two breaths, thirty compressions, two breaths. Out of breath ourselves, all six of us managed to appear relatively poised, but it was not a perfect performance. The rescue board holding Annabelle was lying at a slightly odd angle in the sand, and I couldn't tell how well we did with oxygen or securing her neck. I was worried we might not pass and would, at the very least, have to do it again.

But then I looked up and saw Nicolette. She was smiling and nodding.

"These are really tough conditions," she said. "You worked as a team. You worked it out."

After a wait by the lifesaver tent while the assessors worked out our final grade, Nicolette delivered the news: pass. We all whooped, hollered, and jumped in the sand, throwing hugs and high fives around with a mix of relief and excitement. We took photos in various permutations, not noticing that Ruk had disappeared. He returned with a white plastic bag and a long yellow rescue board.

"One more swim," he said, leading the way with a fast paddle into the rip.

We all dived into the water, wondering what was going on. Ruk had gone out pretty far, past where most of the waves were breaking. This time, I swam slowly, enjoying the water and the power of the rip to deliver me to where I wanted to go.

"As is the Bronte tradition, your swim out is your last swim as a Bronzie," Ruk said once we reached him. "Now you're a lifesaver."

He dug into the white plastic bag and pulled out a red-and-yellow cap. They'd always looked so terribly dorky to me, but as he started tossing them to us one by one, I was as keen as everyone else to grab mine. Until Bronte threw one more surprise our way. Ruk, distracted by the ceremonial gift giving, was sitting on the board facing the shore and didn't see the giant set coming. Just starting to break as it reached us, the first wave to roll in scooped up Ruk and his board, knocking him over and sweeping him toward the shore. The bag with the caps went flying as we submarined under the heavy surf.

For a moment, we were worried we'd have a real rescue to finish the day, but Ruk bobbed up again. He collected his board and bag and paddled back out to us. I swam right up to him to get the cap I'd earned.

Suddenly, putting it on while treading water, I felt a surge of enthusiasm just as surprising as Ruk's wave. Pride didn't quite cover it. The cap felt like an entry pass to another world I'd only seen in glimpses. Just floating there, deep in the waves of Bronte, I was in a part of the ocean and an ocean community that I never would have imagined joining before I came to Australia. I was amazed and a little intimidated. This was suddenly a territory I was expected to be able to handle?

None of us were professional lifeguards. None of us belonged on reality TV saving lives. But we were competent. We were proficient. I loved those words. Not victor. Not hero. Competent, proficient, "skilled in doing," as the dictionary said—a little bit more able to handle whatever the beach and life could throw at us. We'd put in the time with risk. We'd endured. We'd passed. Together.

After a few minutes, we ran up the beach for one last photo, where we threw our arms around each other. I didn't mind being close to them. It was an honor. "If you can swim in Bronte, you can swim anywhere." If Sergeant Major Bond had been there, I'd have given him a hug too.

It was not yet noon, but we already had plans to celebrate with a barbecue and beers at Cam's. His house was a classic Eastern Suburbs affair, understated out front, with a nicely renovated kitchen in the rear opening to a small backyard.

Sitting around a long table together without the pressure of studying or proving ourselves, there was a gradual outpouring of gratitude and an attempt to put the experience in perspective. Now that the tension of training and testing was over, it felt like we could see lifesaving and each other more clearly. Teenagers, young women, dads from different countries, a handful of trainers who were all different in their own rights—we had coalesced by reaching for something that was a little scary, thrilling, and not just for personal gain.

Annabelle, a few drinks in, compared the experience to her mom's faith in religion. "It's something you feel passionate about. It's about caring about other people," she said. "Ultimately, realistically, it's not that different."

Even Jon, after admitting that he'd always been a bit iffy about group things, acknowledged that he'd found more than he expected in the experience.

"My wife is getting such a fucking kick out of it," he said. "She's like 'Oh, did you take your pie for the party with all your new friends?'"

Really, though, he had joined (like me) to be a better father. And lifesaving was already changing how he guided his five-year-old daughter through life.

"She doesn't really like Nippers," he said. "So I've stopped saying to her, 'Hey, this is fun,' and I've started saying that you're just learning how to do things you don't want to do, which I think is a real life skill. That's how I'm framing it, and it's really good for me to able to say, 'Well, I'm doing this and I'm a bit nervous.' She comes down to the beach when we're doing training and sees me come off the beach and she says, 'Oh, Daddy did good.'"

"My daughter was down there today," I told him. "I didn't really want her to see me do this whole thing, but then I thought, why not?"

Hearing myself talk through the past couple of years with someone who had only recently been a stranger, I realized how far our entire family had come. I'd started exploring risk to understand fear. What made us afraid of some things, not others? What would life be like if we tried harder to embrace what excites and scares us with loved ones and strangers?

But in our attempt to work that out, we had learned not just how to be bolder, healthier, and more resilient. Those were the improvements I was hoping for. What surprised me was that we also learned how to belong. Australia has taught us something we did not know we needed—how to make "community" a verb.

Diana, already organizing her days according to the tides, was about to join a monthly surf contest with other women who cheered for each other in the waves and supported each other on land. She was editing a new draft of her novel and had started working part-time for an Australian book publisher that, it turned out, offered access to a writing course. She also had a new website for Kendishna and a few friends in Australia buying and promoting the product.

Amelia was now the one pushing her friends with surfing and in Nippers. In a few months, she would move to a new school to get a head start on learning new languages: Italian, then Chinese. Even though she was young (she'd be turning ten more than halfway into fifth grade), she was more confident and emotionally savvy than many of her peers. Every time she said "cute," she sounded completely Australian.

Baz was changing too. He was still in Nippers and thriving, even as the swims reached a level not far from what we were doing with the Bronze training. He'd become a decent debater who worked well with a team of boys and girls, and he was thinking of running for a school leadership position with a few of his mates. Instead of fearing food and his tree nut allergy, he'd even become a halfway decent cook. With his eleventh birthday still a few months away, he made a killer schnitzel that he served up like a chef.

And me? I was a *lifesaver*. I'd lost about twenty pounds and could swim farther in the ocean than I ever thought possible. I could read a rip at any beach, respond to most injuries, and surf waves (at least sometimes) that stood taller than I do.

There was still a lot that I feared, still a lot where the best I could do was mediocre. But the sense of calm and alertness I found in the water kept me at a more even keel dealing with unexpected events in every area of my life. Especially with the kids, I was like the trained animals in those psychological studies or the soldiers I'd seen in combat: I'd developed an ability to keep a low heart rate in stressful moments.

Just as importantly, I was less of an ambition-driven workaholic. I'd soon have a regular patrol to join, one weekend a month in Bronte. I'd started saying yes to every social gathering that involved deepening friendships—including with several people whose politics did not match my own—and when asked to speak to students or contribute to something that would improve or diversify journalism behind the scenes, without much or any credit, instead of pushing it off and saying no, I also said yes.

With Diana, too, I was more conscious, more present. I got out of her way more often in the surf, and I even gave her the better seat in restaurants. I started to really enjoy trying to be more selfless, discovering I was happier the more I did to make others happier too.

Sitting in Cam's backyard, half listening to the chatter, I drafted in my mind what soldiers call an "after-action report" on what it took to reengineer my faults and defaults around risk and community. First I had to look back, to understand the history of risk and the psychological framework that leads so many of us to blindly pursue and purchase our way to as much safety and comfort as possible.

I also had to look inward. I had to recognize the insecurities that held me back—my fear of being the worst at something, my fear of weakness and social judgment. And I needed to accept that the cure was not avoidance but exposure. I had to dive in without knowing where it would lead, and I had to keep going, through failure, far longer than I wanted. The ocean was my coliseum for many rounds of discomfort. It was where my ego and body were beaten down. It was where I learned to value minor pain and hardships, physical and emotional, to see them in the kind of context that Brock Bastian or Richard Dienstbier saw them, as stairs on the climb toward mastery, toughness, and even a stoic humility that might be called wisdom.

Most of all, I needed to give up faith in myself for trust in others. To actually embody, not just admire, Pascal's proverb: "We are something, but we are not all." That was the hardest part. I had to stop trying so hard to be a colossus, stop prioritizing my very American desire to be right and self-satisfied. To belong, to evolve, I had to become comfortable with my own insignificance. I had to submit to group dynamics when they subscribed to positive values, join others on others' terms, and try to grow with people rather beside them or in opposition.

Why? I thought again of Diana's question. Because, sitting there, looking around at everyone, I could see the obvious—it works. Because a better life is not a life just with more comfort or pleasure or greatness. A good life is a life with community, risk, and adventure.

I knew my own path was not for everyone. Some people in Bronte resented the surf club because they felt it was not friendly enough or that it took over too much of the beach. Listening to a council meeting about the planned club expansion, I could see that the culture I joined sits at the center of a class conflict between the "old battler" Bronte of retirees, gritty surfers, and people who work in the trades, like plumbers or carpenters, and the new Bronte, which is usually shorthand for fitness-first

bankers, lawyers, and well-paid creatives. Both sides could probably learn to be more inclusive; I bet their kids, especially the
young ones, could teach them all a lesson or two.

But in the moment of our Bronze triumph, I saw our squad
and trainers as a community model. While the group would
need more diversity to fully represent Australia, we had corporate recruiters, students, defense contractors, IT workers, a
writer, and students. We came from different countries, backgrounds, and generations. As an American who rarely saw that
kind of close interaction outside an office or place of worship, I
was impressed. Maybe a little amazed. And I wasn't alone. Ruk,
an urban planner who worked all over the state in all kinds of
communities, told me later on that most of the Bronze classes
tended to include more people of similar age and demographics.
Our group was a bit of a social experiment.

"We didn't really know if it was going to work," Ruk said.
"We were kind of worried."

And what if anything might our experience reveal? Maybe
that people are better at learning to belong than we often think?
Or maybe, Ruk said, people are more welcoming, especially
when passion, risk, and the natural world are combined. That was
Diana's experience with surfing, and Ruk said in his own Bronze
group, most of the people had grown up in the area, but rather
than be cliquey or standoffish, they embraced him completely.

"I think they saw that I was new and from Canada and didn't
really know what I was doing in the ocean in terms of rips and
stuff. And they welcomed me.

"Now I go down to the surf club, and I run into at least ten
people I know every single day," he said. "Because the people

who come down, they love the water. They love staying fit. They love supporting the cafés and local businesses. You see them everywhere. It's just felt more like home than anywhere has ever felt, even in Canada."

I'd been seeing references recently on Ruk's Instagram to having had a tough but ultimately empowering year. I asked what had been going on.

He said he had recently come out as a gay man. It was something he had been thinking about since high school, but Australia helped him transform those notions into personal change.

"Do you think it had anything to do with the club?"

"I'd never actually considered that. Maybe it is a factor of having never really had a community," he said. "The surf club was just this incredibly accepting community, as were my friends at home."

"I wonder," I said, "if throwing yourself into something new in one area of life helps you throw yourself into other things too."

"It's very different, obviously," Ruk said with a laugh. But he agreed that there was a connection. Maybe it was Martin Seligman's hope circuit—get good at one thing, and you start to believe you can take on bigger challenges. Or maybe seeing people model strong behavior in one arena helps us transfer the energy to another—like a series of circuits wired together.

"I think it comes down to the bonds that you make," Ruk said. "I think it's those bonds that give you strength."

Nippers. Day one for my water safety debut. I'm in the moment, the present tense, with Amelia near the Bronte Express, the rip to end all rips, and I'm ready to help. It's a sunny day at the bend of summer, and the water is clear enough for me to see the green sea grass attached to the rocks at the outer edge of the bogey hole.

The girls are going out on boards, and Amelia is in the first group to depart. She takes off heading toward me, and I grab the board and propel her over a wave before it breaks, giving her a push that speeds her toward her goal. I float out with the rip as she paddles away, letting myself be carried by an ocean force I used to fear. When she comes back a few minutes later—now she's the one doing long journeys, not just her brother—I can see her waving her arms at me and looking excited, or is it scared?

As she gets close enough for me to see that she's on a board painted like a rainbow, I can finally hear her yelling. "Daddy, Daddy, we saw dolphins!"

She and two of her friends paddle next to me near where the waves are breaking and tell me the whole story in quick little-girl succession.

"There were three dolphins, and they were far away."

"And then they came up to us."

"And they were right there," Amelia shouts, pointing to the short distance between us. "Right there! They were, like, two meters from me!"

A wave arrives, lifts the girls, and gently puts them back down without breaking.

"At first it was scary," Amelia says. "There were fins and everyone was yelling 'shark shark,' and I was like, that's not a shark. Then we saw their noses!"

Floating out there with them, I'm feeling stronger and

happier than I've ever felt. Ecstasy is a pod of nine-year-old girls shouting about paddling beside wild dolphins. I can almost hear what Amelia would tell her own children: *You can't experience the awe of dolphins if you live your life afraid of sharks.*

But it is just a moment. A lull. I can see a large set of waves heading our way.

"Okay, girls, paddle in," I tell them. "Go tell everyone."

My time with Amelia over, I jog down the beach to be with Baz's group as the older boys get started. There are no dolphins, but it's just as satisfying to be out there. Al and Guy start with boards. I rush into waves standing tall over my head. We're farther north than Amelia was, closer to the Twins that took the life of the Hachette publisher, but the boys all know what they're doing. They go out and back three times. On the last one, Baz rides a wave in perfectly, holding the straps at the back, pointing himself and the board toward shore without anything close to a major crash. I don't even need to help him onto the sand. But he doesn't get much of a rest. Now for a swim—Baz and I are back on the sand.

"I don't want to do the swim." He says it in a whisper.

"Just try to do it once," I reply.

I can see that he's tired, and the waves are of middling height for Bronte, chest high, dumping half kilos of weight or more. Getting through the break may exhaust us both.

"We're going to swim a square," Guy says.

"How far out past the break?" asks another dad doing water safety.

"Maybe a little farther. Next week is the club champs. They'll have to do it then."

I try to clock the degree of difficulty: 200 or 250 meters of swimming, into a rip, north, and back into shore, with a 150-meter run on soft sand back to the start. Baz is ten years old. It's probably the hardest thing he's ever been asked to do in Bronte.

Al sends me out to be the corner at the north end, right where the biggest waves are breaking. I grab a flotation tube so I can hold it up in the air for the boys to see (or hold it myself if I need a rest). The first batch of Nippers comes through looking like Olympians, fast and strong. A few weeks later, one of them goes on to win a gold medal in the state lifesaving competition. The next group is a little slower, but everyone is moving well—including Baz. I'm thrilled to see him swimming.

"Good job!" I shout as he swims past me and starts back to shore. I look to the beach, and the first group is just returning. And then they're off again. I move out deeper to avoid the surf break and watch to make sure they all survive. *Is that Baz?* It is. Again.

"I'm so tired," he says as he swims around me.

"You got this," I tell him, breaststroking beside him just like I did at our first lesson in the Bronte pool. "Swim at your own pace. You don't have to win. You don't have to be the best. Just finish strong."

I watch him reach the shore, wait for the other boys, and then swim back in myself, enjoying the cold water and the waves pushing me forward. I no longer see our patch of ocean as a noisy enemy or an ever-present threat—it's like the land we walk on, a part of my world both banal and worth appreciating. And the kids are on their way to a similar conclusion.

I can't believe Amelia has become so confident in the water

and out and that Baz pulled off that swim not once but twice. And as I follow the boys in, I'm amazed to see an empty beach. All of them did it. All of them chose to take a risk, overcome their fears, and swim together. If anyone had stayed on the beach, they would have felt left out. Instead, they learned, as a group, that they were stronger than they imagined. The expectations were high. The peer pressure was for strength and solidarity, for joy and for humility. It's what we had to leave America and come to Australia to learn. *Dive in and do well. For yourself and others.*

Epilogue

*Combine and conquer: what
Australia's experience of fires and a
pandemic can teach the world*

In the first few months of 2020, Australia faced two historic crises that fortified my thinking about the importance of grappling with risk at the community level: the Black Summer fires and the coronavirus pandemic. Like the Christchurch attack, the back-to-back disasters pointed to blind spots in societal risk calculation, and they required a wrenching public and private recalibration of how to interact with each other and with our surroundings.

There was a monstrous and confusing quality to the fires that left many people stunned. I heard it first in the tearful cries of a woman walking through her burnt-out home on the South Coast, crunching through charred family mementos, asking why the flames left her neighbor's house untouched. I also saw it in the eyes of volunteer firefighters like Michael and Edmund Blenkins, a father and son in Batlow who, with just a few others, saved their town from a perfect storm of two giant blazes converging.

"My helmet melted," Edmund told me. He was eighteen years old. He looked like a soldier and he smelled like a fireplace. "Inside the truck melted too."

The politics of the bushfires were not pretty. Prime Minister Scott Morrison was on vacation in Hawaii when the worst blazes hit, and upon return, he tried to put a positive spin on the expanding catastrophe without acknowledging the role of a warming planet.

Many Australians felt frustrated and abandoned, bringing to mind one of Donald Horne's most famous lines, tied to his book's title: "Australia is a lucky country, run mainly by second-rate people who share its luck."[i]

The people I met all over Sydney and in the fire zones were not second-rate or lucky. They were angry and in touch with the disaster's impacts—nearly 80 percent of Australians said the fires affected them in one way or another, whether through smoke or flame, disrupted plans or anxiety.[ii] It was the summer that was no summer. The area that burned was larger than many European countries. On one day after another, the pollution levels in Sydney were worse than Delhi or Beijing.[iii]

But while Australians may be tolerant of mediocrity

(according to Horne), they are also (as he put it) adaptable "when a way is shown."[iv] And the Australian people showed the way.

They started out with simple resistance. In early January, when Morrison visited Cobargo, a dairy town near the New South Wales–Victoria border, furious residents refused to shake his hand.[v] The blazes were still burning nearby, and they wanted nothing to do with his posturing. A few days later and one hundred kilometers north, a volunteer firefighter leaned out of his truck and passed on a red-faced message through a TV reporter: "Tell the prime minister to go and get fucked."[vi]

Other Australians felt compelled to shout beyond their borders. In late January, Lynette Wallworth, an award-winning Australian filmmaker, traveled to the Davos confab for international executives and politicians and stood on a stage before the global elite, trying to shake them to their senses.

"I am standing here a traveler from a new reality, a burning Australia," she said. "We have seen the unfolding wings of climate change."

When I interviewed Wallworth afterward, she told me that what disappointed her most was that her own country's leaders were not rolling up their sleeves and joining with Australians willing to do more.

"We respond really well to a crisis," she said. "We know how to pitch together and put differences aside, and this seems to me a moment to call on the best of us, what is the best of us, and that's what isn't happening."

By then, Australians were already in the streets. Throughout the spring and summer, there were climate protests in all Australia's major cities, many of them led by kids too young to vote. Our own public school in Bronte emptied out once or twice as children pressed their parents to march and confront the global risk of a warming planet burning up with the use of fossil fuels.

I was just as impressed with the quieter acts of adaptation. Political protest was far from the only option Australians pursued; they didn't wait for any one political party to solve the problem, nor did they waste all their time arguing about why the other side was wrong. Maybe because the calamity touched so many people and did so during the holidays, a lot of Australians, regardless of their politics or backgrounds, found their own ways to treat the fires as a shared experience.

The response that started with anger did not get stuck there, as the reaction to tragedy so often does in the United States. It evolved into something more deliberate, like a Georges Seurat pointillist painting, with each dot representing a moment of thoughtfulness that altogether produced a scene of beauty.

Homes were opened up indefinitely for the suddenly homeless. Food, clothes, generators, and trucks full of helpers to clear debris—all of it flowed to fire zones or from one battered place to another. The community centers and fire sheds that I visited were always full of volunteers and generosity.

There were also smaller, less obvious kindnesses. In early January, I was standing in a field with a couple of volunteer firefighters watching a bulldozer cut a containment line when they started talking about how their brigade split up duties on Christmas Day. The parents with small children stayed home in the morning to open presents and fought fires in the afternoon; the parents with older kids flipped the schedule to be home for Christmas dinner.

It was a simple thing, but I recognized in it some of the same

altruism I'd seen with surf lifesavers. The firefighters were looking out for each other without even noticing. That was the social
norm. Serving as an unpaid volunteer and taking care of your
neighbors, said Brad, a ruddy dark-haired dad who worked at a
wind farm, "It's just the bush way."

About a half hour after that conversation, a photographer (Matt
Abbott) and I were traveling in a Toyota Hilux over a paved country
road when I heard a familiar *thump, thump, thump*. Matt pulled over
by a field of cows grazing on grass as dry as sand. There wasn't a
house in sight. We could see bushfire smoke in the distance, and the
back left tire was hissing like a snake. It was flat a few seconds later.
And the jack we had? A factory-issued plaything for smaller tires.

While we searched in the grass for rocks to prop the truck
up, an SUV pulled over.

"Need any help?" asked the older gentleman behind the wheel.

Before I could ask if he had a bigger jack, a truck driver pulling a load of timber stopped as well, and a man with tattoos on
his arms and legs hopped out of the cab. His name was Craig.
He had a mullet and fast hands. Within minutes, he'd found a
better place for our little jack, placing a rock or two under the
base while lying on the ground and getting to work.

In the time it took Craig to change our tire—with Matt and
me watching in utter astonishment—a half dozen other cars
drove down the track. Every driver stopped to offer assistance.
Every. Single. One.

The fires reminded Australians of a lesson that studies of risk
wholeheartedly support: we can't do this alone. It's not enough

for one person, one community, or one country to deal well with a crisis. More people need to be involved. More people need to know how to manage risk and make good decisions to prevent the worst-case scenarios from happening, save the most vulnerable, and ease the collective burden all over the world. Risk requires a degree of unity and fraternalism from one and all.

Psychologists have found that what Lynette Wallworth asked for actually works. The best way to motivate as many people as possible is not with fear or negative messaging but rather with appeals to shared pride, the idea that you are part of a group and a solution.[vii] Working on problems with others tends to counter some of our internal settings that act as impediments to problem-solving, like the "single-action bias," which refers to the tendency to take only a single action to solve a problem when a portfolio of responses is needed.[viii] In simpler terms, if you're teaming up with people and organizations that prioritize shared problem-solving, you're less likely to do just one thing and move on. In-person involvement creates deeper commitments and greater impacts.

"It's not something that lets us just check off a box," said Elke Weber, a professor of psychology and public affairs at Princeton University who has spent thirty years working on how to get people to take climate change more seriously.[ix] "Maybe it adds some meaning to our lives as well. Now that there is less religion in people's lives all over the world, maybe we're looking for something else that's about the meaning of life."

At times, of course, it can be hard to see how something as small as a few hours as a volunteer lifesaver or firefighter or paramedic or mentor does any good. When I first put on the

red-and-yellow lifesaving uniform, I felt like a nuisance, whis-
tling for kids and unsuspecting tourists to move out of the rip. It
also felt and still feels small, too small to do any good.

And yet it's more than I did before. It's something visible that my children and their friends can see. It's helped me
stay calm during emergencies—when I sliced off the tip of my
thumb while cooking dinner, when Baz broke his arm. And there
is continued room for growth. My role in society has evolved
to be just a little bit braver, along with more collaborative and
compassionate.

Weber, like so many others I'd talked to about risk and community, said that is exactly the direction more of us need to be
heading. What we need for any complex threat can be found in
a phrase she coined in 1984, "combine and conquer."[x] Instead
of arguing or waiting for our leaders to save us, we need to find
ways to participate and encourage others to do the same.

"It's important to acknowledge that there is expertise, that
experts know something, but also it's important to see that
nobody has all the expertise," Weber said. "Everybody has a
contribution to make. No single person, no single discipline, no
single country can solve these large collective problems."

COVID, obviously, has been one of those problems. It was and
is the biggest test of risk management that humanity has faced in
a very long time—possibly since the seventeenth century, when
the idea of risk first emerged alongside the bubonic plague.
Especially in the first few months, the coronavirus pandemic
was like climate change but more urgent: it proved that our

actions are interconnected, and it demanded an immediate shift in almost everyone's behavior.

Nearly all of us needed to make many small changes for the collective good, and in Australia, we even knew how many of us had to be on our best behavior. A study from the University of Sydney published on March 25, 2020, showed that if 80 percent of the population obeyed quarantine orders, Australia could suppress the virus in thirteen weeks.[xi]

Like most of our neighbors and friends, Diana and I took that call to action seriously. Eager to join what we hoped would be the majority, we stayed home. We tried to balance managing school for the kids with our own work projects and left the house only to exercise or buy food. Everyone we knew—everyone—followed the rules.

As Americans living abroad, we also watched what was happening in the United States with shock and dread. A former professor of Diana's from Columbia film school, Milena Jelinek, had just died from COVID; so had another former reporter for the *Times*, while several colleagues had fallen seriously ill. Diana and I both reached out to our parents more than usual, pleading with them to take the risk seriously. Thankfully, they were being careful, though the diligence of my father, stepmother, and one of my brothers faded. After easing back into their routines, they caught the virus, suffering for weeks before recovering.

In my family and others, there seemed to be a lot of confusion about what to do or who to believe. When I emailed Paul Slovic to ask if COVID might wake Americans up to risk and provide a crash course in the need for improvement, he was candid and dark.

"I don't think our risk assessment wires are up to handling this very well," he said. "I think people will disagree strongly on what is right. In the United States, partisan divisions will be very strong."

Diana and I had many sleepless nights in early 2020, filled with dreams of friends dying, jobs lost, and futures downsized. Baz, surprisingly, seemed to be the one struggling the most. He had always been self-motivated with schoolwork, a teacher's pet who liked to achieve, but without the structure or socializing of a classroom, he slipped into hiding. He'd disappear into his room claiming to do his work only to reemerge two hours later with barely anything done. One night after dinner, I saw him on the couch, deep in the corner, on his side in an almost fetal position, with headphones on watching something on YouTube.

"Look at him," I said to Diana. "He's literally curling into himself."

To help him cope, I tried to recall past experiences when he successfully managed fear and uncertainty. After talking about how much he'd grown in Nippers, I landed on the feeling we both had during earthquakes in Mexico City. We'd lived there until he was just about six years old, and I knew his memories were sharp, so I reminded him of those moments when we would start to feel the shaking but were not sure how bad it would get. We'd stand there, arms out, balancing and swaying in our apartment on the eleventh floor, as time slowed down and we tried to work out what to do.

Run outside? Dive under something? Huddle in a doorway? The entire world felt woozy. There was no control. And then, suddenly, it was over.

"Do you remember what that was like?" I asked him.

"Yeah, it was kind of weird," he said. "But usually it wasn't that bad."

"Exactly," I said.

Within the rules, we also did what we could to stay calm and active. Sydney's beaches were closed for the first time since surf bathing became legal in 1903, turning even Bondi into a haven for shorebirds and sand patterns blown by itinerant winds. To combat our miserable and dry existence, I ran for longer distances, and so did Diana, often past the fences in Bronte that said "beach closed." She missed the water even more than me or the kids, almost to the point of tears.

The best we could do was take Baz and Amelia down to the park by the water with a Frisbee to toss around. Mostly we just stayed home. We made family TikToks (bad). Diana and I started trying out new cocktails and new recipes (better). Amelia became a master at baking cookies (best), taking them in and out of the oven by herself even after a minor burn.

Amelia was the only person I knew who actually seemed to be handling the quarantine well. About a month in, her teacher asked her class in a group chat to identify one positive thing to emerge from having to be at home, and she could easily count several.

"Sleeping late, definitely," she said. "And doing school on my own time and not having to put on clothes."

There were others, including, "I'm learning how to be more independent."

Good old Australian socializing also found a way to adapt.

At the urging of friends, we started gathering on Fridays in an alley behind one of our neighbors' houses for very socially distanced drinks—on opposite sides of the alley—while our children rode bikes and skateboards back and forth. They got some exercise; we got a chance to laugh and commiserate.

Some of the parking lots at the closed beaches also filled up with parents teaching their children to ride bikes, scooters, and skateboards. Outside an apartment complex in a neighborhood south of me, someone had hung a sheet with a painted message that said, "Single, bored, SEND WINE."

Even Baz started to emerge from his cocoon. It started with video games. I never thought I'd appreciate hearing him yell with his friends as they tried to kill their enemies, but it was a glorious symphony for at least the first few times it happened. And that led to other adventures. One day, I took him for a long swim in Gordons Bay, just south of Bronte. While all the other beaches were closed, Gordons's rocky shore made fencing difficult, and without a sandy spot for people to gather, the authorities (correctly) calculated that the risk of spreading the virus was low enough there to let a few of us get our fix in the sea.

The day I went with Baz, the air was cold, the water colder, but we both found more joy and peace than we expected. Seeing him smile in an ocean that had bewildered us both for so long, diving deep together to see tropical fish the color of crayons, crossing large distances of the salty seas—my lungs seemed to fill up with pure oxygen, my heart with delight. Finally, I had learned to enjoy swimming for swimming's sake, with the boy who started it all by refusing to finish those first few laps in the pool.

Before long, Baz was venturing farther without supervision.

He became one of those kids biking through Bronte with his friends, flying high on homemade jumps in the middle of parks and streets. One afternoon, he came home out of breath and told me that there were some boys who came and dropped trash in the park by the beach—candy wrappers, soft drink cans, the usual.

"We surrounded them and made them pick it up," he said. "There were, like, six of us."

"Were the kids your age or younger?" I asked. I wasn't sure the rules allowed for six people to gather, but I was more worried that he and his mates might have been picking on toddlers. Baz looked at me a bit confused as if it should be obvious.

"Older," he said. "Like by a couple of years."

So a group of ten- and eleven-year-olds stared down a couple of teenagers until they did the right thing? I was skeptical. He was proud.

That may have been the first quarantine's high point. One of the dads I knew from our boozy lunches called all the bike riding and collective freedom a rare upside to the lockdown. He cherished seeing "kids all charting their own paths of carefree randomness."

Diana and I discussed whether Australia might emerge from the pandemic stronger. Whenever Australians asked about our families in America, we had a hard time processing the pity. *Guess we're no longer a model for the world.* But we both heard ourselves echoing the obvious about Australia: "We're so glad we're here."

Neither of us considered the place to be perfect, nor was the COVID response. The police had occasionally been heavy handed, with fines disproportionately applied in lower-class areas filled with immigrants.[xii] The fight over when to return to school had become exhausting, with teachers and a crop of concerned parents insisting on an impossible elimination of risk. Thousands of Australian citizens were also stranded overseas and blocked from coming back.

But Diana and I, strangely, felt optimistic. We had started to regrow something we hadn't even realized we nearly lost—trust, in the people around us and in the idea of a democracy with more agreement than conflict. Instead of 80 percent compliance with the lockdown and social-distancing rules, Australia reached a level of 90 percent or more.[xiii] In the parks, where more people were walking, and in the cafés, where baristas happily served takeaway coffee in masks under a policy that allowed some businesses to stay open, we could see that the momentum was with collective concern and moderation.

In late April, with a somewhat humbled prime minister pleading with teachers and after six weeks of home schooling, New South Wales announced a plan for reopening schools. It would just be a few days a week at first, but there was no denying it. We had flattened the curve, beating expectations. It was a triumph of the commons. The kids screamed and cheered when we told them they would be heading back to class. Diana and I pumped our fists and jumped up and down. The last time I felt that excited about a team effort, the Boston Red Sox beat the New York Yankees on their way to the World Series in 2004.

Over the next few years, as the pandemic spread around the world and surged multiple times, Australia mostly stayed on a successful path. When the United States started to approach one million deaths from COVID, my editors in New York looked around for a country with similar demographics and far less suffering that would show Americans what might have been—and they chose Australia.

Here, the death rate per capita settled at a fraction of what America endured. If the United States had a death rate like Australia's as of early 2022, nine hundred thousand lives would have been saved.[xiv]

In policy terms, the extraordinary disparity can be explained with a single sentence: Australia restricted travel and personal interaction until vaccinations were widely available, then maximized vaccine uptake, prioritizing people who were most vulnerable before gradually opening up the country again.

But it worked because of something more amorphous. Dozens of interviews that I did with officials, doctors, nurses, and epidemiologists, along with survey data and scientific studies from around the world, all pointed to a lifesaving trait that Australians displayed from the top of government to the hospital floor and that Americans showed they lack: trust, in science and institutions but especially in one another.

What we had noticed in our own community proved to be scientifically significant. Trust led to a more nonpartisan response across Australian government. Trust led hospitals to work together. And most of all, trust led Australians to stay home, wear masks, and get vaccinated. They believed others would do the same, and they did not want to break those bonds by ignoring sensible science.

Countries with the X factor of more "interpersonal trust," a study of COVID death rates from 177 countries published in

2022 in *The Lancet* found, simply did better with COVID.[xv] A lot better. Trust, the research showed, mattered even more than smoking prevalence, health spending, or form of government. It worked in New Zealand, where Jul's imam emphasized relationships, and in Norway, Kenya, and South Korea. But in Australia, the process of turning trust into action began especially early.

Mikhail Prokopenko, a Ukrainian computer scientist who directs the Center for Complex Systems at the University of Sydney, which put out the lockdown modeling with the target of 80 percent, told me Australians were among the first worldwide to recognize the strength of shared good conduct.

"Once people started doing it and once they saw the numbers really going down, they realized they are controlling the disease rather than thinking the disease was controlling their lives," Professor Prokopenko said.

"Their engagement with these measures was quite sincere," he added. "Despite all the economic sacrifices, it was quite clear that people wholeheartedly adopted this."

The Australian way of risk assumes that life should be lived with enthusiasm, trust, and optimism despite potential hazards, and then it tries to manage the uncertainty with education, exposure, and a sense of collective responsibility that insists on humility and competence. Especially visible when Australians engage with nature—from remote national parks in Western Australia to Sydney's urban beaches—the philosophy is not applied to everything Australians do, in part because all societies (like all individuals) are inconsistent with risk.

But Australia's reaction to the coronavirus built on its collective response to risk in other areas. Australia would never have done as well with the pandemic compared to other countries if it hadn't first built and supported local clubs and volunteer organizations, for lifesaving, firefighting, and swimming, while also pushing children to confront their fears in the bush, in the water, and in the classroom.

Deep down, I think a lot of Australians know there's something in their approach to life that has helped them avoid the COVID death spirals of Europe and America. Again and again, I heard Australians express an understated pride in their country's pandemic response while explaining their own behavior with versions of the phrase "I'd hate to be the one to let everyone down."

That was the line I heard repeatedly from parents, nurses, construction workers, bartenders, Uber drivers, and chorus singers at the Sydney Opera House, along with some of the country's icons, including Jane Harper, the bestselling novelist, and pro surfer Mick Fanning. Even when harsh snap lockdowns became the norm, the vast majority of Australians, regardless of class and wealth, shrugged and did what was most likely to benefit the most people.

From an American perspective, it was no small achievement. So many of the people I knew back in the land of the free kept traveling even during the worst months of the pandemic while complaining about the idiocy of others. One side said it would all be fine (even as they saw people get sick and die); the other demanded that schools stay closed or masks stay on (even as evidence showed the negative impact on children's mental health).

And while the right's disinformation campaigns were far more dangerous than the left's overprotective errors, there was more than enough self-delusion and misplaced moral outrage to go around.

It all added up to something that I had come to see as a fundamental difference between the two countries competing in our hearts to be called home. At the risk of being shouted down by Australians who understandably demand more from their country, Australia is set up to pull people together into the middle, between the flags (to use a lifesaving reference), with high expectations for personal and community conduct.

The United States pushes people to the fringe of individualism. At the risk of being shouted down by "patriots" who believe the American way is the only way, money, speech, and an individual's feelings still mean far too much in the United States. Inequality defines family life at conception, with wide disparities in prenatal and postpartum care depending on parental wealth. The never-ending pressure to compete along with a culture of defensiveness—a worst-case mindset that stems in part from a fear of being sued and in part from a weak safety net—makes risk aversion and distrust feel like requirements for survival.

Sadly, as part of that, children are being taught that selfishness and a negative view of the world is justified and necessary. For families that can manage it, kids are steered away from danger at all times or guided toward activities based on what they can excel at right away. They are not pushed nearly as often to take chances just for the hell of it or to do what might make them better people even when it requires pain and patience or faith in someone they might not know very well.

Many of their parents are modeling myopic behavior too—glued to their screens or working crazy hours, they can barely see what's being lost in an era of catastrophizing and looking out for number one. Angry at all that's gone wrong in America, they avoid and condemn anyone who disagrees with them and pull deeper into a bubble of personal, political, and consumer identity. If they volunteer to help, it tends to be short lived and maximized for convenience—with a protest, a mission trip with a church, or by giving money online.

I recognize that such sweeping generalizations include some papering over of caveats and exceptions. America is a very big, messy, heterogeneous place, and many Americans are civic-minded citizens who embrace challenges and their neighbors, or who have no choice but to work ridiculous hours to survive. So many people I know in the United States are also wildly creative, makers of beauty for many. And the pandemic, for all its horrors, appears to have created and strengthened the bonds of some communities.

Meanwhile, there are plenty of Australians putting their own needs and biases first. At times, the country can feel far too clubby or cruel, with a sense of community that can be too quick to exclude based on race, gender, or other differences. With greater wealth, driven by a mining boom, Australia is also drifting toward American disconnection, with rates of loneliness and depression increasing.[xvi]

But despite some similarities and related struggles, the pandemic has made the gulf between Australia and America wider than ever. Personally, I keep returning to what works for most people, most of the time. I'm reminded of something that Richard

Flanagan, the Australian novelist, told me before I came to Sydney in 2017: "Don't underestimate the differences between your country and mine." I did make that mistake then, but I never will again. Because the signs are everywhere once you start to look.

It's not just that Australia is a country of pragmatic policy, with its budgeting and taxes, safety net, infrastructure, and removal of threats like guns after a mass shooting in the '90s. It's not just that its minimum wage is high or that healthcare is nationalized and a four-year university education costs roughly a tenth of what it costs in the United States.

It's also the way people behave and interact. Instead of prioritizing the feelings of the free and fragile and framing nearly every decision as a conflict between two warring sides—the current American model—Australians demand participation and proficiency from as many people as possible. Voting is compulsory and has been for nearly a century. Instead of individualistic Americanisms like "the squeaky wheel gets the grease," "have a blast," or "pull yourself up by your bootstraps," Australia's slang tilts toward "she'll be right, mate," "don't get too big for your boots," and "fair dinkum," which I had to look up to learn that it's affirming what Australians (collectively) see as genuine.

Yes, there are things that still rub me raw. I wish Australians would get better at enabling and celebrating talent, especially new and diverse talent. I still have a hard time being patient when restaurant service is slower than any New Yorker could stomach, and I struggle with whether to bite my tongue when I hear Australians express parochial views or try to justify what looks to me like mediocrity and laziness.

But at some point, after COVID started revealing just how

mad and divided America could be, Diana and I started to ask ourselves: Which set of values most matched our own? Were we still American if we prefer Australia's ideals, irritations included? Where, ultimately, can the world's democracies and our children find the healthier model? In the United States or with humbler countries like Australia, Norway, Iceland, and New Zealand?

Most of my life, I have been convinced that America was what my grandfathers believed it to be: the best nation on earth, a place with unmatched opportunity, where everything you could ever want or imagine was possible with hard work and confidence. Covering the world taught me to question pronouncements of American virtue (American foreign policy has messed up a lot of lives in Latin America and the Middle East), but I never fully lost my belief in the aspiration of America's Declaration of Independence: "We hold these truths to be self-evident, that all men are created equal, that they are endowed by their Creator with certain unalienable Rights, that among these are Life, Liberty and the pursuit of Happiness."

There is a lot of hope in that line. When critiqued, it is usually because its goals have not yet been achieved. Racism has kept American society unequal; the meritocracy that my grandfathers admired has morphed into what the Harvard historian Jill Lepore calls a toxic plutocracy. But with some time and distance from America, while living in a country that was clearly much healthier, I imagined a rewrite of that founding principle with other kinds of human rights and goals. The right not to liberty but solidarity. The right to pursue not happiness (or property in John Locke's version) but strength and purpose. The right to a life together with those you love—and with people you sometimes disagree with—not a life alone seeking some dream of individual wealth and attention at the expense of connection.

One night over cocktails (there were a lot of cocktails in the COVID era), Diana and I talked about the America we no longer wanted. I was telling her about something Brock Bastian had told me—that any experience that makes us think of death will cause people to contemplate life's priorities. Offering an example, he said he went for a walk by Waverley Cemetery, just south of Bronte, with a psychologist who worked on experiments showing the clarifying power of confronting our mortality. They both agreed that just passing through that location with its tombs and views would be enough to trigger that introspective impulse.

For most of my time in Australia, I've run past that cemetery three or four times a week. Just talking about the idea seemed to clear away the fog surrounding my own goals for the second half of my life. If America wouldn't change, then I would.

"I don't want to be great. I want a great life," I told Diana. "I just think sometimes that's very Australian and maybe better."

Sitting there with Diana on a breezy night during some COVID surge or another, with Baz and Amelia happily asleep, I felt like I was saying goodbye. To my former self and to the country where I was born. I'd come to Australia as an observer, but several years in, I seemed to have become an immigrant, and like most immigrants, I felt a sense of loss and gain. In the background, that night and on most nights, I still played a soundtrack of American songs I loved. There was a little bit of *Hamilton*, the hip-hop musical by Lin-Manuel Miranda that Diana had been playing on repeat for months, making it something we often turned to as a family when America broke our hearts. There was some Beyoncé, some Bruce Springsteen, some Nirvana, some Alicia Keys.

I still loved that the culture we came from could do that, lead a Jay-Z and Beyoncé to royalty status, lead an adopted son of a Syrian immigrant like Steve Jobs to become one of the most influential technologists of the modern era. I know many Australians admired American culture as well. They marveled at the creativity the United States produced, and in what I was starting to romanticize as community in Australia, many of my Australian friends saw too much blind obedience. Some of them would have happily traded a less great life for international greatness and influence. They saw in American business and popular culture a taste for risk-taking and innovation, and they were right—entertainment and tech are arenas where failure and resilience are celebrated. Americans do take risks to get rich and famous. It's just that many of them have lost their ability to stretch beyond their comfort zone with nearly everything else. We've become like so many of the American embassies I've seen all over the world since the 9/11 terror attacks: hidden behind walls, obsessed with protocol, suspicious of serendipity.

Maybe the future will come down to the kind of people we try to emulate. I asked Elke Weber, the psychologist at Princeton, about the role models she thought were doing a good job of moving the world to a healthier place. Her research had already shown that political leaders who changed their own lifestyles to address climate change are more able to influence public opinion on the issue, but she said the most important thing to remember is that role models do not need to be universally well known— they can also be smaller-scale figures or people who are only well known to smaller groups or communities. The important thing is that they practice what they preach.

The psychology of modeling tells us that trust grows from observed behavior. Whether it's children or adults, seeing someone's actions repeatedly is especially powerful. A pop star on Instagram encouraging recycling has less influence than a neighbor who goes around every Sunday picking up plastic and sorting trash at the corner. A protest against abusive policing, even when it includes hundreds of thousands, may do less to change people's lives than a single police station that refuses to tolerate discrimination and punishes officers for abusing their power. While obvious, it's easy to forget that actual behavior in real life does more to produce healthy families and societies than anything said or shared on the internet.

My own gaze continues to shift. I still admire successful people like Jay-Z, whom I met in a recording studio once, but I also find myself less interested in those at the top and in the media's relentless discussion of who's up, who's down, or who should be promoted or canceled. Instead I'm thinking more deeply about what can be learned from my neighbors and people like Alta and Jul in Christchurch.

I stayed in touch with them even after my story about their recovery was published a year after the shooting. Slowly, along with other victims, they were improving. Alta had a new job with a mental health center, trying to do for strangers what she did for her family—get people the help they needed. Jul was painting and smiling more, while Roes's tantrums had mostly subsided. It was starting to look like they would come out of the tragedy stronger, but in the middle of 2020, pandemic and all, they had one more hurdle to overcome: the shooter was scheduled to appear in court one final time for sentencing.

It was expected to be an emotional moment. Survivors and relatives of the dead would be delivering victim impact statements before he was sent to prison for life without parole. Alta had written an account of their difficult journey and provided it to the judge, figuring that would be enough, but then something happened. In court, it was as if the relatives' room from the hospital came to life. Dozens of people, men and women, young and old, stood and spoke to the killer, expressing anger, sadness, hope, and, most of all, resolve. Together and alone, they chose effort and trust over helplessness and anger.

One of most moving accounts came from Aden Ibrahim Diriye, a regal man in a dark suit with a goatee who was the father of the massacre's youngest victim, three-year-old Mucaad Ibrahim.

"I would like you to know that your atrocity and hatred did not turn out the way you expected," he told the killer. "Instead, it has united our Christchurch community, strengthened our faith, raised the honor of our families, and brought our peaceful nation together."

At the last second, inspired by the bravery of others, Alta decided to speak. I couldn't be there because of COVID travel restrictions, so I wrote to her afterward. "Hope it felt as empowering for you as it seemed to be for others."

A few hours later, she sent me a long message. A generally private person, an American like me who had been taught to value the cocoon of individualism, she'd taken a risk by pushing herself into public alongside other victims. I worried it would be too much, but she described a breakthrough, a moment, finally, when all that pain turned to optimism.

"Last night after putting Roes to bed, Jul and I read through the sentencing minutes," she wrote. "Even though I had watched it in court and he had watched it at home, it seemed important to revisit. We talked about the stories that touched us the most and how we felt at different points—both during the events of March 15 and continuing to the present. He started sobbing, so I held him close.

"I feel like our wounds have healed just a bit more since having reached this legal milestone. The sentencing was everything I hoped it would be, and more. Being present there at court was so important for me. Likewise, I feel seen, no longer isolated, like I am finally a real part of the Muslim community here. Against the backdrop of grief, there is hope, and I've been able to forge relationships with so many wonderful people in unexpected ways.

"My heart says 'what's next?'"

What is next, for us and for the world? It's something that pain may help us see more clearly.

There's a scene in Part IV of Albert Camus's *The Plague*, when Rieux, the novel's stoic hero, swims in the sea with a friend under a starlit sky. "For a few minutes they swam on with equal strokes and equal strength, alone, far from the world, finally free of the town and the plague."[xvii]

After a pandemic that has infected millions and killed more than any war in our lifetimes, how many of us have craved that sense of escape and calm? No matter where we live, we've learned to be isolated. We've learned to be afraid, and we've learned to be more careful. But the best way to be safe—and to find joy and awe and strength—is not to bolt the lock and buy life insurance but rather to throw open all the doors, jump back out into the world, and deepen the connections that have frayed with friends and strangers alike.

I asked Martin Seligman what he thought might happen if and when the pandemic ended, and he sounded surprisingly hopeful. He reminded me that there are often "agentic" moments in history, when technological advancements improve the world and inclusiveness expands. He was in a hotel room self-isolating at the time because his entire family had caught COVID-19. Still he maintained that the future could be bright.

"The black plague led to the Renaissance, almost directly," he told me. "That was the first time there was social mobility in Europe for hundreds and hundreds of years because there were positions to be filled. It upset the apple cart. So I think we're in labor. The pandemic has put us in labor. And I think what's going to emerge from this—for the optimistic, hopeful people who do it—is a world that's better."

Could he be right? Seligman is a believer in imagination, in future outcomes created by people who seize a moment to build knowledge, do well, and create new ways of working through challenges. At some point, when COVID really does fade into oblivion, or perhaps when the fever of American partisanship finally breaks, maybe everyone will look at life's potential with fresh eyes; perhaps we'll all grab our kids and embrace what scares and excites us and join arms with those we thought we loathed in domains that are less politicized—to model toler-ance and persistence for our children. But in his comment, I also heard a familiar call to action—"for the optimistic, hopeful people who do it."

It takes determination to defeat helplessness, pathological prudence, and distrust. None of us is trapped with the nation we come from or the values we picked up along the way.

Reading Group Guide

1. In the introduction, Damien mentions that his family needed help with community as well as with risk taking. How does community support individual risk-taking? What do the Christchurch shootings teach us about the relationship between bravery and trust in community-building?

2. How would you compare Australian schools and American schools based on Damien's first impressions? How does each school reflect the values of its country?

3. Damien has to unlearn the indiscriminate urge to "try harder" when faced with any challenge. What are the drawbacks of increasing effort without evaluating the true problem? What prevents you from taking breaks and coming back to your challenges later?

4. Australian parents are often directly involved in their children's activities as chaperones and fellow participants. How

do communities benefit from this structured intergenerational socialization?

5. When Damien starts his own surf lessons, he gradually begins to enjoy the experience even though his failure is constant. What changes to make those failures absurd and entertaining rather than unpleasant?

6. What role do mentors play in making risk engagement enjoyable? Why are we so afraid to ask for help from people who clearly know more than we do and therefore have the most to teach us? Do we need to be better students to become better teachers and parents?

7. Damien notes that participation in volunteer firefighting and other emergency service corps have decreased in America. What unexpected values do those programs, like the Port Campbell Surf Lifesaving Club in the book, add to communities? What other problems might they solve?

8. American society increases independence (as opposed to community) in tandem with wealth. How does erosion of community contribute to wealth inequality?

9. What risks do you want to brave in the coming year?

A Conversation
with the Author

What inspired you to turn your experiences in Australia into this book?

I was inspired first by my kids, as I saw them struggle with fear and find ways to manage it in a community group that felt very far outside my own experience. The way Australians engaged with nature and risk just felt special in a way that Australians didn't even notice—and I wanted to highlight that because, well, I needed what my kids were getting out of it, and I thought maybe other people might benefit from reading about our family's journey.

It's clear that regular engagement with risk is the best path towards resilience and bravery, but so much of American society is designed to remove risk. How can people find new activities and challenges to stretch outside their comfort zones even in highly controlled environments?

There are a lot of disaster preparedness and emergency services groups that are desperate for help, like volunteer firefighters. First aid training itself is one way to engage with risk in a new way. Beyond that, I'd encourage people to seek out groups that are apolitical, cross-generational, and physically challenging, from hiking to swimming clubs. These often lead to new adventures in risk and community.

Modeling is an extremely effective way to familiarize kids with growth mindsets. What have been your biggest challenges in modeling risk management, and how have you worked through those challenges?

The biggest challenge I've faced in modeling is maintaining motivation and following through. I find it's easier for me to start something new but harder to persist. To help, I try to set goals in time or achievement—I'll do X until the end of the year, or Y until I reach a particular milestone. So far, it's helping, though my kids would tell you my own "growth" is more uneven than I demand of them!

What challenges are you trying these days?

I've been spending more time in Taiwan lately for work, so I've decided to try and learn Mandarin. I don't know if I'll ever be fluent, but I want to get to a point where I can engage in conversation and understand a joke or two. My kids are already learning the language, so once again, they'll be my tutors as I try, fail, and try again.

Acknowledgments

This book could not have happened without the person to whom I am always most grateful—my wife, Diana. No one I have ever met is a bigger adventurer or more adaptable. Her insights, patience, and lived experience were invaluable, and she offered the very best advice that any anxious creator could receive: just keep going.

My kids, Balthazar and Amelia, were the book's spark. They taught me so much about risk and resilience while putting up not just with my constant pushing and failures but also with all the weekends and nights when Dad was *once again* stuck in the bubble writing. I hope they nonetheless look back on this time and their experiences with the pride that comes from a job well done and well documented. I hope this book captures some of their wit and wisdom.

A special thanks goes to Jeffrey Gettleman, who—on a hike through the hills of Hong Kong—encouraged me to tackle a book when I was still uncertain about trying. He is one of many colleagues at the *New York Times* who have been a constant source of inspiration with their own acts of journalistic bravery.

Since this book is, in some ways, a love letter to a life of foreign correspondence, I should also thank the first person who sent us overseas—Susan Chira. If she hadn't taken a chance on posting Diana and me to Baghdad, my thoughts about risk would have never gone anywhere. Same goes for Lydia Polgreen, Michael Slackman, Jodi Rudoren, and Joe Kahn—if they hadn't all supported our move to Sydney, well, there would be no *Parenting Like an Australian.*

Here in Oz, our neighbors Andy Kuper and Bassina Farbenblum opened their doors and hearts to us from the moment we arrived. To our friends in the water—the Nippers crew, the Bondi regulars surfing with a smile, the Let's Go Surfing instructors, the Waverley Council lifeguards, and of course all the dedicated members of the Bronte Surf Club—thank you for modeling and sharing the benefits of ocean life. If we conquered a few of our fears or reduced our selfishness just a little, and if this book helps others do the same, then it's in large part due to the small acts of bravery that we witnessed and tried to adopt alongside those we met in our own community.

There were also the Australians farther afield who helped me understand this very big country, from the volunteer firefighters and farmers to the novelists, from the oceanographers and historians to the dads of the Bronte Bubble and the oft-defeated Buzzcocks. I'm grateful to them for putting up with all my questions.

I spoke to many more experts than I was able to quote in these pages. I'm grateful to everyone who helped me chew over the past and present era of risk studies. I'm also deeply grateful to all the people in Christchurch who opened their lives to me and helped me see the power of trust in recovery from trauma. Alta, Jul, Roes: may peace always be upon you.

Elias Altman, my agent in New York, has been a patient partner through the entire process. The team at Sourcebooks, especially Anna Michels, provided sharp insight and helped me see the book in a new way after it first published with Simon and Schuster Australia. I'm eternally grateful to her, and to my publisher in Australia, Ben Ball, for seeing value in the book's mix of memoir, cross-cultural dispatch, and social science.

My first crop of readers, Michael Luo, Andy Kuper, and Andy Parsons, also deserve a shout out for their constructive critiques.

And finally, I want to thank my own parents. My mother's life was messy but filled with the kind of creative risk-taking in music and art that somehow still inspires. My stepmother took a big chance on us when my father was a struggling single parent. Her disciplined strength saved us both. And Dad? What can I say about the brave soul who drove cross-country with his young son to start a new life, about the runner and newspaper-loving storyteller who always pushed me to do for work what I would want to do for free? Thank you. Yes, we have often disagreed, as parents and children do, but as this book hopefully shows, it's the hard work of love, boldness, and connection that counts.

Endnotes

All web sources are accurate as of April 2021.

INTRODUCTION

i   **A program called Nippers:** "The Social and Economic Value of Surf Life Saving Australia, the Nation's Largest Volunteer Organisation," Deloitte, March 2021, https://www2.deloitte.com/au/en/pages/economics /articles/social-economic-value-surf-life-saving-australia.html.

ii   **Australians are less lonely:** "Social Isolation and Loneliness," Australian Institute of Health and Welfare, September 11, 2019, https://www.aihw.gov.au/reports/australias-welfare/social-isolation -and-loneliness; Elena Renken, "Most Americans Are Lonely, and Our Workplace Culture May Not Be Helping," NPR, January 23, 2020, https://www.npr.org/sections/health-shots/2020/01/23 /798676465/most-americans-are-lonely-and-our-workplace-culture -may-not-be-helping.

iii   **A community group or club:** "General Social Survey: Summary Results, Australia," Australian Bureau of Statistics, September 30, 2020, https://www.abs.gov.au/statistics/people/people-and-communities /general-social-survey-summary-results-australia/latest-release.

iv   **Australians' real-life social networks:** Xianbi Huang et al., "Social Networks and Subjective Wellbeing in Australia: New Evidence from a National Survey," *Sociology* 53, no. 2 (April 2019): 401– 21, https://doi.org/10.1177/0038038518760211; interview with lead author, Xianbi Huang, confirmed comparisons with the United States.

v   **Nippers and surf lifesaving:** Surf Life Saving Australia, accessed June 16, 2022, https://sls.com.au/about-us/.

vi   **Worldwide, roughly 40 percent:** "Factsheet: People and Oceans," (fact sheet, United Nations Ocean Conference, New York, NY, June 5–9, 2017), https://www.un.org/sustainabledevelopment/wp-content /uploads/2017/05/Ocean-fact-sheet-package.pdf.

vii   **In Australia, roughly 85 percent:** G. F. Clark and E. L. Johnston, "Coasts," in *Australia: State of the Environment 2016* (Canberra: Department of the Environment and Energy, 2016), https://soe .environment.gov.au/theme/coasts.

CHAPTER ONE

i   **When Mark Twain visited in 1895:** Mark Twain, *The Wayward Tourist* (Melbourne: Melbourne University Press, 2006), 5.

ii   **Most scholars start their accounts of risk:** Peter L. Bernstein, *Against the Gods: The Remarkable Story of Risk* (New York: John Wiley and Sons, 1996), 11–18.

iii   **But it's not until 1661:** *Oxford English Dictionary Online*, s.v. "risk (*n.*)," accessed December 2020, https://www.oed.com/view /Entry/166306.

iv   **An outbreak of the bubonic plague:** "Great Plague of 1665–1666," National Archives, accessed June 17, 2022, https://www .nationalarchives.gov.uk/education/resources/great-plague/.

v   **"For after all":** Blaise Pascal, *The Thoughts of Blaise Pascal*, trans. C. Kegan Paul (London: George Bell and Sons, 1901), https://oll .libertyfund.org/title/paul-the-thoughts-of-blaise-pascal.

vi   **In 1654, working with a lawyer from Toulouse:** Bernstein, *Against the Gods*, 63–70.

vii   **The person who introduced the problem:** Gerda Reith, *The Age of Chance: Gambling in Western Culture* (London: Taylor & Francis, 2005), 25–26.

viii   **Pascal's breakthrough involved:** "Pascal's Triangle," Math Is Fun, 2020, https://www.mathsisfun.com/pascals-triangle.html.

ix   **Today, weather forecasts, economic models:** Charles M. Grinstead and J. Laurie Snell, *Introduction to Probability*, 2nd ed. (Providence, RI: American Mathematical Society, 2006), vii, https://math.dartmouth .edu/~prob/prob/prob.pdf.

x   **At the peak of his career, he fled:** *Encyclopedia Britannica Online*, s.v.

"Blaise Pascal," by Lucien Jerphagnon and Jean Orcibal, last modified August 15, 2021, https://www.britannica.com/biography/Blaise -Pascal.

xi **Locke believed every citizen:** Emily C. Nacol, *An Age of Risk: Politics and Economy in Early Modern Britain* (Princeton, NJ: Princeton University Press, 2016), 112.

xii **"Men can never be secure":** John Locke, *Two Treatises on Government* (London: C. and J. Rivington, 1824), 261.

xiii **"Hobbes is the weird outlier":** Emily Nacol, in discussion with the author, March, 2020.

xiv **"solitary, poor, nasty":** Thomas Hobbes, *Leviathan* (New York: Penguin Classics, 2017).

xv **"Men," he wrote:** Hobbes, *Leviathan*.

xvi **"One thing that's been true":** Nacol, in discussion with the author, March, 2020.

xvii **The section on life insurance:** Lorraine Daston, *Classical Probability in the Enlightenment* (Princeton, NJ: Princeton University Press, 1988), 169–82.

xviii **The company that set the template:** Daston, *Classical Probability in the Enlightenment*, 174–82.

xix **The prospectus explained:** Daston, *Classical Probability in the Enlightenment*, 178.

xx **"They're selling a vision":** Lorraine Daston, in discussion with the author, September 2020.

xxi **The company's leaders promised cold calculation:** Daston, *Classical Probability in the Enlightenment*, 179.

xxii **"Pathological prudence":** Daston, *Classical Probability in the Enlightenment*, 181.

xxiii **In 1898, a ten-year-old named Alick Wickham:** "Alick Wickham," International Swimming Hall of Fame, accessed June 16, 2022, https://www.ishof.org/honoree/honoree-alick-wickham/.

xxiv **Some historians argue the stroke is ancient:** "The History of Front Crawl Swimming," Swimming.org, 2016, https://www.swimming.org /sport/history-of-front-crawl/.

CHAPTER TWO

i **It was formally organized in the 1960s:** Damien Murphy, "Nippers Clubs Booming 50 years from Inception," *Sydney Morning Herald*,

December 18, 2015, https://www.smh.com.au/national/nsw/boys
-and-girls-of-summer-20151130-glb8wn.html.

ii   **A lot of them were run by rowdy chauvinists:** Douglas Booth,
"In-*Between the Flags*: Reflections on a Narrative of Surf Life Saving
Australia," *Rethinking History* 12, no. 2 (2008): 165–87, https://doi
.org/10.1080/13642520802002125.

iii   **Women were admitted in 1980:** "Celebrating Women in Surf Life
Saving," Surf Life Saving Australia, July 1, 2020, https://sls.com.au
/celebrating-women-in-surf-life-saving/.

iv   **Some of the first photos from Bronte's surf club:** Stan Vesper,
Bronte: The Birthplace of Surf Lifesaving (Caringbah, New South
Wales: Playright, 2006), 47.

v   **"Be like a duck":** Reader's Digest, "'Be Like a Duck,' says Michael Caine,"
Reader's Digest, updated January 29, 2019, https://www.readersdigest
.in/conversations/story-quotable-quotes-be-like-a-duck-says
-michael-caine-124615.

vi   **It was as if the very American:** Robert D. Putnam, *Bowling Alone,*
(New York: Simon & Schuster, 2000).

vii   **Some of it arrived with modernity:** Linda M. Austin, "Children
of Childhood: Nostalgia and the Romantic Legacy," *Studies in
Romanticism* 42, no. 1 (Spring 2003): 75–98, https://doi.org/10.2307
/25601604.

viii **By the 1880s, child labor was outlawed:** "Child Labour," National
Archives, accessed June 17, 2022, http://www.nationalarchives.gov
.uk/pathways/citizenship/struggle_democracy/childlabour.htm.

ix   **In 1909, he came to Clark University:** Perry Meisel, "Freudian
Trip," *New York Times*, January 24, 1993, https://www.nytimes.com
/1993/01/24/books/freudian-trip.html.

x   **"the source of it all":** Meisel, "Freudian Trip."

xi   **According to Freud and psychoanalytic theory:** Ericka N.
Dennis, "The Influence of Risk-Taking Personality on Behavior in
Romantic Relationships," *Scholars: The McKendree University Journal
of Undergraduate Research*, no. 5 (Winter 2005), https://www
.mckendree.edu/academics/scholars/issue5/dennis.htm.

xii   **Seligman opened my eyes:** Martin Seligman, *The Optimistic Child*
(New York: Houghton Mifflin, 1995), 27.

xiii **"The self-esteem movement":** Seligman, *Optimistic Child*, 28.

xiv   **He was Canadian, precocious, and tall:** William Yardley, "Nathaniel

Branden, a Partner in Love and Business With Ayn Rand, Dies at 84," *New York Times*, December 8, 2014, https://www.nytimes.com/2014/12/09/us/nathaniel-branden-ayn-rands-collaborator-and-paramour-dies-at-84.html.

xv   **One of the first self-help classics:** Tom Butler-Bowden, *50 Psychology Classics* (Boston: Nicholas Brealey, 2007).

xvi   **"How we feel about ourselves":** Nathaniel Branden, *How to Raise Your Self-Esteem* (New York: Bantam, 2011).

xvii   **A year earlier, a colorful California politician:** "Now, the California Task Force to Promote Self-Esteem," *New York Times*, October 11, 1986, https://www.nytimes.com/1986/10/11/us/now-the-california-task-force-to-promote-self-esteem.html.

xviii   **Newspapers, magazines, and television news programs:** "Low Self-Esteem Called Major Reason Women Often Pick 'Wrong Man,'" Associated Press, November 12, 1987; "Former Bank Teller Says Low Self-Esteem Led Her to Steal," Associated Press, October 10, 1985; Abigail van Buren, "Body Odor May Be a Sign of Low Self-Esteem," *Chicago Tribune*, July 16, 1989.

xix   **Children in primary school:** Jesse Singal, "How the Self-Esteem Craze Took Over America And Why the Hype Was Irresistible," *The Cut*, May 30, 2017, https://www.thecut.com/2017/05/self-esteem-grit-do-they-really-help.html.

xx   **Grade inflation in the United States:** Seligman, *Optimistic Child*, 28.

xxi   **The skit from *Saturday Night Live*:** "Daily Affirmation: Stuart Smalley's (Al Franken) Halloween Story," *Saturday Night Live*, October 20, 2017, YouTube, 5:52, https://www.youtube.com/watch?v=bd3g0K9KlBI.

xxii   **Then I stumbled on an interview:** Oprah Winfrey, "Adult Children of Emotional Abuse," May 26, 2020 (originally aired March 28, 1989), in *The Oprah Winfrey Show: The Podcast*, podcast, MP3 audio, 26:39, https://www.oprah.com/own-podcasts/adult-children-of-emotional-abuse.

xxiii   **Many psychologists now believe:** Roy F. Baumeister, Brad J. Bushman, and W. Keith Campbell, "Self-Esteem, Narcissism, and Aggression: Does Violence Result from Low Self-Esteem or from Threatened Egotism?," *Current Directions in Psychological Science* 9, no. 1 (February 2000): 26–29, https://doi.org/10.1111/1467–8721.00053.

xxiv   **Even as self-esteem levels increased:** Roy F. Baumeister et al.,

"Does High Self-Esteem Cause Better Performance, Interpersonal Success, Happiness, or Healthier Lifestyles?," *Psychological Science in the Public Interest* 4, no. 1 (2003): 1–44, https://doi.org/10.1111 /1529–1006.01431.

xxv **A comprehensive review of thousands of self-esteem studies:** Baumeister et al., "Does High Self-Esteem."

xxvi **"Required reading first":** Martin Seligman, email message to author, Nov. 23, 2020.

xxvii **"Depression is at least partly":** Martin Seligman, in discussion with the author, Dec. 8, 2020.

xxviii **Seligman's entire career, from his first experiments in 1967:** Martin Seligman, *The Hope Circuit: A Psychologist's Journey from Helplessness to Optimism* (North Sydney: Penguin Random House Australia, 2018).

xxix **For ninth grade at Geelong:** "Timbertop," Geelong Grammar School, accessed June 16, 2022, https://www.ggs.vic.edu.au/learning /campuses/year-9-at-timbertop/.

xxx **In 1966, Prince Charles spent six months:** "Prince Had Happy Time at Timbertop," *Canberra Times*, January 31, 1973.

xxxi **There is scant evidence of grade inflation:** Andrew Norton, "Is Grade Inflation a Problem in Australian Universities?," Andrew Norton (website), March 12, 2020, https://andrewnorton.net.au/2020/03/12 /is-grade-inflation-a-problem-in-australian-universities/.

xxxii **Iceland is another nation where the environment:** Sumarliði Ísleifsson, "Iceland: Self-Image after Crisis," Open Democracy, April 27, 2009, https://www.opendemocracy.net/en/iceland-self-image-after -crisis/.

xxxiii **In the *New Yorker* a few years ago:** Nick Paumgarten, "Life Is Rescues," *New Yorker*, November 1, 2015, https://www.newyorker.com /magazine/2015/11/09/life-is-rescues.

xxxiv **All these countries, it's worth noting:** OECD Better Life Index, accessed June 11, 2021, https://www.oecdbetterlifeindex.org /#/11151151511.

xxxv **The ranks of volunteer firefighters have fallen:** Justin Strawser, "Pennsylvania Fire Departments Facing Volunteerism Emergency," *U.S. News*, December 25, 2021, https://www.usnews.com/news /best-states/pennsylvania/articles/2021-12-25/pennsylvania-fire -departments-facing-volunteerism-emergency.

xxxvi **More recently, though, he concluded:** Seligman, *Hope Circuit*, 376.

xxxvii **In a 2021 study of 185 parents:** Jeremy D. W. Clifton and Peter Meindl, "Parents Think—Incorrectly—That Teaching Their Children That the World Is a Bad Place Is Likely Best for Them," *Journal of Positive Psychology* 17, no. 2 (December 2021): 182–97, https://doi.org/10.1080/17439760.2021.2016907.

xxxviii **"Learned industriousness":** Seligman, *Hope Circuit*, 369–76.

xxxix **"Early experience with control":** Seligman, *Hope Circuit*, 538.

xl **What the Australian surfer Dave Rastovich calls "meaningful play":** Berry Liberman, "Dave Rastovich Surfs with Soul," Dumbo Feather, June 7, 2018, https://www.dumbofeather.com/conversations/dave-rastovich-surfs-soul/.

xli **How Jack London felt after he mastered his first wave:** Jack London, *The Cruise of the Snark* (New York: Macmillan, 1911), 86.

CHAPTER THREE

i **I'd written something for our bureau's weekly Australia newsletter:** Damien Cave, "Why I Love the Managed Risk, and Rewards, of Nippers," *New York Times*, March 14, 2018, https://www.nytimes.com/2018/03/14/world/australia/nippers-beach-surf-life-saving-risk-and-rewards-letter49.html.

ii **In America, from *The Graduate* (1967):** Ryan Reft, "A Dive into the Deep End: The Importance of the Swimming Pools in Southern California," KCET, May 16, 2013, https://www.kcet.org/history-society/a-dive-into-the-deep-end-the-importance-of-the-swimming-pools-in-southern-california.

iii **With a name like Icebergs:** "How We Began," Icebergs, accessed June 17, 2022, https://icebergs.com.au/about-us/heritage/.

iv **"Here's an example that still":** Daston, in discussion with the author, September, 2020.

v **"The predominant emotion":** Thalia Gigerenzer, email message with the author, Sept. 16, 2020.

vi **"Parents began to be afraid":** Lisa Hammel, "Dr. Spock as a Father—No Mollycoddler," *New York Times*, November 8, 1968, https://archive.nytimes.com/www.nytimes.com/books/98/05/17/specials/spock-father.html.

vii **As Friedrich Nietzsche famously said:** Kayla Stoner, "Science Proves That What Doesn't Kill You Makes You Stronger," *Northwestern Now*,

October 1, 2019, https://news.northwestern.edu/stories/2019/10/science-proves-that-what-doesnt-kill-you-makes-you-stronger/.

viii   **"Living in an environment":** Brock Bastian, interview with the author, September, 2020.

ix   **In one of his most cited papers:** R. A. Dienstbier, "Arousal and Physiological Toughness: Implications for Mental and Physical Health," *Psychological Review* 96, no. 1 (January 1989): 84–100, https://doi.org/10.1037/0033-295x.96.1.84.

x   **In studies of rats, the adrenal glands grew:** Dienstbier, "Arousal and Physiological Toughness."

xi   **Small doses of pain pointed even more clearly:** Dienstbier, "Arousal and Physiological Toughness."

xii   **He found that painful events enhanced the interaction:** Brock Bastian, *The Other Side of Happiness* (Sydney: Penguin Random House Australia, 2018), 328–32.

xiii   **A study of Norwegian paratroopers:** Bastian, *Other Side of Happiness*, 221–22; B. Ellertsen, T. B. Johnsen, and H. Ursin, "Relationship between the Hormonal Responses to Activation and Coping," in *Psychobiology of Stress: A Study of Coping Men*, ed. H. Ursin, E. Baade, and S. Levine (New York: Academic Press, 1978), 105–24.

xiv   **"The Anti-Phobic Effects of Thrilling Experiences":** Ellen Beate Hansen Sandseter and Leif Edward Ottesen Kennair, "Children's Risky Play from an Evolutionary Perspective: The Anti-Phobic Effects of Thrilling Experiences," *Evolutionary Psychology* 9, no. 2 (April 2011): 257–84, https://doi.org/10.1177/147470491100900212.

xv   **Mixing personal experience with research:** Bastian, *Other Side of Happiness*, 274–75.

xvi   **His research on pain as "social glue":** Bastian, *Other Side of Happiness*, 287–94.

xvii   **"We need to endure":** Bastian, *Other Side of Happiness*, 235.

xviii   **A study of risk from 2002:** Elke U. Weber, Ann-Renée Blais, and Nancy E. Betz, "A Domain-Specific Risk-Attitude Scale: Measuring Risk Perceptions and Risk Behaviors," *Journal of Behavioral Decision Making* 15, no. 4 (October 2002): 263–90, https://doi.org/10.1002/bdm.414.

xix   **Women and men have similar affinities for risk:** Thekla Morgenroth et al., "Sex, Drugs, and Reckless Driving: Are Measures Biased Toward Identifying Risk-Taking in Men?," *Social Psychological* *and Personality Science* 9, no. 6 (August 2018): 744–53, https://doi.org/10.1177/1948550617722833.

xx   **Trump was being accused of threatening to freeze aid:** Maggie Haberman et al., "Trump Said to Have Frozen Aid to Ukraine Before Call with Its Leader," *New York Times*, September 23, 2019, https://www.nytimes.com/2019/09/23/us/politics/trump-un-biden -ukraine.html.

xxi   **"There's a freedom here":** Matt Zurbo, interview with the author, July 2019.

CHAPTER FOUR

i   **Post-traumatic stress syndrome (PTSD):** Isaac R. Galatzer-Levy, Sandy H. Huang, and George A. Bonanno, "Trajectories of Resilience and Dysfunction Following Potential Trauma: A Review and Statistical Evaluation," *Clinical Psychology Review* 63, (July 2018): 41–55, https://doi.org/10.1016/j.cpr.2018.05.008.

ii   **Even among the families of 9/11 victims:** Kim Armstrong, "Remarkable Resiliency: George Bonanno on PTSD, Grief, and Depression," Association for Psychological Science, January 29, 2020, https://www.psychologicalscience.org/observer/bonanno.

iii   **Another study Bastian turned me on to:** Bastian, *Other Side of Happiness*, 208.

iv   **A psychology professor at the University of Delaware:** M. Zuckerman et al., "Development of a Sensation-Seeking Scale," *Journal of Consulting Psychology* 28, no. 6 (December 1964): 477–82, https://doi.org/10.1037/h0040995.

v   **The tension between expertise and public opinion:** Farooq Ahmed, "Profile of Paul Slovic," *PNAS* 114, no. 10 (March 2017): 2437–39, https://doi.org/10.1073/pnas.1701967114.

vi   **Slovic and his colleagues developed a questionnaire:** Sarah Lichtenstein et al., "Judged Frequency of Lethal Events," *Journal of Experimental Psychology: Human Learning and Memory* 4, no. 6 (1978): 551–78, https://doi.org/10.1037/0278–7393.4.6.551.

vii   **He worked out a matrix of mental shortcuts:** David Ropeik, "Understanding Factors of Risk Perception," *Nieman Reports*, December 15, 2002, https://niemanreports.org/articles/understanding -factors-of-risk-perception/.

viii   **Risk psychologists ascribe this:** Elke Weber, "What Shapes

Perceptions of Climate Change?," *WIREs Climate Change* 1, no. 3 (May/June 2010): 332–42, https://doi.org/10.1002/wcc.41.

ix   **"Attention is akin to a spotlight":** Paul Slovic, in conversation with the author, March, 2021.

x   **These low-risk white males (LRWMs):** Melissa L. Finucane et al., "Gender, Race, and Perceived Risk: The 'White Male' Effect," *Health, Risk & Society* 2, no. 2 (2000): 159–72, https://doi.org/10.1080 /713670162.

xi   **They support interventions known as "nudges":** Daniel Kahneman, *Thinking, Fast and Slow* (New York: Farrar, Straus and Giroux, 2011), 412–14.

xii   **We're more likely to change our habits:** Claudia R. Schneider et al., "The Influence of Anticipated Pride and Guilt on Pro-Environmental Decision Making," *PLoS ONE* 12, no. 11 (2017): e0188781, https:// doi.org/10.1371/journal.pone.0188781.

xiii   **In Gigerenzer's version, it's a triumph of trust:** Gerd Gigerenzer, *Risk Savvy: How to Make Good Decisions* (New York: Penguin Books, 2014), 63–66.

xiv   **As Donald Horne wrote:** Donald Horne, *The Lucky Country* (Melbourne: Penguin Books, 1964), 6.

CHAPTER FIVE

i   **Royal Life Saving Society in England:** James Robert McClelland, *The Bronze Medallion and Lifesaving Story* (Bribie Island, Queensland: Victory Press, 2016), https://www.caloundracity.org.au/Books/The -Bronze-Medallion-and-Life-Saving-Story.pdf.

ii   **Around the same time, volunteers:** Ed Jaggard, ed., *Between the Flags: One Hundred Summers of Australian Surf Lifesaving* (Sydney: UNSW Press, 2006), 29.

iii   **"the water-proofing of America":** "Wilbert E. Longfellow Water Safety Crusader" *American Red Cross*, May 14, 2006, https://web.archive.org /web/20060514225914/http://gso.redcross.org/WilbertLongfellow .php.

iv   **The Jacksonville Beach volunteer corps:** Maggie FitzRoy, "American Red Cross Volunteer Lifesaving Corps," *First Coast*, August 8, 2014, https://web.archive.org/web/20140808033247/ http://firstcoastmagazine.com/american-red-cross-volunteer-lifesaving -corps/.

v   **Sergeant Major John Bond:** "Life-Saving Demonstration," *Sydney Morning Herald*, April 16, 1894.

vi   **Swimming clubs and volunteer lifesaving clubs:** Jaggard, *Between the Flags*, 32–34.

vii   **The early surf clubs:** Jaggard, *Between the Flags*, 37.

viii   **Tommy Tana:** A. M. Lowe, *Surfing, Surf-Shooting and Surf-Lifesaving Pioneering* (self-pub., 1958).

ix   **He set a world diving record in 1918:** W. F. Corbett, "Alick Wickham's Sensational Dive," *The Referee* (Sydney), April 17, 1918, https://trove.nla.gov.au/newspaper/article/120301703.

x   **When Sydney hosted the Olympics:** *Sydney Morning Herald* "Kylie Minogue is carried through the crowd on a giant thong," *GettyImages*, October 1, 2000, https://www.gettyimages.com.au/detail/news-photo/kylie-minogue-is-carried-through-the-crowd-on-a-giant-thong-news-photo/539735037.

xi   **His social learning theory:** Saul McLeod, "Albert Bandura's Social Learning Theory," *Simply Psychology*, February 5, 2016, https://www.simplypsychology.org/bandura.html.

xii   **Bandura's most groundbreaking experiments:** Albert Bandura, Dorothea Ross, and Sheila A. Ross, "Transmission of Aggression through the Imitation of Aggressive Models," *Journal of Abnormal and Social Psychology* 63, no. 3 (1961): 575–82, https://psychclassics.yorku.ca/Bandura/bobo.htm; Albert Bandura, Dorothea Ross, and Sheila A. Ross, "Imitation of Film-Mediated Aggressive Models," *Journal of Abnormal and Social Psychology* 66, no. 1 (1963): 3–11, https://www.uky.edu/~eushe2/Bandura/Bandura1963JASP.pdf; Albert Bandura, "Influence of Models' Reinforcement Contingencies on the Acquisition of Imitative Responses," *Journal of Personality and Social Psychology* 1, no. 6 (June 1965): 589, https://www.uky.edu/~eushe2/Bandura/Bandura1965JPSP.pdf.

xiii   **More recently, researchers have found:** "Children of Anxious Mothers Twice as Likely to Have Hyperactivity in Adolescence," ScienceDaily, September 9, 2019, https://www.sciencedaily.com/releases/2019/09/190909095021.htm.

xiv   **Parents who are physically active:** Lynn L. Moore et al., "Influence of Parents' Physical Activity Levels on Activity Levels of Young Children," *Journal of Pediatrics* 118, no. 2 (February 1991): 215–19, https://doi.org/10.1016/S0022-3476(05)80485-8.

xv   **"There was a moment":** Angela Duckworth, in conversation with the author, October, 2020.

xvi   **One enterprising psychologist, Andrew Meltzoff:** A. N. Meltzoff, "Born to Learn: What Infants Learn from Watching Us," in *The Role of Early Experience in Infant Development*, ed. N. A. Fox, L. A. Leavitt, and J. G. Warhol (Skillman, NJ: Pediatric Institute Publication, 1999), 145–64.

xvii **One study, highlighted by Duckworth:** Julia A. Leonard, Andrea Garcia, and Laura E. Schulz, "How Adults' Actions, Outcomes, and Testimony Affect Preschoolers' Persistence," *Child Development* 91, no. 4 (July/August 2020): 1254–71, https://doi.org/10.1111/cdev .13305.

xviii **In one of Dweck's best-known experiments:** Carol Dweck, "Developing a Growth Mindset with Carol Dweck," Stanford Alumni, October 10, 2014, YouTube, 9:37, https://www.youtube.com/watch ?v=hiiEeMN7vbQ.

xix   **Dweck's book:** Carol Dweck, *Mindset: The New Psychology of Success* (New York: Random House, 2006).

xx   **Schwartz theory of basic values:** "Values: Schwartz Theory of Basic Values," Australian National University, last modified April 2020, https://i2s.anu.edu.au/resources/schwartz-theory-basic-values.

xxi   **"physical fitness, enterprise, tenacity":** "A Powerful Force for Good since 1962," *Outward Bound*, updated June 11, 2022, https:// www.outwardbound.org/about-us/history/.

xxii **The ocean takes up 72 percent:** "Oceans: The Great Unknown," NASA, October 8, 2009, https://www.nasa.gov/audience/forstudents /5–8/features/oceans-the-great-unknown-58.html.

xxiii **Matthew Richell, a forty-one-year-old father:** Michael Koziol, "Matthew Richell from Hachette Australia Dies Surfing at Tamarama Beach," *Sydney Morning Herald*, July 2, 2014, https://www.smh.com .au/national/nsw/matthew-richell-from-hachette-australia-dies-surfing -at-tamarama-beach-20140702-zstzu.html.

xxiv **"The sea, once it":** Jacques-Yves Cousteau, GoodReads, updated June 7, 2022, https://www.goodreads.com/quotes/292757-the-sea-once -it-casts-its-spell-holds-one-in.

CHAPTER SIX

i   **Gigerenzer talked a lot about checklists:** Gigerenzer, *Risk Savvy*.

ii **In their language:** Frances Morphy, "Invisible to the State: Kinship and the Yolngu Moral Order" (paper presented at Negotiating the Sacred V: Governing the Family, Monash University, August 14–15, 2008), https://www.researchgate.net/publication/251797299_Invisible_to _the_state_kinship_and_the_Yolngu_moral_order.

iii **By the time the first European settlers arrived:** Nicolas Peterson, in discussion with the author, March 2021.

iv **The story Bruce Pascoe tells:** Bruce Pascoe, *Dark Emu: Black Seeds: Agriculture or Accident?* (Broome, Western Australia: Magabala Books, 2014).

v **A phrase he used in an old interview:** Nicolas Peterson, "Finding One's Way in Arnhem Land," in *Up Close and Personal: On Peripheral Perspectives and the Production of Anthropological Knowledge,* ed. Cris Shore and Susanna Trnka (New York: Berghahn Books, 2013), 108–24.

vi **"from the kind of close-knit group":** Sebastian Junger, *Tribe: On Homecoming and Belonging* (London: Fourth Estate, 2016), 93.

vii **Citing a global survey:** Junger, *Tribe,* 20.

viii **"The mechanism seems simple":** Junger, *Tribe,* 20–21.

ix **"Spiritual furniture":** Maia Szalavitz, "Q&A: Positive Psychologist Martin Seligman on the Good Life," *Time,* May 13, 2011, https:// healthland.time.com/2011/05/13/mind-reading-positive-psychologist -martin-seligman-on-the-good-life/.

x **"it's because there's no expectation":** Sebastian Junger, in conversation with the author, February 2020.

xi **The pain of losing is more powerful:** Kahneman, *Thinking, Fast and Slow,* 282–86.

xii **In 1969, 89 percent of children:** "The Decline of Walking and Bicycling," Safe Routes to School Guide, accessed June 18, 2022, http://guide.saferoutesinfo.org/introduction/the_decline_of _walking_and_bicycling.cfm.

xiii **And those numbers have continued to decline:** Eleftheria Kontou et al., "U.S. Active School Travel in 2017: Prevalence and Correlates," *Preventative Medicine Reports* 17, (March 2020): 101024, https://doi .org/10.1016/j.pmedr.2019.101024.

xiv **Kids who get to school on their own are healthier:** Manuel Herrador-Colmenero, Emilio Villa-González, and Palma Chillón, "Children Who Commute to School Unaccompanied Have Greater Autonomy and Perceptions of Safety," *Acta Paediatricia* 106, no. 12 (December 2017): 2042–47, https://doi.org/10.1111/apa.14047.

xv   **Americans already lead shorter:** Max Roser, "Why is life expectancy in the US lower than in other rich countries?" *Our World in Data*, October 9, 2020, https://ourworldindata.org/us-life-expectancy-low.

xvi   **Our children are spiraling:** Matt Richtel, "'It's Life or Death': The Mental Health Crisis Among U.S. Teens," New York Times, updated May 3, 2022, https://www.nytimes.com/2022/04/23/health/mental -health-crisis-teens.html.

xvii   **Spending time with people and opinions:** Stefano Balietti et al., "Reducing Opinion Polarization: Effects of Exposure to Similar People with Differing Political Views," *PNAS* 118, no. 52 (December 2021): e2112552118, https://doi.org/10.1073/pnas.2112552118.

CHAPTER SEVEN

i   **On November 9, I wrote:** Damien Cave, "At Least 3 Dead as Fires Rage Across Eastern Australia," *New York Times*, November 9, 2019, https://www.nytimes.com/2019/11/09/world/australia/fires-two -killed-climate-change.html.

ii   **Two days later, I wrote:** Damien Cave, "Australian Fire Officials Say the Worst Is Yet to Come," *New York Times*, November 11, 2019, https://www.nytimes.com/2019/11/11/world/australia/fires-sydney -new-south-wales.html.

iii   **Road fatalities per capita:** "International Road Safety Comparisons—Annual," Australian Government: Bureau of Infrastructure and Transport Research Economics, November 2, 2021, https://www.bitre.gov.au/publications/ongoing/international_road _safety_comparisons.

iv   **Advocating for the removal of monkey bars:** Joe Hinchliffe, "No More Monkeying Around: Push to Remove Dangerous Play Equipment," *Sydney Morning Herald*, November 26, 2018, https://www. smh.com.au/lifestyle/health-and-wellness/no-more-monkeying- around-push-to-remove-dangerous-play-equipment-20181121 -p50hea.html.

v   **"Never be rigid":** London, *The Cruise of the Snark*, 99.

EPILOGUE

i   **Horne's most famous lines:** Horne, *Lucky Country*, 233.

ii   **Nearly 80 percent of Australians:** Nicholas Biddle et al., *Exposure and the Impact on Attitudes of the 2019–20 Australian Bushfires*, ANU

Centre for Social Research & Methods, February 2020, http://dx.doi
.org/10.26193/S1S9I9.

iii **The pollution levels in Sydney:** "Wildfires Cover Sydney in Smog
Worse than Delhi; Residents Asked to Stay Indoors," *BusinessToday
India*, November 10, 2019, https://www.businesstoday.in/current
/world/wildfires-cover-sydney-in-smog-worse-than-delhi-residents
-asked-to-stay-indoors/story/390706.html.

iv   **But while Australians may be tolerant:** Horne, *Lucky Country*, 247.

v   **When Morrison visited Cobargo:** Janek Drevikovsky, "Bushfire
Victim Slams Scott Morrison for Walking Away," *Sydney Morning
Herald*, January 3, 2020, https://www.smh.com.au/national/nsw
/bushfire-victim-slams-scott-morrison-for-walking-away-20200103
-p53omq.html.

vi   **"Tell the prime minister":** 7NEWS Sydney (@7NewsSydney),
"For days we've been warned it was coming, and tonight,
communities across New South Wales are fighting to save their
towns, as the bushfire emergency roared back to life," Twitter, January
4, 2020, 2:08 a.m., https://twitter.com/7NewsSydney/status
/1213356579971420161?s=20.

vii **The best way to motivate people:** Schneider et al., "Influence of
Anticipated Pride."

viii **"Single-action bias":** Jon Gertner, "Why Isn't the Brain Green?," *New
York Times*, April 16, 2009, https://www.nytimes.com/2009/04/19
/magazine/19Science-t.html.

ix   **"It's not something":** Elke Weber, in conversation with the author,
March 2020.

x   **"Combine and conquer":** Elke Weber, "Combine and Conquer:
A Joint Application of Conjoint and Functional Approaches to the
Problem of Risk Measurement," *Journal of Experimental Psychology:
Human Perception and Performance* 10, no. 2 (1984): 179–94, https://
doi.org/10.1037/0096–1523.10.2.179.

xi   **A study from the University of Sydney:** "Greater Social Distancing
Could Curb COVID-19 in 13 Weeks," University of Sydney,
March 25, 2020, https://www.sydney.edu.au/news-opinion/news
/2020/03/25/greater-social-distancing-could-curb-covid-19-in-13
-weeks.html.

xii **The police had occasionally been heavy-handed:** Melissa Davey,
"Victoria Police Powers Under Scrutiny After Fines Issued for Exercise

and Going to Supermarket," *Guardian*, September 3, 2020, https://www.theguardian.com/australia-news/2020/sep/03/victoria-police-powers-under-scrutiny-after-fines-issued-for-exercise-and-going-to-supermarket.

xiii   **Australia reached a level of 90 percent:** Mikhail Prokopenko, in discussion with the author, July 24, 2020.

xiv   **If the United States had a death rate like Australia's:** Damien Cave, "How Australia Saved Thousands of Lives While Covid Killed a Million Americans," *New York Times*, May 15, 2022, https://www.nytimes.com/2022/05/15/world/australia/covid-deaths.html.

xv   **Countries with the X factor of more "interpersonal trust":** COVID-19 National Preparedness Collaborators, "Pandemic Preparedness and COVID-19: An Exploratory Analysis of Infection and Fatality Rates, and Contextual Factors Associated with Preparedness in 177 Countries, from Jan 1, 2020, to Sept 30, 2021," *The Lancet* 399, no. 10334 (April 16, 2022): 1489–1512, https://doi.org/10.1016/S0140-6736(22)00172-6.

xvi   **Australia is also drifting toward American disconnection:** Andrew Leigh and Nick Terrell, *Reconnected: A Community Builder's Handbook* (Carlton, Victoria: Latrobe University Press, 2020), 14–22.

xvii   **For a few minutes they swam on:** Albert Camus, *The Plague*, trans. Robin Buss (Melbourne: Penguin Random House Australia, 2009), 198.

About the Author

Damien Cave has worked for the *New York Times* since 2004, starting in New Jersey and going on to cover several regions of the United States and more than a dozen countries. He and his wife, Diana, were finalists for the Pulitzer Prize in international reporting in 2008 with a team in Baghdad when covering the Iraq war. Australia bureau chief since 2017, he lives in Sydney with his wife and two children.